THE
INCREDIBLY STRANGE
FILM BOOK

THE
INCREDIBLY STRANGE
FILM BOOK

Jonathan Ross

S I M O N   &   S C H U S T E R

LONDON·SYDNEY·NEW YORK·TOKYO·SINGAPORE·TORONTO

First published in Great Britain by Simon & Schuster Ltd, 1993
A Paramount Communications Company

Simon & Schuster Ltd
West Garden Place
Kendal Street
London W2 2AQ

Simon & Schuster of Australia Pty Ltd
Sydney

A CIP catalogue record for this book is available from the British Library.

ISBN 0-671-71097-4

Typeset in Avant Garde Gothic & Palatino
by Florencetype Ltd, Kewstoke, Avon
Printed and bound in Great Britain by the Bath Press

To my wife and daughter, with love forever.

Contents

Acknowledgements

It's not at all strange that a project as large and as lengthy as this one could only come about with the help, understanding and hard work of many. However, it should be noted that I am more than happy to take full credit for other people's work. That's why this list of tireless editors, picture researchers, publishers, friends, agent, business partners, film critics and assorted losers is written in very small type inside the book and only my name is displayed in huge letters on the cover.

Thank you to my wife Jane L A Ross for everything. And to my daughter Betty K Ross for everything else.

Family hugs to Mum, Dad, Paul, Simon, Miles, Adam, Liza and James Ross for not sniggering when I said I was going to write a book. Big warm in-law cuddles to Amanda, Stu, Bunker, and Kinny for the very same reason.

Thanks also to Gary Farrow, who deserves a medal for his support and guidance throughout the project, but will have to settle for twenty per cent.

A cheap but ever so cheerful thank you to friend, inspiration and movie star Ric Meyers. Congratulations and thanks also to proud father of two and fellow traveller Andy Harries, and a tip of my figurative fedora to number one film writer Kim Newman. Thanks for lending me so many movies – you'll get them back soon, honest.

A big brotherly pat on the shoulder to Tris `mofo' Burns – thanks for spending so many fruitful hours in the BFI photo-copying articles on dirty movies. I know you loved it really.

Heartfelt thanks and firm, manly handshakes to: Big Nick Webb, Martin `the charmer' Fletcher, Jenny Olivier, Daphne Bien and everyone else at Simon and Schuster, including of course the person who kept the fax machine full of paper. I really couldn't have done it without you.

Hugs and kisses (of the most professional kind) to Hazel Southam, for tirelessly hunting down stills from films that she would rather not have known existed. Similar gushing thanks to Clare Wheatley for taking such excellent shots from my own collection. Neither of us will ever work with front projection sets again.

Big wet kisses of thanks to Alan Marke, Kenton Allen, Heather Hampson, Katie Lander, Mike Bolland, Pete Orton, Jack Barth, Meena Sud, and many many other people at Channel X for consistently believing me when I said I couldn't make an important meeting because I was finishing the book. Even when I wasn't.

And finally, a cheery cockney `Gawd Bless You Guvner' to the artist who painted the front cover, for giving me such a fabulous physique.

Introduction

There are hundreds of books about films available, I know, I've got most of them. So why write another? And why expect people to shell out nearly ten quid for it, even if it does have a rather garish and titillating cover?

Here's why. Over the last ten years, I've tracked down and watched as many cinematic curios as I could find from Filippino Kung-Fu films to early sex and drugs shockers via the real life story of Siamese twin sisters locked in a courtroom battle. Watching them was fun but, as I discovered, not quite as much fun as talking about them afterwards. I am ashamed to admit that I turned into that worst type of conversation hog: a strange-film bore. Out of all the dull species of talkative film-buffs, the strange-film bore is the most persistent and deadly. Not only do we ramble on for hours about films, actors, directors and genres that most people have not and probably will never see, but there is always the sneaking suspicion in the back of our victim's mind that we could have made it all up. Maybe none of this junk exists! After all, what adult in his or her right mind would really believe that anyone would have been sick enough to make a film about a crazed enema bandit? Or that a man with virtually no acting ability could get to star in a whole series of films purely because he suffered from a rare disease, enabling him to play monsters without any make-up? But it's all true, and I've taken inordinate pleasure in recounting these stories to dozens of friends and casual acquaintances over the last few years.

SADLY IT WASN'T ENOUGH! I *had* to spread the word further. I felt the noble call to educate complete strangers about the more ridiculous cinematic gimmicks that were dragged along in the wake of the wide-screen boom in the 1950s. I wanted to explain the myth surrounding the `dismal failure' of 3-D. I felt the urge to corrupt (in a loving way, of course) by recounting the history of the porn flick and the sleazy joy of exploitation films. And finally I felt, perhaps foolishly, that I could uplift the human spirit by singing the praises of those who had previously gone unsung: the writers, directors and would-be stars who had been sadly overlooked or, even worse, deliberately neglected by the composers of more straightforward love letters to the movies.

The better travelled, the more wordly-wise, yes, I'll say it, the *sophisticates* amongst you will be aware that I am not alone in my love for the more obscure cineastes and their products. Over the last fifteen years or so, dozens of fan publications and a handful of reassuringly successful books have appeared which cover similar ground. Michael Weldon, with both his *Psychotronic Encyclopedia of Film* and his excellent *Psychotronic* magazine, was a trailblazer to whom we are all indebted. Likewise, Jim Morton for his *Trashola Newsletter* and his contribution of V Vale and Andrea Juno's *Research* Publication *Incredibly Strange Films*.

But despite the joy with which I greeted each new foray into the world of strange film-making, I felt that many of the books available were a tad pretentious in their desire to bestow critical respectability on all low-budget film-makers, regardless of their actual ability, purely because they worked outside the mainstream. Also, many of the books and magazines were of little use to anyone encountering these films for the first time, relying heavily on previous knowledge. I hoped that, as a comparatively knowledgable fan of unusual films, I could write a book that would gather the more exciting and interesting aspects of off-beat films into one, easily absorbed volume and tempt people who might otherwise not want to get within a hundred yards of anything so down-market, to browse, buy and then broaden their cinematic horizons.

So this is it. A history, of sorts. All encompassing? No, of course not. But hopefully you'll enjoy reading about the films and personalities that have helped to keep me such a happy soul for years. Conclusions drawn throughout are mine, so if you find yourself horribly offended by either the tone or just my gross stupidity, I'll offer a blanket apology now: Sorry.

And so the book lies open before you, like open books do. Dive in. Wallow in the mire. Get yourself good and dirty. Fold over the corners of favourite pages. Scribble important looking notes in the margin. In fact feel free to treat this as if it were a real book on the history of cinema, which of course, it very nearly is.

Happy Reading,

Jonathan Ross.

Part One

Sex

1 The History of Porn Films

It's important, early on, to make clear the difference between sex in films, and films which only exist to show sex. The problem that you immediately encounter when attempting to deal with this subject is that of definition. What characterises a blue movie, a porno film, from, for example, a mainstream successful film that happens to have explicit sex in it? Are *Last Tango in Paris, Don't Look Now* and *Basic Instinct* pornographic films because they are unflinching in their depiction of the sexual act? Alternatively, are *Deep Throat* and *Debbie Does Dallas* somehow better than other skin flicks because they have decent production values, and were exhibited in proper first-run movie theatres rather than in speciality cinemas?

The traditional answer is in the portrayal of the deed itself. If sex is simulated than it isn't porn. If it's for real, then it is. But where does that leave us with films such as the recent piece of French twaddle *The Lover*, or the previously mentioned *Last Tango in Paris* and its infamous butter scene? Both were films that thrived on the publicity generated by 'did they or didn't they' speculation.

This time, the answer lies in intent. If the sex is there to spice up the plot or add another dimension to the on-screen characters, I'll give the film the benefit of the doubt and happily bestow legitimacy upon it. But if the sex is the driving force of a picture, the only real selling point or theme, then it's a sex movie. And if what is shown is actually happening, if the actors and actresses are really doing it, then it's pornography.

The history of porn is no less fascinating than that of sex in legitimate cinema, but due to the clandestine and shady nature of the beast itself, it's a lot trickier to pin down. One of the reasons why pornography is a difficult subject is because pornography is a difficult word. It carries a certain amount of emotive luggage with it wherever it goes. To some, it brings to mind images of rather sad, lonely men shuffling around Soho or Kings Cross at night looking for something to, er, get excited over. To others, it immediately sets off alarm bells, sexually explicit movies being seen as an evil, corrupting influence. Interestingly, Britain is one of the few Western countries that still prohibits the open sale or distribution of pornographic films and I don't see that we're much better off than other less repressive nations that do. But fortunately I don't have to argue the case for or against this stuff. All I have to do is tell you how porn on film came to be the multi-million pound industry that it is today.

Maria Schneider pouts sexily for a mainstream audience in *Last Tango in Paris*.

An ALBERTO GRIMALDI Production MARLON BRANDO in "LAST TANGO IN PARIS" X A Film by Bernardo Bertolucci with MARIA SCHNEIDER · MARIA MICHI · GIOVANNA GALLETTI and with JEAN PIERRE LEAUD Also starring MASSIMO GIROTTI   Produced by ALBERTO GRIMALDI Directed by BERNARDO BERTOLUCCI
A Coproduction   PEA Produzioni Europee Associate S.A.S. - Rome   Les Productions Artistes Associés S.A. - Paris
This copyright advertising material is licensed and not sold and is the Property of National Screen Service Ltd. and upon completion of the exhibition for which it has been licensed it should be returned to National Screen Service Ltd.

Porn movies have, over the years and in different parts of the world, been known by many names, from the rather quaint-sounding 'stags' or 'smokers' (named after the kind of all-male gatherings where they would be shown, a 'smoker' being a euphemistic term for a brothel), to the more modern 'skin flicks', 'blue movies' and, perhaps most direct and basic of them all, 'dirty films'. The very first examples are believed to have originated in Buenos Aires around 1904. They were shipped to wealthy private clients or to brothels and private boudoirs. These early South American exports were simple little one-reelers, graphically depicting one or another of the sexual acts. No attempt was made to elaborate upon the deed itself, no time wasted on scene setting or character development. None was needed. Just a few years before, the novelty of seeing moving pictures of even the most banal event had been enough to pack in the crowds. So, for the smaller audiences gathered around these films, one reel of straightforward rumpy pumpy was much more than enough.

Genuine porno movies of the more modern variety, by which I mean they at least made a nod in the direction of a little story or plot, began in France around 1907 or 1908. This would make sense in more ways than one. Firstly, we have the Frenchman's fondly held reputation as the world's greatest lover. How fitting, then, that he would seek to capture his favourite movements and moments for future generations. Secondly, there was the issue of technology. Since day one, the French had led the way in the development of the moving picture.

In 1895, the Lumiere brothers introduced a new method of recording images, the *cinematograph*. Weighing only five kilograms (about one-hundreth of the weight of Edison's bulky *kinetoscope*, which had been marketed the year before) the Lumieres' invention was also hand-cranked, needing no fixed power source, making it the perfect choice for capturing those saucy moments as they happened, *au naturel*. Although I've yet to find any evidence to support this, I'm positive that the phrase 'aving a queek and crank' must have emerged around this time as the newest euphemism on the block, or arrondisement. *Vive La France!*

This new wave of film-makers were producing items for a speciality market, and a small, but lucrative, industry soon developed. Gentleman's magazines and those catering to cinema enthusiasts were soon filled with discreet but obvious advertisements for (piquant) films and Lantern slides. A 6d stamp would bring you a richly illustrated catalogue by return post, and presumably, many happy evenings thereafter.

Although notably more relaxed morally than the generation before, cinema-goers in the Edwardian era were still far too upright and strait-laced to accept open and graphic portrayals of sex and nudity outside of the all-male atmosphere of a stag club or brothel. So from virtually the very beginning of the history of cinema, porn existed as a separate industry, sharing in the technical and creative developments of mainstream film-making, but operating surreptitiously. At times throughout their respective histories the two would touch and absorb some of the new ideas and techniques employed in the other (such as the close up and, of course, sound), as well as the conventions and clichés. But ultimately the sex in films produced for mainstream pictures, intended for and eagerly consumed by the mainstream audience, would always remain less explicit and far less honest (or obvious, depending upon your point of view) than that found in its openly pornographic cousins.

The oldest known porno movie to have been made in the United States is thought to be a 1915 short called *A Grass Sandwich*, also known as *A Free Ride*. In most respects the film was similar to the far less saucy one-reelers that preceded it. There was next to no plot, with the entertainment value deriving solely from the deed itself: A man picks up two women in his car. They go for a drive. He stops to relieve himself behind a bush. The women get excited watching him go and, inevitably, they wind up getting it on.

Although, as I pointed out earlier, the history of porno films ran parallel with that of conventional cinema in terms of technique, in other ways it lagged woefully behind. Acting has never been a strong point, and with a couple of notable exceptions porn movies have always suffered from bad writing. I guess that it's inevitable, bearing in mind that the majority of people watching are only interested in seeing the participants get their clothes off and get into action as soon as possible. Why waste time on characterisation or in setting the scene convincingly?

In his 1973 book, *Contemporary Erotic Cinema*, porn director William Rostler noted that even as late as the mid-1970s there were still only about five plots used in porn films:

- Plot One starts with a male visitor, maybe a plumber, the milkman or a salesman, being invited inside by a woman, alone at home. Sex takes place.
- Plot Two has a rural feel. Down on the farm or just out in some fields, a woman will see animals copulating. This will inevitably excite her. A farmhand or travelling salesman (again!) will benefit from her arousal.
- Plot Three involves a more elaborate indoor setting, maybe a doctor's or dentist's surgery. After a routine examination or treatment, sex will follow.
- Plot Four is a little more fantastic. A masked burglar or bandit will encounter a lone but usually randy woman after breaking into a property. Undoubtably, sex will seem the natural thing to do.
- Finally, Plot Five. A woman sunbathing or secretly skinny-dipping will be surprised by a male onlooker. Sex happens.

Apart from the sex, there's nothing in these plots to get remotely excited about. But that of course was the whole point. As long as these films were offering something that could be got nowhere else, there was no need to waste money or other resources on unnecessary frills like a screenplay. Just sketch in the basic framework and get on with it. As times changed, so did the excuses for sex. Plumbers and door to door salesmen were gradually phased out in favour of pizza delivery boys and television engineers. Farm frolics occasionally involved animals as well as people.

Despite the similarities in the early stag films, national preferences were easily spotted. In America it was most commonly the lonely frustrated housewife or the doctor's surgery scenario. Titles like *Oh Doctor, Doctor Penis*, and *Doctor Hardon's Injection* were typical. In Britain a teacher–pupil set up was far more common, or occasionally farm-worker and Lord or Lady of the manor. In the Catholic parts of Europe a priest or nun might well get involved. But the consistent theme was one of sex occurring in everyday situations, often involving a betrayal of some professional or personal code of behaviour, adding, I suppose, a little extra spice to the proceedings.

It's not absolutely necessary to have this many beautiful women in a movie to sell it - but history has taught us that it certainly helps.

The history of mainstream porno, by which I mean that produced for a relativly large audience, is largely devoid of the more unpleasant aberrations. Although there are a handful of films that deal with or hint at such things as bestiality, paedophilia (more often than not implied by costume and scenario rather than the real thing) and extreme sado-masochism, they played next to no part in the formative years of the undergound cinema, only really surfacing in the Seventies as the video peep shows spread throughout America and much of Europe. One theory for the gradual spread of such material is the need for films of this type to appeal to a sense of guilt, of the taboo. As sex in cinema and most other forms of modern mass media became more widespread and acceptable, the slimier individuals, who had prospered by selling what was unavailable elsewhere, found they had to break new ground to appeal to their jaded clientele.

Pornographic films have been produced in every country where there is reasonable knowledge of and access to cinema technology. But like so many other twentieth century art forms (the comic book, jazz, serial killers), it found its spiritual and financial home in America. In their quest for new tricks to be played upon a very old theme, pornographers quickly turned to parody. Explicit and theoretically humorous versions of established films, stars and genres soon appeared. Nothing was sacred, not even Disney-esque cartoons.

Animated movies had obvious advantages over real films: no need to pay performers or indeed persuade them to perform, and in a genre where appearance is very nearly everything, it was a positive advantage being able to draw your leading man and lady as big or small as you liked. But the cost of animating a full length feature that would receive only limited exposure was prohibitive, and so fewer cartoons exist than you might suppose.

Buried Treasure, one of the more famous animated sex films, appeared in the late Twenties or early Thirties. It followed the adventures of Everready, a character with a detachable penis that gets him into all sorts of trouble, much of it pleasurable of course. Episodes involve a donkey, a woman with a crab in her vagina (I didn't promise you clever humour, did I?) and a fencing duel with a Mexican using their two penises as swords.

Another well known porno cartoon was a direct spoof on Disney's *Snow White and the Seven Dwarfs*. Believed to have been made in the Fifties or early Sixties, *Snow White the Cutie* played off the original in every way you might suppose, group sex being the most obvious. I saw part of this film in a tourist trap 'Sex Museum' in Amsterdam and I seem to remember that they changed the dwarfs' names. (How do Droopy, Itchy, Stiffy, Gropey, Licky, Happy and Doc grab you?)

The broader humour of the early porno films gradually gave way to a more sophisticated type. Less play on words, more attention to plot and narrative. Films like the very broad and very lewd sex-comedy from the Thirties, *Matinee Idol* (featuring such characters as Lord Fuckem and Sir Rattling Nuts), were replaced by less amusing but perhaps more genuinely erotic pictures. So far so good. Just as in mainstream cinema, sex movies had appeared initially as a gimmick and then developed at a solid pace, growing out of the initial juvenile stage as the novelty of what they had to offer wore off. One might have supposed that they would have continued developing and improving over the next few decades, but instead they were to suffer a major developmental set-back: the amateur.

The spread and proliferation of 16 millimeter cameras and projectors, and the development of 8 millimeter technology, allowed a greater number of inexperienced and talentless wannabes to try their hand at film-making. For many, porno was an ideal choice, for no matter how bad the script, actors or direction, the films were still assured some kind of an audience. In their book *Dirty Movies*, Al Di Lauros and Gerald Rabkin noted that the quality of the goods on offer plummeted after the Second World War for this reason. By the mid-Fifties, not only had just about all attempts at humour disappeared, but so too had any gesture towards making actual full-lengths films. In their place were amateur vignettes, short movies that existed only to show the act of intercourse or related activities. There was also a greater degree of secrecy surrounding the productions that inevitably affected what was seen on screen. The sight of actors completely naked except for masks or other disguises became very common.

The boom in home photography and film-making created an obvious new market for films which still weren't able to receive open and public screenings: mail order. Providing you could avoid having material seized and held for prosecution, there was money to be made by selling prints direct to the home audience.

The generic term for the cheaper and poorer quality porn movie of this period is the 'motel film'. The most basic requirements were rarely altered: a camera, some film, a couple of performers and a motel room. The majority of these films don't warrant a mention beyond the fact that they existed, but as always there were exceptions. One which achieved a certain notoriety was *The Smart Aleck* (1951). It has survived and received attention over and above its contemporaries solely due to the fact that it 'starred' a name performer, a pretty 16-year-old called Juanita Slusher, who went on to achieve a degree of fame in America as a stripper, working under cover as Candy Barr. (Candy Barr was recently portrayed by Sherilyn Fenn in the 1992 film *Ruby*.) The only other interesting thing about *The Smart Aleck* was the scene in which Ms Barr, 'lured' into the ubiquitous motel room by a businessman who plies her with booze, refuses to administer oral sex. Barr later commented that this was largely because she was not even aware that such a practice took place.

There has always been speculation that other stars – Monroe, Joan Crawford, even Barbra Streisand – appeared in hard-core movies before they became better known and presumably more choosy about their work. I've seen the film that supposedly starred the young Monroe, rolling an apple and then a coke bottle over her naked form. Conventional wisdom on the subject agrees that in fact it wasn't her, but it had me fooled. (I myself have no such skeleton in my cupboard, but purely because I was never asked.)

The late Fifties saw an increase in the amount of nudity seen in the non-mainstream pictures of the day, but no attempt was made to even simulate the kind of sex seen for real in the stags. Nor was the porno market noticeably affected by the rise and spread of television. Consequently, porn films had no need to experiment with gimmicks like wide-screen or 3-D.

The scene remained pretty much the same from the late Fifties until the late Sixties. The gradual increase in the amount of nudity and the greater sexual content of main-stream movies impacted upon what had become the soft-core movie industry, but had no discernible immediate effect upon hard-core. The importance of the change in attitude in cinemas the world over was to be felt further down the

Who needs full-frontal when you can pout like that? Before hard-core, films could be sexy and wholesome!

line. The relaxation of censorship and the move toward a permissive attitude prepared the stage, and more importantly, the screen, for hard-core to finally cross over.

One of the first breakthrough, cross-over movies was produced by Alex De Renzy, a successful pornographer from San Francisco. *Sexual Freedom in Denmark: A New Approach* (1969–70) was a documentary examining the rise and spread of the pornographic film industry in Europe. Shot mostly at a sex industry trade fair in Denmark, it included a few minutes of genuine hard-core footage, filmed at a porno cinema while punters were watching. It claimed, with good reason, to be showing the action to make a point rather than for the audience's enjoyment.

Seeing as *Sexual Freedom in Denmark* was a documentary, merely reporting this new phenomenon, not exploiting it, the film got shown at cinemas and art houses outside of the normal grind-house circuit. Its success and acceptance was of crucial importance in paving the way for other films containing hard-core to break out of the pornographic ghetto. It also served the industry well by revealing explicit material to those who had not yet been exposed to it, and by setting the record straight that pornography was nothing to be ashamed about, at least according to people who lived in Copenhagen and San Francisco.

Other 'documentaries' followed. De Renzy produced another, more interesting film, *A History of the Blue Movie* (1971), which covered much of the same ground as this chapter, only in a much more exciting way. Clips were shown from most of the landmark movies, including *A Grass*

Hollywood Blue. Adam (Batman) West and Phil (Bilko) Silvers bestow an odd sort of legitimacy on one of the better soft-core porn-fests.

Sandwich and *The Smart Aleck,* and the film detailed such historical moments as the first of what is lovingly referred to in the porno industry as the 'cum shot'. *Hollywood Blue* (1971) was another such big screen documentary on the dirty film, courtesy of another hip San Franciscan, Bill Osco. Although not quite as good as De Renzy's, it was still a quality production, certainly better than other imitations, such as the spurious documentaries *Pornography – Prostitution USA* or *Sex Freedom in Germany.*

The emergence of porn from the all-male stags and private parties into the glare of the great outdoors could not have happened before the early 1970s. The attitudes toward censorship had been steadily eroding since the Second World War and, most importantly, the birth and growth of a genuine sub-culture that openly pursued pure sexual pleasure provided a new and far healthier audience for sexually explicit material. Previously, those producing or using hard-core pornography had hidden the fact, and it had been necessary to keep such activities secret to avoid legal as well as social persecution. (It probably also heightened their enjoyment of the material, illicit pleasures often seeming the sweetest.) But by the early Seventies, anything went, and they went to the cinema to see hard-core.

This brings us to the most famous and probably most important movie in the history of porn, Gerard Damiano's *Deep Throat* (1972). As porn goes, it was above standard. The acting was consistently good, with the exception of Harry Reems as Linda Lovelace's doctor, and the plot itself, though ludicrous, at least supplied the audience with a reason for the constant on-screen humping and sucking.

In brief, the film presents Linda Lovelace as a young, swinging, sexually liberated, very 1970s kind of chick – with a problem. The earth doesn't move. Fireworks don't go off in the sky. The London Symphony Orchestra doesn't burst into music when the train finally enters the tunnel. In short, Linda's sex life is nowhere near as satisfying as she thinks it ought to be. Her roommate suggests various different positions, situations and partners in an attempt to help her reach the level of orgasm that seems so readily available to

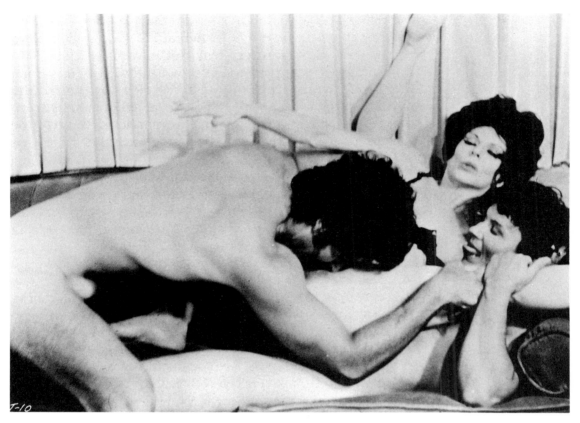

Deep Throat actors hard at work.

everyone else. Eventually, her quest leads her to a specialist doctor, who immediately and correctly diagnoses her problem: her clitoris is in the wrong place. It is at the back of her throat. Doctor prescribes a lengthy blow job, in which Linda not only gets to finally achieve orgasm, but also to demonstrate the famed Deep Throat technique that gave the film its name. She takes the doctor's not inconsiderable penis into her mouth, and presumably throat, right down to its base. 'How far does a girl have to go to untangle her tingle?' asked the posters. 'All the way', was the predictable answer.

Deep Throat wasn't, as is occasionally reported, the first full length hard-core feature film. That credit belongs to Bill Osco's *Mona* (1970), which also made money. But what was noteworthy and important about the film was its audience. *Deep Throat* heralded the beginning of 'porno-chic', a short but telling phase in the history of cinema when it actually became hip and cool and fashionable to watch dirty movies, ideally with your partner, then talk endlessly about them afterwards at dinner parties. This was a huge improvement on the past, when it was merely sad and feeble and pathetic to watch dirty films on your own then sneak home to masturbate before talking endlessly about them at dinner parties.

Deep Throat wasn't just a hit. It was a *cause célèbre*. It became the rallying post for those opposed to censorship and the old hypocrisy that the sub-culture of the Sixties had set out to destroy. Its huge success was, ironically, thanks to those who attempted to ban it. It opened at a cinema in New York, the New World Theater. Inevitably, the film encountered resistance, and attracted considerable litigation. The whole business came to a head with the famous New York trial, towards the end of 1972, where the judge concluded that the film was essentially without merit and therefore should not be publicly shown. He concluded his decision by saying: 'This is one throat that deserves to be cut.' The World Theater was subsequently fined $3 million. Not suprisingly, it appealed the decision, and the ruling was overturned, paving the way for a new wave of hard-core movies to get screened throughout America and making an international impact on what could and what little could not, be shown on screen.

If anything, the legal struggles endured by the film's makers helped to publicise the movie. It became a genuine cultural happening, something that intelligent people felt the need to see in order to be able to talk about it. *Variety* reported on 10 January 1973 that 'Grosses at the World Theater continue in record breaking proportions as a result of the trial coverage, but the real impact is measured not so much by the spinning turnstiles as by the types of folks being introduced to theatrical hard-core fare. A visit to the World on Friday revealed the house fully sold out for a mid-afternoon show and a line outside composed of elegant unaccompanied ladies, young couples, middle aged couples and at least three silver haired matrons with shopping bags.'

Linda Lovelace, the world's first porno star.

An inevitability of such success was the impact it would have on the life of its leading lady. The success of *Deep Throat* with its respectable audience turned Linda Lovelace into the porn industry's first real star, and only household name. She appeared on television and was interviewed on radio. Early stag films starring her were dug up for re-release to cash in on the public's fascination with this wholesome looking but apparently insatiable all-American gal.

Years later, Lovelace produced a book about her life in films. Called *Ordeal*, she alleged that her appearance in these movies was entirely involuntary. Her then husband beat her until she agreed to appear, she claimed. Her films, however, are so convincing that the story is a bit hard to believe. Nevertheless, it does make the movie difficult if not impossible to enjoy, leaving a kind of nasty taste in the mouth. Figuratively.

I recently attempted to watch the movie again. I'd only seen it once, in the mid-Eighties in a sleazy cinema in LA. So on one of my visits to the States I picked up a copy on

Laserdisc from Tower Records. I shipped it home with a box of stuff that I'd been using for work, only to find that even today, some twenty-odd years after it was shown in cinemas all over America, *Deep Throat* is illegal in England. I wrote to Customs asking why it had been seized. This was their answer:

> As you have been made aware, the importation of indecent or obscene material is prohibited by the Customs Consolidation Act 1876. The material you attempted to import has been examined, and the laser disc titled *Deep Throat* was found to contain scenes of troilism, buggery, masturbation, ejaculation, cunnilingus, fellatio and intercourse.

No wonder they didn't want to let me have it back.

The golden age of the hard-core movie industry appeared to have dawned. *Deep Throat* was followed by a number of other hard-core but successful adult hits – *Behind the Green Door*, and *The Devil in Miss Jones* being two of the most popular. But despite their success, and despite the appearance of clean, well run theatres devoted to porn, like the famous O'Farrell Theater in San Francisco (nicknamed 'The Carnegie Hall of Sex' by Hunter S Thompson), hard-core sex movies are no longer distributed and shown at normal cinemas. What happened?

A number of factors contributed to, if not exactly the decline, certainly the re-direction of the dirty film. On the legal front, the United States Supreme Court decided in June 1973 that pornography could no longer be judged nationally. In brief, if a film went to trial and eventually won in, say, New York, it could still encounter litigation and all the associated headaches and legal costs in any of the remaining American states. But after the success of the early porn crossover hits, there was no longer any real benefit to be had from such notoriety. So factor number one is that it became too expensive and too risky to risk a proper release.

Secondly, there was the boredom factor. Audiences watching hard-core for the first or second time were prepared to overlook the bad acting, weak plots and poor technical quality that have always characterised porn movies. But as the old saying goes, 'You've seen one, you've seen them all.' Despite the money to be made in porn, the stigma attached to such projects meant, and continues to mean, that first rate talent was reluctant to get involved. Quite simply, audiences got bored with sex being the only consistent factor in these films. And with the release of *Last Tango in Paris* (1973), it became evident that adult scenes and sexual situations could be presented in a way that was realistic and potentially erotic without resorting to the graphic close-ups that are the mainstay of porn.

The final death knell for hard-core in the cinema was the video. With the development and spread of this incredible invention, it has become possible for people to experience the more stimulating movies in the privacy of their own homes. If the *raison d'être* of explicit sex films is to excite, then you might as well be somewhere you can do something about it. Hard-core as a theatrical alternative might be dead, but it thrives handsomely as home entertainment. In 1990 it was estimated that in the United States the sale and rental of hard-core films accounts for one-third of the video market. It is a billion dollar industry. It has its own stars and even its own annual awards ceremony, held in Las Vegas. (I've always wanted to visit just to see what the speeches are like. I mean, who exactly do you thank when you've just won Best Blow Job? Your mother, your father and your dentist?)

Although hard-core operates right in Hollywood's back-yard, and despite an increasing tendency among mainstream film-makers to either deal openly with sex or rely heavily upon sexual titillation to keep audiences awake, there is hardly any cross-over of ideas or talent from the world of pornographic film-making to Hollywood proper. One or two brave souls have tried. Brian De Palma's admittedly lacklustre *Body Double* was initially to have been Holly-wood's first big budget properly distributed hard-core pornographic thriller. De Palma even offered the lead female role to a porn veteran, Annette Haven, before bowing to pressure from the money men and casting Melanie Griffith in the role. He also decided to change the focus of the film,

BODY DOUBLE

Melanie Griffith trying to act sexy in Brian De Palma's ill-fated *Body Double*.

turning it into a mildly sexy cliffhanger set within the milieu of low-budget movies with only the slightest hint at a porno scene.

In the reverse situation, however, the opposite is true. One of the more amusing trends in modern porn flicks is the lightning speed in which their makers lift ideas and subvert the titles of the latest big hits. A couple of years ago I was staying in the Royalton Hotel in New York with my wife and baby. The hotel offered a VCR in every room and a list of movies that guests could borrow from the concierge, including a fair sampling of the kind of hard-core stuff that would get you arrested at customs in England. That night we intended to stay in, order some room service and maybe catch up on a film. After some debate, we settled on

Regarding Henry, the warmhearted, life affirming Harrison Ford flick. We phoned down; they brought it to the room; we settled down in bed and I pressed play. Next thing you know we're staring at the most unpleasant youngish couple banging away at each other in horrific close-up. Thanks to the quality of the video, the man involved appeared to have been painted orange, and the woman possessed a pair of the most shockingly unrealistic and unwelcomingly solid set of silicone titties I've ever seen. Wise to my rather pathetic schoolboy ways, my wife immediately assumed this was a desperate ploy to interest her in a late night tumble. Only after I ejected the tape and revealed the title did she accept my innocence. We had been lent a copy of *Regarding Heiney* instead.

So convincing and well adapted are some of the titles that it's hard to believe they weren't the first choice for the original movie. Spike Lee has been on the receiving end at least twice. His so-so essay on miscegenation, *Jungle Fever,* has inspired the far more upfront *Jungle Beaver*. More recently, his epic *Malcolm X* has reappeared on porn store shelves as *Malcolm XXX*. Kevin Costner's bland but likeable tribute to the loveable thief *Robin Hood* is currently available as *Throbbin Hood* (starring Little Dong and Friar Suck). Perhaps the least pleasant translation is the Tobe Hooper/Steven Spielberg shocker *Poltergeist* which has returned from the dead in its porn reincarnation as *Poltergash*. *The Terminator* has resurfaced as *The Sperminator*, and who knows what clean cut Michael J Fox would make of the homage paid to his big breakthrough, *Back to the Future* under the new title *Backdoor to the Future*. Occasionally the tribute goes further than just a pun about the title. In *Edward Penishands*, a clever takeoff of Tim Burton's sentimental but pleasing *Edward Scissorhands*, the plot actually sticks pretty close to the original, although instead of shears for hands our hero has a fistful of dildoes on the end of each arm. I could go on and on, and I think I probably will. Look at this lot:

Honey I Blew Up The Kid	*Honey I Blew Everybody*
West Side Story	*Breast Side Story*
The Addams Family	*The Anus Family*
Beetlejuice	*Beetlejism*
Little Shop of Horrors	*Little Shop of Whores*
Chitty Chitty Bang Bang	*Titty Titty Bang Bang*

There's a whole wide world of cinematic enjoyment out there that can only be sampled abroad. Happy hunting!

2 Totally Deranged Movie
The Enema Bandit

Although you hear this kind of expression a lot, usually before lacklustre pictures that turn out to be dull and predictable, this time it's for real. Be warned: this movie *really* isn't for the squeamish!

On the surface it could be any one of hundreds of fairly respectable low-budget detective thrillers. A crime is committed and, through the usual combination of questioning, undercover work and male bonding, the cops finally track down the perpetrator. It's well shot, in a kind of moody, shadowy, Martin Scorcese kind of way. But although it sticks fairly closely to the basic conventions and clichés of the cop film, it has the most degenerate and ludicrous gimmick ever.

It's all in the title, of course. If you advertise a film called *The Enema Bandit* then I guess an audience has the right to see both of those in the picture. And of course they do. The eponymous bandit is well played by an Italian-looking, sweaty, nervous guy. We first see him spying on an attractive neighbour, then the camera follows him out to a New York brothel (all loose hand-held shots à la *Mean Streets*). Despite the best attempts of a very nice young woman working there, the bandit fails to get really interested. On the way out of the establishment, which appears to be a fine, clean, well run place, he chats to the Madam. She's been told that he's not an entirely satisfied customer, and suggests that maybe what he needs is a little variety. Why not check out one of the more specialist items on offer? He follows her to a back room where he is allowed to watch another customer at play.

This is where the movie loses all touch with reality and sanity, pulling the rug right out from under the audience and setting the scene for what is to come.

The customer is dressed as a doctor. One of the prostitutes is playing his nurse. A third working girl is then wheeled in on a chair. According to the nut in the doctor's get-up, she's been a very naughty girl, and the only way to actually cure her of her misbehaviour is to flush it out with a good two-quart enema – which, of course, he then proceeds to administer in graphic close up. No cutting away, no special effects, no body doubles, nothing. Just the kind of sight that real-life nurses presumably have to deal with every day.

While this is going on, the putative bandit is acting, in a distressingly convincing way, as if he's finally seen the light, and that the only thing that's been missing from his lacklustre sex life has been a length of rubber tubing, a hot water bottle and a few pints of soapy water. He runs from the house of ill repute in a state of considerable excitement and stews at home for a couple of days, before creeping out to buy himself a full enema kit. Armed with said kit and a small revolver, he then breaks into and terrorises the poor neighbour that he's been spying on, administering an enema to her entirely against her will. This has got to be not just one of the sickest scenes in any movie I've ever seen, but also one of the most unpleasant. It is suprisingly well acted, although I guess if you were a young woman used to starring in more straightforward porno epics, suddenly having an enema given to you in the middle of a working day would be a big enough shock that you wouldn't actually have to act at all.

Obviously pleased with himself, the enema guy beats a hasty retreat, and the next day the papers are full of his exploits, officially dubbing him 'the Enema Bandit'. Two plain-clothes policemen are assigned to the case. They set out to interview the victim and generally try to piece together what happened and why. Just like in a million other cop films, they joke around with each other, eat doughnuts, drink strong black coffee, drive up and down a lot and win the audience over. These are cops we can trust. If anyone can end the terror of the Enema Bandit, it is them. But not soon enough for a few more victims for our man with the problem. Twin sisters are next, and although they giggle rather a lot and rather unconvincingly (even looking into the camera for much of the time), it doesn't seem to spoil the bandit's fun. More newspaper headlines paint the picture of a city under siege. The cops are receiving more and more pressure from their superiors to catch this villain. Finally, as a last act of desperation, they plant a plain-clothes policewoman, who also happens to be the girlfriend of one of the cops, at a site where they think the bandit looks for his victims.

True to clichéd detective movie form, the bandit turns up and goes for the bait. But as they drive off together, the cops lose sight of them! The bandit takes the woman back to his apartment, and appears to have had second thoughts about his anti-social hobby, when he catches a glimpse of her police badge hidden in her bag. Furious that he might have been rumbled, he decides to give her the deluxe treatment. He ties her up, puts a gag in her mouth, places her in the bath and connects her via a length of tubing to a running tap!

The cops are desperately racing to the scene, thanks to a tracing device placed in her handbag. The director intercuts between the car, racing through traffic, sirens wailing, to the poor woman, gradually filling up with water. Of course, the cops arrive in time, bursting into the apartment and yanking the tube out of her back passage. But sadly, the bandit has escaped. The film ends with a somber, written warning: The bandit is still at large. Where will he strike next? All women are advised to be on their guard.

All my attempts at tracking down information about this picture have led nowhere. Not surprising, I suppose, as not many people would actually admit to even having seen the film, never mind knowing anything about it. I did hear one, probably apocryphal story, though. I was told that the film was made not for the porno market, but as an attempt by a porn director to crash into the mainstream. Enemas were his particular kink, and like most slightly loony warped folk, he assumed that there were thousands, if not millions of people like him out there, just waiting for the opportunity to stand up and publicly exclaim, 'I like flushing people's bowels out with hot water, and I'm damn proud of it.' His thinking went that a serious drama which 'just happened' to have enemas as its central theme would provide his closeted friends with the courage to come out. Hence, the movie. This story continues with the remarkable assertion that the film was actually given a genuine release in a normal New York cinema, but was taken off and forced into the porno palaces after the mayor of New York himself insisted that it was Grade A filth.

Assuming you can get over the initial feeling of queasiness, *The Enema Bandit* is a genuinely hilarious movie. Imagine one of the better episodes of an American TV detective series – Kojak, for example – with a town terrorised by enemas. Even down to the ending, where the cops are normally racing to rescue a woman held at gun or knifepoint, it is faithfully and successfully recreated, only with a far more humiliating threat. Sure, the film is degrading to women. It's also degrading to men, and every idiot like me who sat through it. But it was also, I hate to admit, a lot of fun.

3 Russ Meyer

Go Baby! Go! Go!

> Is there then, no American auteur director? Perhaps there is one. One man who thinks up his own stories, and produces his pictures and directs them too. And also serves as his own cinematographer. Not to mention he does his own editing as well. All of this connected with an intensely personal and unique vision of the world. This man is Russ Meyer.
>
> *Adventures in the ScreenTrade. A personal view*
> *of Hollywood and screenwriting*
> *William Goldman*

I encountered Russ Meyer's films completely by chance. I had visited the Scala Cinema, London's leading repertory theatre, intending to catch Jean-Luc Godard's *Pierrot le Fou*, only to find that I was a day too early. On offer in its place was the double bill of *Faster Pussycat! Kill! Kill!* and *Mondo Topless*. Unlike the many other 'serious' film fans who had hoped to catch sight of Jean Paul Belmondo with his face painted blue, I did not mutter in disgust and turn away. Ladies and Gentlemen, I succumbed, and in so doing I became acquainted with one of the most impressive, original, and sadly neglected directors ever to have pointed a camera and shouted action.

Before we proceed, let me clear up one small niggling misconception about the appeal of Meyer's movies. With the notable exceptions of *The Seven Minutes* and *Blacksnake!*, every Meyer movie features the most preposterously proportioned females ever to grace a strip of celluloid. Without doubt, the inclusion of such remarkable female leads in his movies attracts a certain audience. But to dismiss the entire

27

Meyer *œuvre* as a collection of big-tit shows would be a heinous error.

The bodaciously busty women that populate his mini-epics are not there just to satisfy Meyer's obvious predilection. They serve a very valuable purpose. The outrageous humour and wild comic-strip action and dialogue would fall horribly flat without them. So please, I beg of you, suspend your splendid beliefs that copious nudity is a bad thing, and join me in wallowing in the wonderful world of Russ Meyer's movies.

Russ Meyer has created some 23 movies. Aside from the personal vision of the director, they also serve as a potted history of the development of the soft-core nudie film in American cinema. For Meyer was no Johnny-come-lately band-wagon jumping hack. He was a man with integrity, vision, courage and, of course, a love of mountainous flesh!

In person, Meyer delights in giving the impression of being a cross between General Patton and a pit bull. He has achieved his success, his wealth and lifestyle by doing exactly what he wanted in the way he felt best. The handful of financial failures to his name can almost all be put down to the interference of others. As a result, Meyer is rightly proud of his ability to survive and succeed right in the heart of the jealous, obstructive and fickle film business.

When I visited him in Hollywood for the first time in 1988, I had no idea what to expect. I'd spoken to him briefly on the phone, and I'd spoken at greater length to his lawyer, Lee Blackman, about putting together a documentary on Meyer for Channel 4. It looked impossible. Meyer was almost maniacal in his obsession that he not get ripped off, that his work be presented fairly and that we wouldn't just drive him crazy.

After long and painstaking negotiations, however, it looked as though we were set. His house is way up in the Hollywood hills, just a short journey from the famous sign. Meyer greeted me, a tall, thick set man with silver hair and moustache. After small talk and a couple of beers he showed me round his place. I have never seen anything quite like it. Every inch of space on the walls or the sloping ceilings was

covered with Russ Meyer memorabilia: posters from all over the world, photographs of Meyer with his crews and the stars of his pictures, props that would be as valuable to a Russ Meyer fan as the sledge Rosebud is to fans of Orson Welles. There were the black leather gloves worn by Tura Satana in *Faster Pussycat! Kill! Kill!*; the comical straw boater that was the trademark of Mr Teas in his immoral adventures; and even more curious personal items, like the case that held the contraceptive cap of Meyer's lover, Kitten Natividad, when they visited London in the late 1970s – all displayed on wooden shields just as a hunter would display the heads of his greatest triumphs. There also seemed to be a great number of breast shaped objects – breast shaped cups, pens, sunglasses, hats; everything, in fact, except breast shaped

Russ Meyer and guest at his home in the Hollywood hills. You'd never guess he worked in the film business.

breasts. And the shelves were adorned not just with the vast number of gifts that Meyer has received from friends and fans, but also the many awards he has earned as America's leading independent film-maker.

Russ Meyer was born on 21 March 1922 in Oakland, California. His mother, Lydia, was a registered nurse, his father a policeman. He received his first camera at the age of 14, bought for him by his mother with cash she raised by pawning her engagement ring. It was an 8 mm Univax camera with an F56 lens that cost $9.95. During the Second World War he served in the 166th Signal Photographic Corps. He landed in Normandy with the 29th Division, and his job was to cover the day to day activities of the infantry. Some of the footage shot by Meyer can be seen in the movie *Patton*.

He was discharged on 13 December 1945. Despite his ambitions, Meyer was unable to find work in Hollywood and in 1946 he began work as an industrial film-maker in San Francisco. Later, at the recommendation of an old army buddy, he started to shoot cheesecake style pin-ups for men's magazines, including *Playboy*. One of his more popular subjects, Eve Turner, was to become his first wife, and consequently, the star of his second all-American nudie-cutie film, *Eve and the Handyman* (1960).

The genre of nudie films in the late Fifties fell into two categories. The first were the pseudo documentaries of showmen like Kroger Babb, whom we'll talk about in the exploitation chapter. These films existed ostensibly to deal with contemporary social ills such as teenage pregnancy, incest, prostitution and drug abuse, but in fact they fully and gratuitously exploited these subjects for the benefit of the voracious audiences. Secondly came the rather tame and lame nudist colony pictures, live action versions of *Health and Efficiency* magazine, in which nudists interacted with the occasional burlesque star or stripper. It was always pretty easy to tell them apart – the genuine nudists were the ugly ones with the saggy bum cheeks.

Both types of film left Meyer cold, but eventually he gave in to requests that he make a nudie film, on the condition that it be one that he found exciting to watch, something that featured outstanding bodies and that he himself found genuinely sexy. *The Immoral Mr Teas* (1959), shot for a meagre $24,000 over five days did the trick.

The Mr Teas of the title was played by Bill Teas, one of Meyer's army buddies. The simple plot, in itself an historic first in the history of such films, existed only to make full use of Teas's remarkable gift: the ability to see fully clothed women naked. Throughout the 63 minutes of the movie, he is given many fine opportunities to demonstrate this talent. While going about his daily work as a bicycle messenger delivering false teeth, he encounters a fully bosomed psychiatrist, a voluptuous dental assistant, a bikini-clad (and eventually unadorned) pin-up model, a buxom stenographer, and a woman who lives opposite a melon-laden fruit stall, played by the British 'bra-buster' June Wilkinson. All are revealed in their naked splendour not only to the voyeuristic Teas, but also to the equally passive but titillated audience.

Even in this first, and admittedly crude, example of Meyer's cinematic sensibilities, certain trademark devices are evident. *The Immoral Mr Teas* was essentially a silent film, with voice-over narration, a style that Meyer stuck with for the first part of his career, probably more due to economy than art, and then revived in his later films. The use of voice-over, the humour intended by Teas's profession and the situations that he found himself embroiled in enabled Meyer to poke fun at and lighten the whole reason for the film's existence: lust. For the first time, the soiled raincoat brigade could smile while they added fuel to their fantasies. And fantasies, of course, they were.

The brilliance of Mr Teas was that it both pandered to and commented on the appetite of the new breed of American man, the breed that made *Playboy* magazine and its scores of imitators such a success. Like *Playboy*, *Mr Teas* featured gorgeous women, unavailable in real life to your average Joe, but suddenly all there as fantasy objects. Objects being quite the most accurate term for them. With no dialogue and very little to do other than stand in the buff, the women who starred in Meyer's early films were little more than two dimensional pin-ups come to life.

Another Meyer trademark that can be traced back to *The Immoral Mr Teas* is that his films are without exception beautifully made. The colour is crisp, the sound is clear and, unlike most low budget genre films, Meyer's pictures display inventive camerawork and skilled editing. Most skin-flicks exist only to show the audience the flesh and, where possible, the act. Meyer's films, even the later more simplistic documentary-style features like *Mondo Topless*, are characterised by plentiful shots and interesting angles. Although it is accurate to describe Meyer, as he jokingly does himself, as a 'class pornographer', he is also a class film-maker.

The similarities between *The Immoral Mr Teas* and Meyer's later films were not purely stylistic. The film was banned and prosecuted in San Diego, and Meyer was to provoke similar reactions in other states with many of his films. But despite the reaction in San Diego, *Mr Teas* was an unprecedented success. The film broke box office records almost everywhere it played, and went on to gross over $1.5 million on its investment of $24,000.

Meyer followed *Teas* with a series of pictures that were unabashed imitations of the original winning formula. *Eve and the Handyman* (1960) played in theatres with a ten-minute short, *The Naked Camera,* also directed by Meyer. Next came *Erotica* (1961), *Wild Gals of the Naked West* (1962), *Europe in the Raw* (1963) and *Heavenly Bodies!* (1963). The last was also accompanied by a Meyer short, *Skyscrapers and Brassieres.*

All these were of a far higher quality then the plethora of imitations that were churned out by other film-makers to cash in on the phenomenal success of *Mr Teas.* However, in a saturated market even quality goods had a hard time. As profits began to wane, Meyer took a bold step and added an extra ingredient to his pictures: violence.

Lorna (1964) began what is generally agreed by fans to be the second phase of Meyer's cinematic career. Like the three films that were to follow it, it marked a drastic change from the lightweight features that had established him. To begin

with, it was shot in stark black and white, far more suitable for the bleaker more melodramatic mood of the film. Meyer recalls that money itself was the sole reason for his decision, but it's hard to imagine *Lorna* working anywhere near as well in colour.

A definitive Russ Meyer moment in *Lorna*.

The film starred the bounteous and abundant Lorna Maitland. Filled with lots of action, strong characterization, and strong moralising atop a very simple plot, it was the story of a frustrated wife who sought satisfaction outside her marriage. Her husband, the strong but dumb type, doesn't realize that she might want a little more than the one minute touchdown he throws her once a month. While strolling through the woods, Lorna is raped by an escaped convict. But far from minding, she takes him home where they carry on lovin', until hubby returns. A fight ensues, and

Lorna is inadvertently killed. Oh, and a preacher pops up throughout, warning that the characters are on the road to ruin.

The highly moral ending to this film enabled Meyer to infiltrate a wider market then previously, but even so, *Lorna* was banned in Florida, Pennsylvania and Maryland. Once again, however, Meyer hit paydirt. The film was a huge success and earned him some respectable reviews – one critic dubbing Meyer the 'Tennessee Truffaut'. In fact, more appropriate comparisons would have been Fellini or De Sica, and there's even a bit of Bergman thrown in for good measure when the Grim Reaper puts in a timely appearance.

Meyer followed *Lorna* with *Mudhoney* (1965) also starring Lorna Maitland. Set in Missouri in the 1930s, the posters sold it as, 'A film of ribaldry and violence made from the juice of life!' But *Mudhoney* was even bleaker than *Lorna*, and unlike its predecessor it fared badly at the box office. In retrospect Meyer attributed its commercial failure to its complexity. In place of the simple almost clichéd characterization of *Lorna*, *Mudhoney* featured far less straightforward people. Fittingly, the film is considered by many Meyer fans to be his best work, and although I can't say I agree, rarely a week goes by when I don't think fondly of one particular scene, in which the rustic mute Eula, played by the bodacious Rena Horten, takes an alfresco bath in a tin tub. *Vavoom!*

Motorpsycho (1965) was the next slice of the Meyer psyche targeted to hit and score at drive-in screens. The poster promised 'Bike Riding Hoodlums Flat Out on Their Murder Cycles'. Probably because of budgetary constraints, the hoodlums in *Motorpsycho* were forced to look menacing while cruising around on rather weedy looking mopeds. But really Meyer was looking out for their own interests, as the riding of the more threatening and recognisable Harley-Davidsons did not form part of his cast's limited acting repertoire.

Despite their low horsepower, the gang assembled by Meyer still managed a pretty convincing job of bringing terror, rape and mayhem to a small community. Ultimately, of course, they paid the price for their sordid hi-jinks at the hands of the husband of one of the women they've systematically dispatched during the film's 74 minutes running time. One feature worth noting, in what was essentially one of Meyer's less memorable flicks, was the motivation given to the lead heavy. He was an ex-Vietnam vet who suffered from flashbacks that convinced him he's bumping off Vietcong rather than natives of California. All this some 20-odd years before Oliver Stone began to bore us all rigid with his rambling apologies for the war.

Motorpsycho was really nothing more than an hors d'oeuvre to Meyer's first real masterpiece, the near legendary *Faster Pussycat! Kill! Kill!*, a movie of such deranged perfection that I've singled it out for special notice. Probably the most widely seen and talked about of all of Meyer's films, *Faster Pussycat!* marked the end of his gothic period and the beginning of the faster paced, wilder pictures that were peculiar to him alone. Everything about it was extreme: the plot, the acting, the editing, and, of course, the casting. The show was well and truly stolen by possibly the most *fatale* of all screen *femmes*, Tura Satana, whose menacing sexuality enabled Meyer to create an unforgettable picture.

Like so many other cinematic milestones – Capra's *It's a Wonderful Life*, for example – at the time of its release *Faster Pussycat!* was a box-office disappointment. Driven, as always, by the need to make a buck, Meyer shifted direction again. He moved away from the dark and melodramatic to the colourful and almost contentless. And in that genre he scored a huge smash.

Mondo Topless (1966) capitalised on the topless craze that was sweeping the clubs and bars of the US at the time. The film was little more than a string of topless go-go girls dancing in pleasant outdoor locations. But as always Meyer chose his stars well. The posters proclaimed, 'You've only dreamed about these kind of women. . .'til now.'

Today, Meyer dismisses *Mondo Topless* as mere Bosomania, but fondly recalls that it starred the biggest-busted woman ever to appear in one of his movies, the British Darlene Ercy. Although there's little in it to tickle a cineaste's fancy, the Meyer trademarks of fast paced editing and hilarious voice-over narrative ensure that it stands out from others of its ilk.

The film came along at exactly the right time. It gang-banged them in the drive-ins and made Meyer and his partner/wife, Eve, a lot of money. But despite its huge success, Meyer abandoned the documentary approach and returned to real film-making for his next outing.

How Much Loving Does a Normal Couple Need (1967) was retitled *Common Law Cabin* after local theatre owners complained that the original title wouldn't fit on their marquees. Starring Babette Bardot and Alaina Capri, it was, for the most part, a variation on a familiar theme: sexually frustrated men and women flung together at a rundown and isolated tourist resort, lusting after each other before succumbing to temptation and, inevitably, paying penance. Meyer's strong instinct for exploitation was evident in the promotional material for the film. He released photographs featuring the three stars, Capri, Bardot and Adele Rein, claiming that they shared identical body measurements of 44–24–34. Needless to say, advertisements for the film exploited their abundance, referring to the three women as 'the big six'.

Once again, Meyer collected a healthy box-office profit, but critical appreciation eluded him. Writing in 1986 in the *Guide for the Film Fanatic*, Danny Peary concluded that if Meyer had been a European director and his films been made in a language other than English, then *Common Law Cabin* would probably have been hailed a masterpiece and shown on double bills with Polanski's *Knife in the Water*. I'd love to agree, but in my humble opinion Polanski has never produced a scene as memorable as the fire dance and swan dive performed as a tourist attraction by the boisterously buxom Babette Bardot.

Good Morning . . . And Goodbye (1967) returned to the basics of a situation drama exploiting sexual desires, wants and shortcomings. Even in 1967, Meyer's effort to make an uncompromising drama about the lives and loves of rural folk met with some opposition. The film was confiscated from a theatre in Kentucky, and the projectionist arrested.

But the times, of course, were a changin'. Mainstream films had themselves begun to feature 'adult' topics and the occasional nude scene, and Meyer, the trailblazer, was suddenly running at the head of the pack. With the release of his next picture, *Finders Keepers, Lovers Weepers*, in 1968, he suddenly found one of his pictures getting booked into first-run 'family' cinemas when previously they had been shown only in drive-ins and art houses.

Finders Keepers, Lovers Weepers was one of Meyer's more consistent movies, with the wild sex and visual ideas adding immeasurably to his by now standard schtick of 'lusty-woman-trapped-in-an-unsatisfying-relationship'. This time, the sex hangs around a robbery attempt in a go-go bar and, as ever, adulterers, criminals and all other ne'er-do-wells are suitably punished by the end of the movie. In fact, the film contained more moralizing than normal, and even the sex scenes contained portentous symbolism.

In one memorable clinch, shot in Meyer's own swimming pool between the predictably bountiful Anne Chapman and leading man Gordon Westcourt, Meyer combined close-ups of the pair's submerged bodies slamming together in a sexual frenzy with shots of cars smashing into each other at a demolition derby. In one broad stroke, he managed to hint at the destruction that illicit and casual sex would wreak on their lives, while also undercutting the intensity of the scene and hence avoiding censorship. The film worked well, its stronger plot adding coherence and believability that was lacking in many of Meyer's more basic soft-core pieces.

The Sixties were drawing to an end, and the rules that governed what could and could not be shown in the cinemas of America and the world were changing rapidly. Although it would not be until the early 1970s that 'hard-core' sex films would affect mainstream movies, they had already surfaced in the peep-show booths in red light districts in the bigger cities, notably New York and San Francisco. Meyer was undoubtably aware of their existence, but had always been a film-maker first, a pornographer second, if at all. Despite the relaxation in what would be allowed on screen that was to follow, Meyer would never make a hard-core movie.

Instead, he responded to the popularity of such imported hits as *The Fox* with his most successful picture, *Vixen* (1968). Just as *Faster Pussycat!* showcased the remarkable Tura Satana, so too did *Vixen* feature an extraordinary star. Erica Gavin was not quite as ridiculously pneumatic as Meyer's earlier leading ladies, but she was the perfect choice for *Vixen*, which marked a shift away from the more histrionic mix of sex and violence back toward good old sex and more sex. In fact, out of the entire canon of Meyer's work, *Vixen* is the only film that can really be considered erotic, the only one that actually has the power to sexually excite. In his other pictures, Meyer would undercut the sex with humour or melodrama or violence. With his one genuinely and openly sexy film, he triumphed.

Brotherly and sisterly love Russ Meyer style in *Vixen*. Tom Palmer (Garth Pillsbury) in a clinch with Vixen Palmer (Erica Gavin).

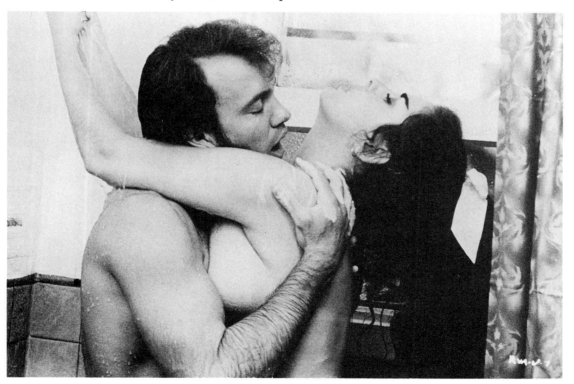

Erica and friend making the most of the weather in *Vixen*.

In place of the accepted morally correct ending in *Vixen*, Meyer attempted to protect himself from charges of obscenity by filling the movie with the correct social values of the day. In *Vixen* he aired his views on his pet hates: racists, communists and draft dodgers. Working with an associate, Jim Ryan, Meyer set out to create 'the sexiest film ever made'. Wishing to shoot somewhere unusual, but as ever keeping an eye on the budget, he decided on Canada. The location gave him the chance to throw a mountie into the mix. As we know, the mountie always gets his man – well, thanks to Meyer, he finally gets his woman as well. As played by Erica Gavin, Vixen is a sexual healer, and she is not mean with her gift. In the course of the 70-minute film she 'heals' several men including her brother, her husband, the mountie, and another woman.

Vixen was the film that made Meyer financially secure. It grossed over $20 million at the box office back in the days when a cinema ticket cost only $1.50. It played for 58 weeks in the city of Chicago, Illinois.

In 1969 Meyer's career was to take a turn that was as unpredictable and unlikely as it was sweet. He was asked to sign a contract with a major studio, 20th Century Fox, to start producing his own kind of films for mainstream audiences. Fox were going through an especially difficult time. They had invested in several big-budget movies that had failed at the box-office, and studio heads were clearly out of touch with what audiences would pay to see. As part of a major shake up, Fox executives looked to the independent sector. One film-maker in particular seemed consistently to deliver huge profits on tiny budgets. Russ Meyer. A deal was struck, one that for Meyer, who had been refused work in Hollywood after the war, was especially good.

Suddenly, he was working with budgets twenty times as large as those he had been used to. Of course, now that he was working within the studio system he would have to abide by Union requirements. But still, to be courted by the mainstream! To have legitimacy as an artist and businessman thrust upon you after years in the wilderness! To have a parking space with your name on it! All of these things, plus the silver Corvette they threw into the bargain, appealed immensely to Meyer.

The first project that he agreed with Fox was to produce a sequel to the successful film version of Jaqueline Susann's trashy novel *The Valley of the Dolls*. Although this might have seemed an unlikely subject for Meyer, die-hard fans need not have worried. In fact, so different was the finished version of the sequel to the original *Valley of the Dolls* that it was forced to carry a disclaimer denying any similarity to Jaqueline Susann's creation.

Beyond the Valley of the Dolls was yet another landmark picture in Meyer's career. In addition to being his first movie for a major studio, it was his first collaboration with the noted American film critic Roger Ebert.

Best known today as co-host of the most popular television movie review show in America, 'At the Movies with Siskel and Ebert', Ebert was at the time a respected film critic for the Chicago *Sun-Times*. More importantly, he had long been a fan of Meyer's work. Working with Ebert on the screenplay for *Beyond the Valley of the Dolls*, Meyer was to discover the style of film-making that he continues to pursue today: mad, overblown, delirious satire – of Hollywood, of modern morality, of turgid soap operas like its prequel, of show-business in general and, of course, of all things American that didn't fit right in with Meyer's peculiar world view.

The combination of Meyer's wild and distinctive cinematic style, and Ebert's more youthful love of cinematic clichés and awareness of what actually was going on in the world resulted in a film which Meyer considers to be his best, and Ebert refers to as a 'camp sexploitation horror musical that ends with a quadruple ritual murder and a triple wedding'.

On paper, the film is in danger of coming across as a mess, with a little bit of everything thrown in for good measure. It centres on the rags to riches story of an all girl band, The Carrie Nations, working their way up the ladder of success and finally making it big in LA. Along the way, there are beach parties, fist fights, attempted suicides, drug-fuelled Hollywood showbiz parties, Nazis in hiding, and mad Svengali agents. The Svengali agent in particular makes

The greatest all girl band that ever existed – The Carrie Nations in *Beyond the Valley of the Dolls*.

a lasting impression. He is Ronnie (Z-Man) Barzell, revealed in a fantastically unpredictable plot twist to be an insane and murderous hermaphrodite who decapitates one of the film's leading men for refusing his advances.

Although each new plot twist and discovery seems so brilliantly unbelievable that you feel it must have been carefully planned, in reality much of what happened was last minute. When I spoke to Roger Ebert, praising the bizarre revelation about Barzell's sexuality, he told me that it wasn't the masterful denouement I had supposed. Rather, the idea about Z-Man Barzell turning out to be either a hermaphrodite or just a plain old woman (I'm still not sure which), only occurred to him and Meyer when the scene was actually being played out. A lot of the picture was added in this way, giving it a wild, free-wheeling spontaneity that most movies, having passed through re-write after re-write, cannot possibly match.

The movie was rescued from being just plain silly or over the top by Meyer's decision to shoot it absolutely straight.

How come I never get invited to parties like this? Fun and games, Russ Meyer style, in *Beyond the Valley of the Dolls*.

The Nazi gets his! Martin Borman meet Z-Man Barzell.

At no time did he tip the wink to the audience that he was sending up what he was superficially portraying. Even the actors didn't appear to know, playing their parts straight down the line. The majority of film critics, accustomed to having their plots and ideas spoon fed, missed the point entirely. Taking it at face value, they wrote it up as the type of overblown badly observed melodrama that it actually subverted, and it received some of the worst reviews of any of Meyer's movies.

But the younger, hipper audience, and reviewers working for less respectable but perhaps more influential journals such as *Rolling Stone*, cottoned on immediately. Word of mouth was rabidly enthusiastic, and the film became a major hit. Ebert says that it could hardly have been more successful than it was, claiming that it grossed about $20 million, which in Nineties terms is like having a $100 million hit on your hands. It was one of the most successful movies of 1968. Meyer had entirely vindicated 20th Century Fox's decision to back a maverick, and had proven that he could, when and where it counted, make movies every bit as big and successful as the studios could.

The possibility of a golden future at Fox, with Meyer cast as the lone genius maverick working from the inside of Hollywood, was ended abruptly with the poor showing of his next epic. It was a strange but understandable choice for a man who had spent much of his professional life fighting the censors. An adaptation of Irving Wallace's book of the same name, *The Seven Minutes* (1971) dealt with the way in which the censorship process works. The lengthy and talky courtroom drama failed, not surprisingly, to appeal to Meyer's normal audience, who had come to expect fast paced satirical comedies featuring well endowed women. It bombed. The critical and commercial failure of *The Seven Minutes* coincided with a change in the top level management at 20th Century Fox. Meyer was out on the street.

Returning to his home territory of low budget independents proved to be slightly harder than anticipated. In a way, Meyer had only himself to blame. Largely as a result of his earlier films and *Beyond the Valley of the Dolls*, most of the major companies were now turning out films which, if not containing out and out soft-core pornography, certainly made an attempt to dabble in it. Breasts would obviously no longer be enough. So, for his return to self-financed pictures, Meyer attempted to cash in on someone else's genre.

Blacksnake (1972) was designed to combine good old fashioned sex and violence with the trend for black action pictures, such as *Shaft* and *Superfly*. In short it was the story of a white plantation owner (Anouska Hempel) who keeps her workers in line with a winning combination of soft sex and her whip. At the beginning of the film, a British agent arrives to find out what has happened to her missing husband. After about an hour and a half of very mild inter-racial sex, torture and intrigue, it's revealed that her husband has been turned into a zombie. It all ends quite happily with the slaves rising up to overcome their oppressors and burning down the plantation, killing nearly everyone inside.

But happy endings do not a hit film make. By the time *Blacksnake* was released, the blaxploitation boom was already on the wane. Like its predecessor, it was a film that could have been made by just about anyone, having very little of Meyer himself in it. As a result, Meyer scored his second flop in a row.

The failure of *Blacksnake* was a blow to Meyer. Growing permissiveness meant that hard-core pictures, those that graphically presented the sexual act, were surfacing and even getting shown by respectable cinema chains. *Deep Throat* and *Behind the Green Door* were both huge hits. Was this to be Meyer's future? The cynical recording of humping and grinding without the merest hint of irony? Never!

Spurred on by the sting of recent failures and by a growing disillusionment for the unsubtle peep-shows that passed for 'adult entertainment', Meyer made a clear and definite decision. He turned his back on 'respectable' film-making and on the whole triple-X industry and concentrated instead on the films he made best: titillating but inoffensive, wildly funny romps with people who resembled pneumatic cartoons in the lead roles. The kind of films that only he could possibly get away with.

After a couple of frustrating years and false starts, Meyer finally got back on top with *SuperVixens* (1975). His fans had nothing to complain about in this film. Everything that Meyer had done in the past he did again, only bigger, faster and better, and, as if to reassure fans that this really was a Meyer movie, for the first time his name appeared above the title: *Russ Meyer's SuperVixens*. Who could resist?

Meyer's characteristic shooting style, (fast paced/breathless editing/strange angles and close-ups) was exaggerated in *SuperVixens*, making it look almost like a parody of a Meyer movie. The plot was convoluted, concerning the sexual adventures of a young man, wrongfully accused of killing a woman and on the run from the crooked cop who actually committed the crime. He finally finds happiness, unknowingly, with the re-incarnation of his dead wife and, in the ultimate triumph of good over evil, witnesses the death of the psychopathic police officer. Along the way he encounters escaped Nazi Martin Bormann, now running a service station, and five women who, even by Meyer's standards, are remarkably proportioned. Shari Eubank (playing the murder victim SuperAngel and playing her again, re-incarnated as SuperVixen), Christy Hartburg, Sharon Kelly, Uschi Digard and Deborah McGuire all contributed to the sense of cartoonish unreality that marked the beginning of the final stage in Meyer's film-making style. Most of these women's bust measurements were up in the '60s! To match their outrageous and over the top physical presence, Meyer found a leading man who not only had the requisite good looks, but could act. Charles Napier, who was later to find semi-stardom as a villain in *Rambo*, played the psychopathic cop with just the right level of insane intensity.

The film roller-coasts along in a delightfully manic and giddy style, but even so there were two or three scenes which

Supervixens – Russ Meyer back on top.

really stood out. In the first, Napier playing Harry Sledge erupts into a remarkably convincing murderous frenzy after being taunted by SuperAngel for his sexual inadequacy. Instead of the usual Meyeresque quick cutting, for this one scene Meyer concentrated on Napier as his rage builds to the point where he smashes down the bathroom door and savagely beats SuperAngel, then hurls her into a bath and electrocutes her with a radio set. The scene sat uncomfortably with the rest of the picture, and, if anything, harked back to Meyer's earlier sex and violence movies, where the melodrama was played straight rather than for laughs. But Napier's chilling performance carried it off.

Another outstanding scene involved the film's hero, the hapless Clint Ramsey (played by Charles Pitts), indulging in his favourite pastime. After the event, the bitch SuperAngel lays into him with her acid tongue, accusing him of everything under the sun, including unfaithfulness. A fight between the two ensues, spilling out of the house, where SuperAngel takes an axe to Clint's pick-up truck. The police are called by a nosey neighbour, and Harry Sledge turns up, to lay into Clint with his nightstick.

The final scene in *SuperVixens* worth blabbing about was, fittingly, the end one. Harry Sledge has Clint Ramsey and the reincarnated SuperAngel, now SuperVixen (and a far nicer person this time around) tied together, spreadeagled on the top of a mountain. Ramming a stick of dynamite between their legs, he strolls off, leaving them to die. As SuperVixen shouts defiantly that he can never destroy their love, the dynamite fizzles out. Completely ignoring the firework code, Sledge goes back to look at the dynamite. Picking it up, he walks back to get a fresh stick, when the fuse sputters back to life. Sledge just has time for a comedy look to camera before he is blown to pieces. In direct homage to the RoadRunner/Coyote cartoons, Meyer then cuts to a nude woman straddling the mountain top shouting, 'Th – Th – Th – That's All Folks!'

Returning to the pure Meyer style paid off. He scored a much needed hit, grossing over $17 million from a budget of about $220,000. Generally speaking, *SuperVixens* was well

Giving them what they want to see.

received critically, the only real flak it attracted was, perhaps justifiably, calling him to task over the brutal murder of SuperAngel.

To counteract such criticism on his next picture, Meyer went all out for laughs, as evidenced in the film's abrupt title, *Up!* (1976). Plotwise, *Up!* both refined and exaggerated the ideas and style of *SuperVixens*. Abundant and sexually voracious women, stereotypically masculine men, always dumb and ever outsmarted by the women, engaged in cartoon violence, comic strip sex and a token Nazi or two. *Up!* was marked by the first appearance of Meyer's star discovery, Kitten Natividad. Kitten not only appeared in all of Meyer's remaining projects, but lived with him for several years, partaking in 'the mutual exchange of wondrous bodily fluids', as a plaque in Meyer's house attests. The plot was so wildly out of control that Kitten's role, that of a kind of nude Greek Chorus of one, was all the more essential to help the audience figure out what the hell was supposed to be going on. She promised a 'cacophony of carnality', but seeing as she spoke in phrases such as 'Pummelling the scrotum with joyous supplication, meting out the vengeance upon the connubial oppressors' – it was still every man for himself.

As far as I can make out, *Up!* followed the investigation into the modern day murder of Adolf Hitler. Meyer wanted to feature his old pal, Martin Bormann, in the film, but the actor who normally played along, allowing Russ to vent his satirical spleen on his old army enemies, refused due to the homosexual elements in the movie. Instead, Meyer cast a Hitler look-a-like whom he called Adolf Shwartz. Shwartz meets his end in a bath tub listening to his favourite German marching tunes as the killer unleashes an especially hungry piranha into the tub.

Up! was probably the only whodunnit in the history of cinema in which it was patently obvious that not even the director really cared about solving the crime. The film overflowed with a legion of insane subplots including a double rape in which the attacker, a super-human lumberjack, was fought off with an axe in his back, sado-masochistic gay sex and a chainsaw murder. In the end it was revealed that Adolf was murdered by none other than his bastard daughter, Eva Braun Jnr.

Even with Meyer's attempts to defuse criticism, the violence, although outrageously over the top and ridiculous, still attracted some negative reviews. The movie was nevertheless a success, and Meyer moved on to a project that would, perhaps, have been the ultimate vehicle for his genius. He was approached by Malcolm McClaren, a big fan of *Beyond the Valley of the Dolls*, and offered the job of bringing the Sex Pistols to the big screen. He collaborated with Roger Ebert on the script and in the summer of 1978, at the height of tabloid fuelled punk mania, flew to London to begin work on *Who Killed Bambi?*

Meyer managed to complete just four days of filming before the project collapsed due to lack of funds. Whether Meyer and the Sex Pistols would have been able to maintain a working relationship for long enough to actually complete a feature film is unlikely. But whatever resulted would have been fascinating. The casting was to have included Marianne Faithfull as Sid Vicious's mum!

Meyer, not used to *not* getting films finished, bounced back in 1979 with *Beneath the Valley of the UltraVixens*. It had one of the most remarkable opening sequences in any of his films. An abundant young woman is taken to an elderly man's house, where she dances seductively in front of him. The twist is that he is lying in a coffin, peeping through two holes cut in a shroud. In a moment that would do Benny Hill proud, he finally attains an erection that lifts the whole sheet up. If anyone was in doubt as to whether or not this was going to be a serious picture, the opening scene soon set them straight.

Like Meyer's earlier films, *Beneath* had a strong moral code. It dealt with a young woman's attempts to steer her husband away from his evil perverse desires for anal sex back toward the true path of good old-fashioned American intercourse. Kitten Natividad played the lead role, but the film was stolen by the remarkable, heavy breasted Ann Marie as local radio evangelist Eufala Roop. Wearing a unique all-in-one crocheted body suit, Ms Roop eventually leads the wayward husband back on the path of righteousness. There was little violence in *Beneath,* and although the plot had similarities with earlier Meyer films, including a return appearance by Martin Bormann (the Nazi from *SuperVixens*), it marked the most extreme and satisfying of his sexual parodies. Meyer himself played a roving cameraman, filming the action and tying up all the loose ends. The loosest end of all, of course, being just how much of what we see on screen is really Russ Meyer.

Beneath was a successful movie for Meyer, but it was also the last film he would release theatrically to date. Instead he has worked almost exclusively on his masterpiece. *The Breast of Russ Meyer*, a film set to run at between six and eight hours in length, and never intended for theatrical release. It mixes moments from his films with new footage of Meyer and some army buddies travelling through Germany, reliving their wartime experiences. Some of the black and white wartime footage shot by a young Russ Meyer is also included, footage shot long before the young man embarked on a career in which his personal sexual preferences and fantasies would turn him into the single most successful and original independent film-maker in the history of cinema.

Roger Ebert told me that he once asked Russ how he would like to be remembered. On his grave, he said, he wants this quote from Charles Keating, the head of the Citizens for Decent Literature:

> More than anyone else in his time, Russ Meyer was responsible for the decay of values in American Society
> Charles Keating

under which Russ wants carved:

> I was glad to do it
> Russ

RUSS MEYER FILMOGRAPHY

THE FRENCH PEEP SHOW (1950)
THE IMMORAL MR. TEAS(1959)
THIS IS MY BODY (1959)
EVE AND THE HANDYMAN
 (1960)
NAKED CAMERA (1960)
EROTICA (1961)
WILD GALS OF THE NAKED WEST
 (1962)
EUROPE IN THE RAW (1963)
HEAVENLY BODIES (1963)
LORNA (1964)
FANNYHILL (1964)
MUDHONEY (1965)
MOTORPSYCHO (1965)
FASTER PUSSYCAT! KILL! KILL!
 (1966)

MONDO TOPLESS (1966)
COMMON LAW CABIN (1967)
GOOD MORNING . . . AND
 GOODBYE (1967)
FINDERS KEEPERS, LOVERS
 WEEPERS (1968)
VIXEN (1968)
CHERRY, HARRY AND RAQUEL
 (1969)
BEYOND THE VALLEY OF THE
 DOLLS (1970)
SEVEN MINUTES (1971)
BLACKSNAKE (1972)
SUPERVIXENS (1975)
UP! (1976)
BENEATH THE VALLEY OF THE
 ULTRAVIXENS (1979)

4 Totally Deranged Movie
Faster Pussycat! Kill! Kill!

If you've already read the chapter on Russ Meyer, you'll know that I'm not exactly an objective critic of his work. I have enormous admiration for his films, and also for the way he has consistently out-performed Hollywood, not just financially, but also by keeping alive a flame of personal, individual movies in these days of cinematic homogeneity. Of his many masterpieces, the film I wish to tell you about now is without doubt my favourite, my Desert Island Choice. Let the house lights dim, settle back, and enjoy.

The screen is black. As the voice-over begins, a white soundtrack striation appears, then multiplies, oscillating in time with the opening speech:

> Ladies and Gentleman, welcome to violence. The word and the act. While violence cloaks itself in a plethora of disguises, its favourite mantle still remains – sex. Violence devours all it touches, its voracious appetite rarely fulfilled. Yet violence doesn't only destroy. It creates and moulds as well. Let's examine closely then this dangerously evil creation, this new breed encased and contained within the supple skin of woman. The softness is there, the unmistakable smell of female. The surface shiny and silken. The body yielding yet wanton. But a word of caution, handle with care and don't drop your guard. This rapacious new breed prowls both alone and in packs. Operating at any level, at any time anywhere and with anybody. Who are they? One might be your secretary, your doctor's receptionist, or a dancer in a go-go club!

As with all of Meyer's mini-masterpieces, *Faster Pussycat!* unfolds at a frenetic pace. The opening montage, for example, cuts rapidly from black to odd-angled shots of three gorgeous go-go dancers doing their thing, to shots of

52

the jukebox playing the title song, to close-ups of eager men watching the girls shimmy, urging them on with cries of 'Go baby! Go! Go! Go baby! Let's go! Harder! Faster!' Cut to a shot of a steering wheel before cutting one final time to the legendary Tura Satana, driving her sports car and laughing maniacally.

The shortest credits ever flash on screen, and we're off. Varla (Tura Satana), Rosie (Haji) and Billie (Lori Williams) are three go-go dancers spending their weekend off driving fast through the desert and looking for things to do. It's quickly established that Varla is the meanest, not to mention butchest, of the bunch, keeping the other two under control with a sneer and the iron will she displays by beating them both at Chicken. (Chicken, of course, being the game in which cars race toward each other head on, the 'chicken' being the first person to realise just how dumb it is and swerve to safety.)

Wearing leather gloves, smoking a slim cigarillo and displaying a Grand Canyonesque amount of cleavage, Varla is

Haji looks on in amazement at the incredible Tura Satana – kill baby, kill!

clearly affronted by the arrival of a clean-cut all-American boy racer and his simpering bikini-clad girlfriend. She taunts and goads him into racing her. She cheats and beats him, but that's still not enough. They fight, and Varla throws in a few keen karate moves before finally locking her knee in his back and pulling – hard. One loud snap later and the plot veers off in a new direction. Now we're looking at the story of a cold-blooded murderess and her two accomplices.

They head off, with the simpering girlfriend unconscious in the front seat of Varla's speedster. They discover a secluded ranch, inhabited by a wheelchair-ridden lecher and his two sons, an academic wimp and an overdeveloped vegetable. The gals get wind of the fact that the old man might have a fortune stashed away somewhere, and decide to hang around to see what they can find. Now the movie really slips into top gear. Billie attempts to seduce the strong but dumb son, while the simperer, having escaped the clutches of the lecherous old man, almost escapes, but is unwittingly brought back to the ranch by the other son. The girls all take alfresco showers, but reveal little. In fact, here's the most shocking thing about the movie: there's no nudity in it at all!

The girls go for lunch at the ranch, and mucho flirting takes place. Varla admits that she likes 'men with big appetites. Only I could never find one to match mine.' To which the old man replies, 'Honey, what you eat seems to settle in the right places.'

After the simperer shouts the truth about Varla's killing ways, the old man breaks down and tells them that his wife died giving birth to the vegetable. ('He was big even then!') After lunch, Varla gets steamy with the bookworm in an attempt to find out more about the hidden loot. The bookworm knows what he's getting into, but can't help himself:

BW: Because you're a beautiful animal. And I'm weak. And I want you. Badly I want you.
VARLA: What's weak about wanting. Everybody wants. That's what makes things run. Your father, he wants revenge. You want me.
BW: And you. What do you want?
VARLA: Everything. Or as much as I can get.

Rosie looks on jealously as Varla looks ready to surrender her ample charms to a mere man, but bookworm's and Varla's coitus is interruptus by the news that the simperer has escaped. Again. They arrive just as the old man is trying to have his way with her aided by the simpleton. They break it up and the bookworm realises how unpleasant the lot of them are and heads off with the girl. After arguing with Billie, Varla throws a knife into her back. The old man and the veggie witness it, and the boy is broken up over Billie's death. Varla, acting more from spite than anything else, runs the old man over, wheelchair and all. From out of the wrecked chair flows the hidden cash. Varla sends Rosie to retrieve the knife that killed Billie. The vegetable, still mourning the death of only decent go-go girl in the bunch, gives Rosie the knife to keep, in her rib cage.

Varla knocks the vegetable down with her car, but up he gets. Varla has him in her sights, and attempts to crush him against a barn. In a superb sequence, his thick musculature holds back her mightily revving motor until it digs itself to a standstill in the desert sand.

The simperer (Susan Bernard) as she appears for most of the film - a simpering wimpette.

Varla doesn't want any loose ends lying around, so she borrows the old man's truck and heads off to dispose of the bookworm and the simperer. She heads them off, but in true movie villain style can't just kill them. She needs to gloat first. 'Your old man's been blasted out of his wheels, and your king size brother's been twisted like a pretzel,' she sneers at the bookworm. 'You're all that's left, lover!'

She's almost finished off the last of her male adversaries, with some more snazzy karate, when the simperer finally finds some pluck, and dispatches Varla with the old man's truck. The End.

On paper, it may seem that there's little to distinguish *Faster Pussycat!* from the handful of other sleazy sex and violence movies aimed at the drive-in audience of the mid-Sixties. But the combination of Meyer's directing and editing style, the extraordinary appearance and performance of Tura Satana and the general amoral tone that hangs over the film have quite rightly earned it a legion of fans. For a team that, on screen at least, made such a great partnership, it's strange that Meyer never worked with Tura Satana again. When I asked him if he regretted the fact he displayed typical candour: 'Dumbest thing I ever did. There was just one girl who could play that role. It was tailor made. She had this monumental figure. She was Oriental and she knew karate.'

In a footnote that will delight fans, I found out from a recent conversation with Meyer that he plans to remake *Faster Pussycat!* toward the end of 1993, working at the same locations and from the exact same shooting script, but in colour and with more remarkably muscled men and outrageously abundant women. The key role of Varla, so memorably performed by Tura Satana, will be more than filled by Meyer's latest discovery, Pandora Peaks. The world waits with bated breath.

5 Forgotten Star
John Holmes

Of all the characters in this book, John Holmes is the saddest. His story probably illustrates the tragedy that can occur when someone gets involved with those vices that we associate most readily with the twentieth century and stardom: easy money, recreational drugs and organised crime.

Many actors achieve fame because they can act. Others because they are handsome or charismatic. Others still have a penchant for comedy, a funny face or voice or quick wit. John Holmes was famous for none of these reasons. John Holmes was famous because of his penis.

As far as I know, John Holmes's penis was never measured in any of the 2,500 or so films in which he appeared. Knowledgeable estimates have it between 11 and 15 inches (when erect, of course). His cock, and his willingness to display it and perform with it under just about any circumstances, were the only remarkable things about him. He was of average looks and intelligence, with a scrawny physique and next to no actual acting ability. But what he lacked as a thespian he more than made up for in sheer size and stamina. His penis really was something.

He achieved his dubious, but legitimate, stardom in the late Sixties and Seventies, appearing initially in the short 'loops' that came out of San Francisco. They were called loops because they were actual loops of film, running for about 10 minutes before beginning again. In the days before video, this enabled sex films to be shown in private booths without needing a separate projectionist for each customer. When you consider the primary, if not only, function of showing porn in private booths, it's easy to see why the presence of a projectionist might be considered a little intrusive.

Loops were always cheaply made and, due to their brevity, had little story-line or plot. Some began with the sexual act already happening, others made a token gesture toward a set up. As the hard-core sex industry grew both in size and confidence, more money was put into longer films, resulting in the appearance of full length pornographic features in the early Seventies.

Holmes's big break came when he met a producer of hard-core features, Bob Chinn. Together they came up with a spoof of the hard-boiled detectives epitomised by Sam Spade, casting Holmes as the 'comically' named Private Dick, Johnny Wadd, in movies including *China Cat, Liquid Lips* and *Blonde Fire*. Like the majority of even the more expensively produced porno movies, they were crudely and cheaply made, but they owed their huge success to the huge Holmes. After the Johnny Wadd series, Holmes went on to make somewhere in the region of 2,000 full length features, including some gay films, a 3-D thriller and the film of his life story, *Exhausted* (1981).

In an interview given by his first wife, Sharon Gebeninni, to Mike Sager of *Rolling Stone* magazine (15 June 1989), she said that Holmes decided to make porn his life's work because 'he wanted to be the best in the world at something, and he thought that pornography was it.' Indeed, for a few years, it was.

Pornography, partly because of its popularity, but largely because it hovers on the fringes of legality, has always attracted a criminal element. In America, those in the industry to whom I've spoken claim that it is largely run these days by organised crime. Mobs own the shops, run the magazines, make the movies. They also supply drugs to those working in the films, either as a bonus or occasionally in payment for work done. That's not to imply that everyone involved in pornographic films uses drugs or breaks the law in any way. It just seems that a fair proportion do.

John Holmes was no different. Cocaine was his drug of choice, and he would ingest it via the method known as freebasing. Using the drug in this way is incredibly costly, and Holmes readily involved himself in other clandestine activities over and above his 'acting' to meet these costs. Hiring himself out as a stud to the sexually adventurous and curious who had seen his movies was one way of earning extra cash. Working as a courier for the mob was another.

As the drugs became a bigger part of his life, he found that they affected his sexual performance in films. He gradually spent less time making movies and more time talking about them while robbing people to fund his habit. By the early Eighties, he had all but given up appearing in films. His life revolved around cocaine. Hanging out with a group of like minded individuals at a place called Wonderland Avenue in Los Angeles, Holmes helped mastermind an armed robbery. Using information volunteered by Holmes, a group broke into the home of another big drug user, Eddy Nash. They were successful, but Nash later 'persuaded' Holmes to lead him to the thieves. All three were beaten to death by Nash's men. Holmes was tried for the murder along with Nash, but got off. Nash was eventually found guilty eight years later.

Holmes served about a year in jail for burglary offences and then returned to porn movies on his release. Thanks to the notoriety brought about by the court case, he was now more of a novelty turn than a star performer. The fame and attention he had once received, back when hard-core was hip and fresh and new, had disappeared. He dabbled with drugs for a while before finally giving up. He lived with the porn star Misty Dawn (probably not her real name), and was diagnosed HIV positive in 1985. Despite the virus, he continued making movies, his last being *The Rise and Fall of the Roman Empress* (1987), co-starring the famous Italian hard-core star and one-time member of parliament, Illona Stalla, La Cicciolina. He died on 13 March 1983, aged 39. His last wish was that his wife check his body was in one piece before it was cremated. He didn't want part of himself, the part that he had exploited and sold to the highest bidder while he was alive, to wind up pickled in a jar as a curio for someone's sick entertainment.

Part Two

Exploitation

6 The History of Exploitation Films

'Exploitation films', is one of those expressions that's bandied around willy nilly, and seems to mean an awful lot of different things to different people. Some use it as a catch-all, to describe any film that is out of the ordinary, that deals with subjects and themes rarely found in mainstream pictures. Others prefer that it be used only to describe a certain type of film that contains an obvious cheap thrill, be it sex and nudity, violence or some other real life aberration – physical or sexual. I'm going to settle for a combination of the two. I believe exploitation films to be those that try to grab an audience by offering something unavailable elsewhere – films that pander to our baser instincts, pique our curiosity, salaciously sell us the seamier side of life, but do so knowingly and for just one reason: to make money. This chapter is about sex, drugs and freaks, by far the most interesting subjects exploited by film-makers.

Sex in all its varied and bewildering manifestations has always been an ideal subject for the exploitation film-maker. Although there was little in the way of enforced and consistent censorship until the introduction of the Hayes Code in 1930, local legislation and pressure applied on cinema-owners by local groups kept the graphic depiction of the sexual act off cinema screens until the 1970s. But sex as a titillating feature has always been available if you know where to look.

Even from the very early days of film-making, directors and producers knew that to avoid prosecution and therefore reach an audience, they had to avoid charges of titillation for its own sake, of appealing *solely* to the prurient interest. To that end, films that played out salacious stories would always adopt a very high moral stance. A host of movies, from the beginning of the century right up until the 1960s, all took the position that the subject of the movie, be it illicit sex, drug abuse, violence – you know, all the fun things – posed a very real and very dangerous threat to all moral individuals and society as a whole. It was the duty of the film-makers, as responsible educators and honest men, to use this great tool, cinema, to educate mankind to the evil that lurked all around. That was the kind of jazz promoters talked when they needed to get a hot little number like *Traffic In Souls*, a 1913 melodrama about beautiful young white girls abducted and forced into a life of unimaginable but damn exciting torment and slavery. Such was its success that the film spawned a slew of imitations; *The White Slave Trade*, *Chinaslaver* and even the outrageous *Trapped By Mormons* followed hot on its heels, although the Mormon Church swiftly took action and prevented the last one from reaching too wide an audience.

Other 'taboo' subjects were soon given the same treatment. Abortion, single motherhood, contraception, all appeared in unassailably correct dramas, intended, claimed their creators, to alert all and sundry to the evils that abound, and never (How dare you, Sir?) to provide cheap thrills. In this respect they were typical of almost all the early exploitation pictures. The audiences, of course, lapped them up. They were shocking enough to appeal, but unlike their more openly salacious and less publicly viewed counterparts, they did not offer open or graphic displays of sex itself. And providing that they all had a few moments of moralising in the last reel, they mostly avoided the wrath of local censors.

From the very beginning, Hollywood was almost as reliable a source of titillating fun as the independents, with a series of what were known as 'Jazz age' movies satisfying the more basic needs of movie-goers. One of the earliest masters of these was none other than Cecil B De Mille. In 1918 he released *Old Wives For New*, a film which sparked a whole wave of films dwelling on the hedonistic lifestyles of that era's young things. Proving immensely popular, he followed it with, amongst others, *Don't Change Your Husband* (1919), *Male And Female* (1919), and *Why Change Your Wife* (1920). But critics were quick to denounce the salacious content of these movies, so De Mille wisely changed tack, and began producing tales that were just as saucy, but came from a source so morally impeccable that no one dare say a word. That source was the Bible and with *The Ten Commandments* he outdistanced his imitators royally.

Essentially, the formula remained the same. Lashings of sin throughout but always with a good, moral Christian ending. So long as Christian ethics won out, it seemed that just about anything could be put on screen. De Mille was to remake *The Ten Commandments* in 1956, but his original 1923 version is far stronger. It contrasted the biblical story with a modern version, revealing what would happen when the same set of rules were disobeyed today (today being 1923 of course).

Although De Mille had cleverly side-stepped the issue of titillation for the 'wrong' reason – i.e. to entertain – by replacing it with titillation for the 'right' reason – i.e. to bring God's word to the masses – others had not been quite as smart or cautious. More and more groups were being formed across America to resist the spread of sex and violence in the movies. They did not go unheeded.

In 1922, bowing to pressure from these religious and concerned groups, the heads of the various studios set up a watchdog organisation, the Motion Picture Producers and Distributors of America, Inc. Ultimately, its introduction was not due to the general standard of morality on display *in* the movies, but rather to the general lack of it on display in the 'private' lives of movie stars off screen. Murders, narcotic related crimes and deaths, wild parties and their aftermath (such as the infamous Fatty Arbuckle 'did-he-or-didn't-he rape young starlet Virginia Rappe with a Coke bottle' court case), all added to the growing feeling that the people behind the movies were debauched crazed sex maniacs. Surely it would only be a matter of time before their values infused their on-screen appearances. What hope the youth of America then? (For the answer, take a good look at the youth of America now.)

Needless to say, the only reason those in power in Hollywood felt the need to regulate their excesses was the fear that if they did nothing, it was surely only a matter of time before the government bowed to the various powerful pressure groups, (the Mormons, the Catholics, the Baptists, various teacher and parents organisations, all of the usual guilty parties), and did it for them. By setting up a body themselves, they would be able to keep a far more useful degree of control.

And so the Hayes Code trundled into being. Henceforth, Hollywood proudly proclaimed to the world, movies will educate, not corrupt. They will enlighten, not degrade. They will, a more cynical observer might have added, bore, not entertain.

Directors wishing to add a little extra spice to their picture had to tiptoe around the prohibitive guidelines of the Code, introduced in 1930, and put properly into effect in 1934. Specific guidelines included: 'Pictures shall not infer that low forms of sex relationships are the accepted or common thing.' 'Scenes of passion should not be introduced when not essential to the plot. Seduction or rape should never be more than suggested.' 'Children's sex organs are not to be exposed.' 'White slavery is not to be treated.' And, 'Sex hygiene and venereal diseases are not suitable subjects for motion pictures'. Hear, hear.

In actual fact, because the Hayes Office was not a governmental agency, its powers were greatly limited. Essentially its effects were felt only by those working for the studios, companies that wanted their movies properly and easily distributed and exhibited in the larger theatre chains. For those who wanted to make a quick buck (the vast majority), or for the handful who genuinely wished to express themselves a little more honestly or openly than was allowed, the options were simple.

Produce the movies yourself. Distribute them the same way. If you can't find a cinema that will show the film, put up a tent, or take it to the local burlesque hall. Local papers won't take your advertising? Stage an event. Some of the smaller operators who had probably financed, produced and directed their film would also travel the country with it, showing the movie anywhere and anyhow they could.

Such 'roadshow operators', as they were known, were common, sometimes working together, sometimes in open competition, but they were all trying to sell something on film that couldn't be got elsewhere – sex. The most consistent group of independent producers became known as 'The Forty Thieves', and with good reason. Not only were they all shrewd businessmen, they were also con-artists of the highest order. Rarely did they deliver on screen what they promised with their advertising copy. Many of the films they distributed were produced by them with their very specific audience in mind. Many more were brought in from abroad, hacked around until they just about fit whatever the new title was, and if the public were dissatisfied, tough. They could still be suckered in to see next week's movie if the title and poster were lurid enough.

For example, a movie called *Sex Madness* would, you might think, at least show a little of the sex promised in the title. But apart from a few coy party scenes and a quick flash of bur- lesque, it essentially offered a melodramatic diatribe against the evils of syphilis and quack doctors. A trip around a syphilis ward was the highlight of the film, where the insid- ious effects of the disease upon the gentle female form were shown to a young show girl, diagnosed with a dose.

To be fair, while most of the roadshow films were of very poor quality, they normally delivered on the most basic level. But promising more than you actually delivered was not without its risks. Roadshow operators were used to dealing with disgruntled punters who, after having accepted the promises made by posters and flysheets, were somewhat peeved to find themselves sitting through a dull lecture on film. To compensate and prevent riots, a straightforward reel of naturists frolicking and playing the obligatory volleyball would be tacked onto the end of another, totally unconnected film to satisfy a flesh-hungry audience. This became known as the 'square up' reel, which would be shown if the opera- tors were sure there were no local police around, to 'square things up' with the audience.

Forgotten movies from this era still make entertaining viewing today, but for entirely different reasons. My favourites include *Tomorrow's Children* (1934), a stunningly hammy piece of work concerning the subject of 'forced sterilization'. It was produced by Bryan Foy who had been one of the 'Seven Little Foys' and went on to produce another classic roadshow attraction, *High School Girl* (1935). His parents must have been very proud.

Another goody is *Honky Tonk Girl* (1937), the story of a hitchhiking ring of prostitutes, matched only by *Mad Youth* (1939) for sheer insanity. For those with more specific tastes there are a handful of real oddities, such as *Lash of the Penitents* (1937) – allegedly based on a true story in which a newspaper reporter stumbled onto a strange cult that worshipped torture and pain. Another unmissable and quite amazing film is *Child Bride* (1941), in which a school teacher tries to start a movement against the practices of ugly old Southern hillbillies taking young (teen and pre-teen!) brides. It was a movie of such ludicrous campness that it managed to avoid being outright distasteful, despite having such unpleasant scenes as an elderly farmer leering as a potential child bride goes skinny dipping. It also had the best fight scene between two hillbillies and a midget that I've ever seen, but that's by the by.

Gradually, the public attitude toward such cinematic fare began to shift. Post-war America and Britain enjoyed greater affluence than before, and society was changing accordingly. A good example of the public's increasing tolerance for more gratuitous titillation was *The Outlaw*. When first released in the early 1940s it had been trimmed so as to avoid local censorship. Consequently, Jane Russell flopped in her first outing. But when re-released intact in 1950, it became a major hit. A more important landmark was the release in 1952 of Otto Preminger's *The Moon is Blue*. It contravened the Hayes Code by allowing words like 'virgin', 'seduction' and 'mistress' to remain in, but the studio released it even without approval of the Hayes Office. They billed it 'Adults Only', which presumably helped to turn a rather tedious picture into the hit it was.

Film-makers and exhibitors were responding to the demands of their audience with ever more revealing pictures. First up came the burlesque movies, filmed performances by some of the biggest burlesque stars of the day; Lilli St Cyr, Blaze Starr and Tempest Storm all enjoyed their short burst of celluloid glory, and didn't have to pay the piper at the end! These films were sold as tributes to all-American beauty and grace, innocent but lovely performers. Many of them also included routines by the crude comics who would play the same clubs as the girls and keep the audience from dozing off in between acts. One such film, *Strip-O-Rama*, even went so far as to introduce itself as 'a hilarious story that un-blushingly answers the prude that says gorgeous girls aren't good enough for him. A shameless revelation of the shamming prigs who say they're shocked by legs, laughs and a lavish display of lovelies. You'll see them all, and we mean *all* of them, in *Strip-O-Rama*!'

The success of the burlesque film paved the way for a second development in sexploitation, nudity presented as serious documentary. Films claiming to reveal the honest wonder and joy of naturism had been around since the early Thirties, but in the Fifties they re-appeared as a fully fledged craze. Semi-dramatised accounts of what goes on behind nudist camp walls became the rage.

A classic nudist shot, correctly judged to be devoid of erotic content.

For a while people just couldn't get enough of watching partially undressed folks play volleyball, shuffleboard and run around a lot. Films with titles as diverse as *Nature In The Raw*, *Naked As Nature Intended*, *This Nude World* and *Garden of Eden* all packed them in, despite being some of the least sexy movies ever made. In fact, the lack of any real sex in the nudist camp films is the reason for their survival and proliferation. They were ruled to be devoid of erotic content after a lengthy legal case in New York in 1957, and it was therefore far easier for distributors to persuade the cautious theatre-owners that they could get away with showing a little skin.

Among the more interesting of what is a consistently boring genre were those films produced by one of the few female directors to work in this part of the biz, Doris Wishman. Wishman has directed just about every type of exploitation picture, beginning with the nudies, dabbling with violent sexy thrillers, gratuitously cashing in on topical stories about sex-changes and capitalising on the almost freakish proportions of her most famous star – Chesty Morgan.

Now in her late sixties, Wishman is a petite, silver-haired lady, rather shy and certainly modest about her extraordinary career. She jumped on the sexploitation bandwagon in the early Sixties, riding in the wake of Russ Meyer's groundbreaking *The Immoral Mr Teas*. Wishman started with fairly straightforward stories, in films like *Gentlemen Prefer Nature Girls*, *Diary of a Nudist*, *Nature Camp Confidential*, and *Blaze Starr Goes Nudist*. Although they all look tame today, these films, in which an 'innocent' would normally get seduced into the totally wholesome joys of nudism, were considered hot stuff back in the early 1960s. 'The incomparable marvel of the female form at play, and at rest' was considered a big enough attraction to hang many a film around.

As the initial novelty of naked people playing volleyball wore off, Doris looked to spice her films up with imaginative and highly creative concepts. My favourite is *Nude on the Moon*, in which two scientists land on the lunar surface to discover that it looks remarkably like a nudist camp in Florida, and the aliens are not just humanoid, but naked – a strange race of beautiful moon-dolls!

*Diary of a Nudist -
one of Doris
Wishman's less
sleazy moments.*

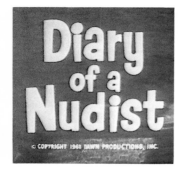

When talking about the cinematic style of low budget film-makers, what you see on screen, and the way in which it got there, is, more often than not, determined by budget and not because of some personal vision. Wishman was no exception, and one of the most endearing characteristics of her movies was the way in which she shot dialogue. To save cash, most of her films were shot mute, with no sound recorded. To avoid costly lip-synching later on, she would always shoot the back of the head of the person speaking, or concentrate on close-ups of the person listening or even unrelated things, like feet, hands, even ornaments! It's almost as if Wishman wasn't quite sure what she wanted to have her characters saying, so she let the camera wander, looking for inspiration.

The growing popularity of television and the threat it posed to the cinema as the primary form of entertainment spurred film-makers and exhibitors into new territories. Television offered the sanitised view of life that had previously been served up at the pictures, so in an attempt to win back audiences, mainstream Hollywood gradually began to ignore the more prohibitive guidelines of the Hayes Code, which inevitably had a knock-on effect on those who had previously staked a claim to that market.

If cinema audiences of the early Sixties were to be treated to their first wide-screen naked breast in *The Pawnbroker* (1964), then drive-in crowds would require something a little spicier. What was at stake was the whole existence of the low-budget sector. Unable to compete with star names, exotic locations and lush soundtracks, the mavericks working on the fringe had succeeded by daring to show what the establishment could not – sex. Now the indies had to find new gimmicks. Imported European movies, early Bergman, for example (*Summer With Monika* was re-titled *Monika, the Story of a Bad Girl!*) and Roger Vadim's love letters to Bardot, notably *And God Created Woman* – exposed American and British audiences to a more realistic and honest sexuality. To keep one step ahead, Russ Meyer introduced a little rough stuff into his low budget films. *Lorna* (1964) showed unbridled lust overflowing into violence. Others moved away from sex altogether. The far less talented but equally shrewd Herschell Gordon Lewis working with his partner, Dave Friedman, created a whole new genre, the gore film. In *Blood Feast* (1963) they took a Playboy bunny and showed her having her tongue ripped out by a madman.

Like most other directors in her field, Doris Wishman also followed the trend towards mixing sex and violence. *Another Day, Another Man, Too Much Too Often, A Taste of Flesh* and *Bad Girls Go To Hell* all came courtesy of the prolific Wishman during the mid-Sixties. But rather than follow the gradual drift toward the excessive violence that Herschell Gordon Lewis had exploited, or the ever more graphic depiction of sex, Wishman found fresh themes to exploit. She really came into her own with a couple of movies cashing in on the perennial interest in sex-changes. The first was a work of complete fiction, but the second was one of the greatest single exploitation pictures, in the purest sense of the word, ever made.

The Amazing Transplant featured a young man called Arthur who both admired and envied his friend Felix's success with the opposite sex. Despite what you might expect, his envy doesn't disappear when he discovers that Felix is dying. Instead Arthur approaches a doctor with a crazy plan: he wants the doctor to graft Felix's overactive penis onto his body, hoping that it will boost his own flagging sex life.

The amazing transplant operation is a big success; in fact it is too successful, with Arthur turning into a sex maniac, embarking on a spree of rapes to satisfy his unnatural, uncontrollable needs. Arthur finally commits a murder, killing his ex-girlfriend when she discovers what he has become. In the end, Arthur turns himself over to the authorities, leaving the audience to imagine what his eventual fate will be.

Let Me Die a Woman was by far the strangest and cruellest film that Wishman ever made. It starts with footage of a young, dark-haired woman getting up and out of bed in the morning. As she strips out of her négligé, revealing her breasts, and into her morning robe, we hear her voice over the picture: 'When I wake up in the morning I'm always a little surprised. This is my life and I'm happy. I used to wear baggy suits, shirts that were concealing. Now I wear things that flatter me, that go with my colouring. I am lonely, yet I feel wonderful, because I'm a woman now.' She now turns to face the camera and says, 'Last year, I was a man.'

Wishman had been looking for some kind of gimmick that would give her film an edge, a selling point that would overcome its low budget and hence poor production values. A chance conversation with an old friend who had began working with transsexuals put her in touch with a Dr Leo Waldman. Together they made a deal that would allow Wishman to film not just the counselling sessions and the doctor talking about his work and explaining the processes used, but to actually film a sex-change operation taking place. It has to be the most gruesome footage ever put into a theatrically exhibited film, and certainly the most extreme gimmick ever used by any exploitation film-maker. Every step, every incision, every horrible, personal moment was captured on film and offered up for the audience to gawp at. Now *that's* exploitation.

The most famous films ever to bear the Wishman name would be the two she made starring Chesty Morgan. They were both hilarious but bizarre, designed solely to capitalise

In the Presence of Greatness 1. Doris Wishman and me.

on Chesty's only assets, her alarming 73-inch bosom. Chesty used her bust to suffocate the men who killed her husband. In *Double Agent 73*, she played a spy with a camera implanted into her bosom, activated by pointing and then squeezing the breast.

During the late Sixties and Seventies, the distinction between the low-budget entrepreneurs, blazing the trail of permissiveness in search of a slice of the action, and the mainstream studios began to fade and disappear. No longer held back by the code of their own creation, the studios started making films dealing with previously taboo subjects, including homosexuality, prostitution and even our old friend the sex-change. For a short time, it looked as though hard-core itself might actually become mainstream. The permissive society was about as open as it was going to get, and the swinging Sixties had swung right on into the Seventies.

The final blow to censorship in the cinema as it had stood until then came when a genuine pornographic film, *Deep Throat*, was not only released and distributed like a mainstream one, but became a success with the otherwise straight, middle-class cinema audiences. For the first time, an explicit sex film, both about and featuring its subject graphically, broke out of the predominantly male, seedy ghetto that such films had previously occupied. Why this particular film managed the extraordinary feat of going mainstream is anyone's guess. Theories abound. One is that it was a simple case of right time, right place (it originally took off in the most liberal city in the States, San Francisco and then word of mouth sold it elsewhere). Others point to the film's humour, or to the obvious and quite heartening pleasure that Ms Lovelace appeared to take from her work. Others still maintain that it was the combination of an honest, open approach, an attractive cast and an amusing if implausible story line. Whatever the reason, *Deep Throat* inspired a host of other porno hits, most importantly *Behind the Green Door* and *The Devil in Miss Jones*. However, the novelty of hard-core pornography was short-lived, and hard-core has now found its rightful and lucrative home with the home video market.

Essentially, the new permissiveness meant the end for those who made sexploitation flics. Some accepted the rise of hard-core and jumped on that bandwagon, one or two survived because their films were more than just crass skinflicks. For a while, certain gimmicks looked as though they might save soft-core sex films from extinction. 3-D in particular looked promising with the success of *The Stewardesses* (1972), *Secrets of Ecstasy '72* and *The Groove Room* (1973), but it too faded from the scene.

Occasional low-budget soft-core hits still emerged. The *Emmanuelle* series in the Seventies for example. Another noble stand-out was *The First Nudie Musical* (1976). Although nowhere near as funny as it would like to think it was, it did have one or two memorable scenes, most notably the big Busby Berkeley style dance number, The Dancing Dildos.

It's safe to say that with the proliferation of sex in just about every movie, soft-core sex as a selling point in and of itself is dead. Take, for example, *Last Tango in Paris* (1972), in which the spectacle of one of America's greatest screen actors simulating anal sex with a busty young French starlet was

Maria Schneider warming up for that infamous butter scene.

enough to turn an otherwise dreary and lacklustre piece of work into one of the most talked about films of its decade. It was also enough to prove that the explicit, graphic shots which had always been the main appeal of hard-core pornography, were not necessary. An adult movie could be erotic and still be considered shocking by simulating sex. The advantages were enormous. Not only could one get actors and actresses of note and genuine talent to appear in the films, but it was possible to avoid much of the expense and stigma attracted by pictures which went past accepted standards and more often than not wound up in court.

In sum, after years of struggle, sex is no longer only to be found in exploitation films, but is a consistent and successful part of our regular cinematic diet. Although it reached a high point with the spread of hard-core into the market, there seems to be more of it on offer in just about every type of film today than ever before. Yesterday's sexploitation is today's mainstream!

If sex is now commonplace, a second type of exploitation film has survived in a totally different way, adjusting to fit our changing perception of the subject matter: drugs. Just as Doris Wishman rather neatly encapsulates the sexploitation film-maker of the Sixties and Seventies, so too does a remarkable man with the equally remarkable name, Kroger Babb, best exemplify the earliest drug exploitation films.

Kroger Babb was one of the very first pioneers. A show-man in the original sense of the word, he was a member of the lost confederation of individuals who worked, at times together, at others in direct competition, in selling the same kind of movies to a sensation hungry public – 'The Forty Thieves'. No detailed history of the man or his films appears anywhere. The most comprehensive attempt at telling his tale appears in the autobiography of David Friedman (*A Youth in Babylon*), one of Babb's many protégés. Friedman, whose own contribution to the sleazier end of the market appears in the section on Herschell Gordon Lewis, described Babb as, 'A combination of flim flam man, P T Barnum and W C Fields.'

Babb's career began when he met up with a couple of car-nival types called Cox and Underwood. They were already travelling the country with a copy of *High School Girl* (1935), by all accounts a fairly staid little pot-boiler. However, Cox and Underwood had spiced up the joint by adding a couple of reels: one showed explicit footage of a woman giving birth, the other being a reel warning against casual sex by showing the various venereal diseases in grotesque close-up to reinforce the point. Both were there for purely educational reasons, of course.

Babb joined forces with Cox and Underwood as their main promotions man, thinking up ever more outrageous scams to get an audience and then fleece them once they were there. His two greatest innovations were the segregated show and the after-film pamphlet.

Babb's segregated shows had nothing to do with those low-budget films starring all-black casts that were made cheaply in Hollywood to show at the theatres segregated by race in the South. His was motivated purely by profit and segregated in an entirely different way. Babb would take a movie like, say, *High School Girl*, and re-title it. *Dust to Dust*, for example. The film would receive three segregated showings: a 2.00 p.m. matinee for women and teenage girls, a second showing at 7.00 p.m. also for women only, and a final late night screening at 9.00 p.m. exclusively for the men of the town. Although all three groups were admitted to the same film, somehow or other word would always get round that the 'men-only' session was the real McCoy, uncensored hot stuff worth queuing round the block for. Which is exactly what they did.

After the showing, a presumably happy but not quite sated crowd made for an easy sales pitch, that was where the after-film pamphlets came in. Babb made sure that there was always a related publication available that could be purchased for 50 cents or a dollar and taken home so that the audience could continue to improve their morals and stave off unnatural cravings long after the last prurient scene had faded from their memory. These books were pitched by a phoney but impressive sounding lecturer who would make an 'exclusive public appearance' with the movie. For example, *Mom and Dad*, a sexploitation flick billed as the ultimate 'birth of a baby' film, was attended by 'the Eminent Hygiene Commentator' Elliot Forbes. His appearance would be heralded in all advertisements for the movie, once again promising more than was actually delivered.

Kroger Babb made his money by capitalising on forbidden, taboo subjects that the mainstream studios were unable to exploit. He had a few doozies, such as *Prince of Peace*, a filmed version of the Passion play, after which Babb would try to sell a four-colour litho of 'Christ the Saviour' and miniature Bibles, and *The Secrets of Beauty*, selling a book and make-up kit right after the show. Obviously these subjects didn't tickle the audiences fancy as much as easy sex or drugs.

The most famous of all the drug movies with which Babb was involved was *Reefer Madness*. Originally sold as a

Reefer Madness – formerly Tell Your Children: don't worry, I will.

warning against the evils of narcotics, the film became very popular with a totally different audience and for totally different reasons in the 1970s. Although it roundly condemned both those who smoked and, especially, those who dealt in the narcotic, it almost played like a beginner's guide on how to get into the business, showing tricks of the smugglers' trade, how the weed is grown, prepared and smoked. The film showed how high school students would be offered their first 'reefers' free, until they were hooked and would pay. Some of them paid in more ways than one, like young Bill, framed for the murder of his girlfriend, Mary – actually killed by an evil pusher.

Babb's Roadshow Attractions Company was also behind the 1937 release of *Marijuana: Assassin of Youth*. In many respects it was similar to *Reefer Madness*, but slightly more saucy. One scene showed a group of giggling, chubby flappers slip their panties off before running into the sea for a session of dope induced skinny dipping. Hardly a warning against drug use, I would have thought.

With the introduction of the Marijuana Tax Stamp Act in 1937, marijuana use and consequently films about marijuana use were stamped out – at least as far as the general public was concerned. Babb went back to touring the country with sexploitation potboilers like *Mom and Dad*. But when marijuana hit the news again, he was right there.

He secured the services of a young unknown starlet called Lila Leeds, who had been partaking of the stuff with Robert Mitchum when Mitchum was arrested for smoking dope in 1948. With no other work available to her on her release, she agreed to star in Babb's loose dramatisation of her life. *Wild Weed* was the result, later renamed *She Shoulda Said No*. The movie established its impeccable aims with a caption that read:

> This is the story of 'tea' or 'tomatoes' . . . the kind millions through ignorance, have been induced to smoke. We are proud to bring to the screen this timely, new film about marijuana. It enables all to see, hear and learn the truths. If its presentation saves but one young girl or boy from becoming a 'dope fiend' . . . then its story has been well told.

Another great moment in *Reefer Madness* - a warning against and a beginner's guide in one easy package.

The movie is set in LA, and the man in charge of seeking out marijuana and its suppliers is Captain Hayes, who relates with disgust how pushers will sell the evil weed to anyone, even college kids, if they can make a buck. We see some innocent high schoolers smoking their first joint. They giggle. One of the girls claims to be on 'A great big purple cloud, and it's real pretty!' The others laugh at her boyfriend – 'You look funny! You've got purple hair!' They drive off to go dancing and then after failing to see another car, crash! Cut to a woman in black at their funeral, screeching, 'My babies! My babies!'

The rest of the movie details the activities of the narcotics squad and Captain Hayes to catch the pusher, but before they do, the pusher has lured a pretty young dancer into his shady world. The weed affects her work, and she's fired. She joins the pusher in peddling dope in order to keep her kid brother in college. He finds out about her sad decline and, in a hugely improbable plot twist, hangs himself.

The police narrowly avoid catching the pusher, Marky, but get the dancer. To warn her off the path she's taken, they take her on a guided tour of junkiedom; a braindead hop head; a needle user with swollen blistered arms; and finally a stop at the psychiatric ward so she can see what lies in store for her at the end of the road. She's convinced, and so are we. She helps the cops catch Marky, and all's well. The message?

> It is high time the public . . . old and young alike . . . know the whole truth . . . the full truth, about Marihuana (sometimes spelled marijuana). Ignorance is a sin. Knowledge is power. Only boys and girls who are fully informed can be expected to resist the Markys of today . . . and tomorrow.

> No one seeing this film could be easily tempted to so wreck their mind and body. But millions won't see it. To enlighten them . . . is your job.

> Cooperate fully with government authorities in stamping out ignorance. Make your nation a better place in which to live . . . and raise a family.

And, of course, don't forget to buy a copy of our book on the way out.

Babb faded from the movie scene in the early 1960s and died in 1983, presumably rich and hopefully happy. With him died the old school of drug movies. But coinciding with the increase in drug use during the swinging Sixties, a new kind of narcotics film was born. Marijuana and cocaine movies were a thing of the past. As youngsters changed their drug habits, so film-makers sought to cash in on the brand new threat to the nation's youth: hallucinogenics!

With LSD achieving its illegal status in America in 1966, it became a natural for movie types to focus on. Albert Zugsmith, a producer who had been a key figure in the boom of rock'n'roll young-gone-wild type of movie in the Fifties, was quick to cash in on the public's interest in the drug by bringing out *Movie Star American Style*, or *LSD, I Hate You* in 1966. Unlike the early drug exploitation pictures, in this one the drug was treated as much as a joke as a menace, with a Beverly Hills doctor prescribing it to his famous Hollywood patients. It concludes with a communal acid trip, shot with colour-tinted lenses.

LSD was shown in a slightly less humorous light in *Hallucination Generation* (1966), directed by Ed Mann. It painted the picture of drug induced murders and acid leading to people losing their minds, running around screaming and generally behaving in a silly way. To mark the different states of being, 'real life' was shot in black and white while the 'trips' were all in colour – another reason why you would probably *want* to do drugs after seeing the film. In *The Depraved* (1967), director Andy Milligan had LSD serving as a kind of aphrodisiac used at wife-swapping parties. Everything was groovy until a pregnant woman on acid jumped to her death from a window. LSD was used again as an inhibition relaxant in *Psychedelic Sex Kicks* (1967) and *Campus Confidential* (1968), but the biggest hit of the period was *Riot on Sunset Strip* (1967), where yet again LSD led to a crazy freak out followed, in this instance, by a gang rape.

One of the key differences between the early drug films and the acid movies of the Sixties is in the terminology; back in the Thirties and Forties, drug users were portrayed as innocent victims, seduced by smooth tongued big-city racketeers. In the Sixties it was much more down to personal choice – experimentation was the buzzword. *The Trip* (1967) starred Peter Fonda as a director of television advertisements who experiments with the drugs in the hopes of sorting his life out. The best bit occurred just after Fonda had escaped from a madly pulsating cupboard and ran to a nearby launderette where he sat and stared into the spinning driers! If that didn't scare the kids away from drugs, nothing would.

The script for *The Trip* was written by Jack Nicholson, who went on to star in an acid movie of his own, *Psych-Out*, the following year. Neither *The Trip* nor *Psych-Out* were as heavily censurious of their subject as other LSD films, and as a result they came far closer to capturing the acid experience in the late Sixties. The same cannot be said of the ridiculous *Wild in the Streets*, in which a teenager named Max Frost made a pile of money selling LSD, became a rock star and, after slipping acid into the drinks of powerful politicians, eventually wound up as president of the United States.

Acid as an evil tool was a popular theme. *Satan's Sadists* (1969), *The Cycle Savages* (1969) and *The Acid Eaters* (1969) all featured gangs of nasty Hell's Angels who slipped acid to their victims before raping them. LSD in films was no longer the joke it had been to begin with – now it was 'the devil's sugarcube', as great a threat as cocaine or marijuana had ever posed. One of the great LSD myths – that it could be, and often was, slipped to people unawares – formed an integral part of the plot in such movies as *Candy Baby* (1969) and *The Dean's Wife* (1970). As ever, wild sexual abandon was the end result.

Although LSD was the drug of choice during the Sixties for low budget film-makers, there were the occasional strays. *The Hooked Generation* (1969) included many scenes of senseless violence and even showed someone injecting heroin into his arm.

Easy Rider (1969) and *Woodstock* (1970) both included scenes of drug use, but weren't *about* the drug. After the initial wave of curiosity and interest LSD, like marijuana and cocaine before it, was relegated to merely a plot twist, never a plot. LSD has come to represent an era, the free thinking and free loving Sixties. Occasionally, in films like *Blue Sunshine* (1976), in which hippies who took a certain type of acid in the Sixties lose their hair and turn homicidal ten years on, it adds a certain something. But the problem with film-makers and drugs these days is that they're so damn responsible.

Panic in Needle Park (1971), starring Al Pacino as a heroin addict and *Drugstore Cowboy* (1990), with Matt Dillon as a small-time addict and hustler, are both excellent movies, firmly set in the modern drug addict's milieu. But compared to the show-all, tell-all exploitation drug-feasts of yesteryear, they're so damn sympathetic and responsible, so . . . good. I live in hope that the next boom in designer drugs (we seem to have missed the boat with ecstasy), will bring with it a rich load of cheap and nasty, 'shocking exposés' and much needed warnings against the evil spread of narcotics – otherwise, how can we gratuitously enjoy them?

If exploitation films featuring sex are the great survivors in the world of sleaze, and if illicit drug use is now shown in a sympathetic rather than exploitative light, then freak films are alone in their inability to weather the changes and survive. They are, rather fittingly, the forgotten ones. It must have seemed such a natural and easy gimmick: find, then exploit, someone who might be described on a lurid poster as 'a genuine oddity of nature', or by a less politically correct observer as a freak. I don't mean the use of midgets in *The Wizard of Oz* as Munchkins, or of exceptionally tall men wearing robot suits in science fiction films. I'm talking about people whose only contribution to the plot, and the only reason for their inclusion in the film, was the unusual way they looked – freaks. And *Freaks* was fittingly, the title of the most famous example of this type of film.

Made in 1932 by talented horror film director Tod Browning, most famous for his many collaborations with Lon Chaney and for directing the Bela Lugosi version of *Dracula*, *Freaks* was banned in Britain until 1963. Although it is exploitative as hell, Browning at least tried to cast his 'freaks' in a sympathetic light. The lead role was taken by a tiny actor called Harry Earles. In the film he is wooed by a heartless

Director Tod Browning enjoys a quiet moment with the cast of *Freaks*. I've seen wedding photos that look like this!

The star of *Freaks,* midget Harry Earles, out for a stroll with his sister Daisy who played his fiancée in the movie.

but otherwise 'normal' trapeze artist, played by Olga Baclanova. He rejects his lover, played by his equally small sister, Daisy, and marries Olga. Her plan is to murder him for his inheritance which she will then share with her lover, the circus strongman. In a rightly famous scene, the freaks welcome Olga into their group by chanting 'one of us, one of us, we accept you, one of us – gabba gabba hey!' – a line later adopted by punk band The Ramones.

Browning used the physical differences of his cast to especially disturbing effect in the climactic scene, the troupe discovers Olga's plan, hunting her down and attacking her during a relentless thunderstorm. Few who have seen the limbless Price Randian crawling toward his victim with a knife held between his teeth can forget it. Other real life circus freaks in the film included 'the living half-boy' Johnny Eck, a thin man, real life pinheads and the Siamese twins the Hilton Sisters. After seeing the 'freaks' of the title, the ending is sadly unrealistic and melodramatic. Olga has been transformed by those she manipulated into one of them – a hideous and, unfortunately, ludicrous looking half-woman half-chicken.

Unlike the other films that exploited real life oddities, *Freaks* was made by a major film company and directed by an established, successful director. Perhaps its treatment of the oddities on display was too sympathetic, or maybe the cinema-going public of the 1930s just wasn't ready for a film of its type (apparently, at the film's première in San Diego, a woman ran screaming up the aisles!), but *Freaks* was not a success, and Browning retired from film-making in 1939. *Freaks* was remade in the Sixties as *She-Freak*, but it could boast neither the real life oddities nor the skill with which Browning created the original.

Two of the performers in *Freaks* were later to star in a movie of their own. *Chained For Life* was one of the most peculiar and saddest examples of the 'human-oddity' type of exploitation film. Produced in 1950 by the Classic Films Company, it starred Victoria and Daisy Hilton, real-life Siamese twins who had led a pretty awful life. They had been sold by their mother, an English barmaid, in 1908, to an American freak show operator. By the time they were in their twenties, and still captive freak show performers, they had

A brace of genuine pinheads exploited for your viewing pleasure in *Freaks*.

been named as correspondents in a divorce suit. The case was dismissed, and the resulting publicity led to their finally attaining their freedom.

Chained For Life was a dramatisation of their life story – an over-dramatisation in fact, as the divorce case becomes a murder trial! Victoria, re-named Violet Hamilton in the film, was tried for a murder she didn't commit and the film includes her marriage, carried out live on stage in a burlesque hall in front of a paying audience. Another key scene was the first passionate kiss between one of the women and her husband-to-be, in which both sisters experienced the same sensations! As surreal cinema experiences go, this one takes the biscuit, and the sight of the sisters, both in their forties, playing themselves as teenagers, only added to the weirdness. The tacky nature of *Chained For Life* was further enhanced by a host of third-rate variety acts – comedy jugglers, a unicyclist, a speed-accordionist and a sharpshooter, shown in their entirety to pad the film out to feature length.

Mutations (1972) and *The Sentinel* (1976) were two more straightforward horror films that mixed real life 'monsters' with those created by make-up men. *Mutations* boasts the most impressive list: a human pincushion, an alligator lady, a monkey woman and, the most impressive by far, a character called Popeye who could indeed pop his eyes, right out of their sockets! *The Sentinel*, courtesy of our own dear Michael Winner, was the more outrageously exploitative of the two; it included real freaks intended to horrify the audience, appearing as the guardians of the gate to hell. Consequently, *The Sentinel* is one of those films that leaves a nasty taste in your mouth.

The Crippled Masters, made sometime in the 1970s, is a cheap and nasty Kung Fu film, in which an armless fighter teams up with a legless one to seek revenge on those who deprived them of their limbs. It looked as though the armless guy was actually a thalidomide, but in the film they hide his arms, insisting that they've been chopped off by the bad guys. Likewise, the 'legless' fellow actually had very small legs, but they too were hidden. The tackiest scenes included those that showed the fighters in action, with the armless guy carrying the legless one into battle.

For Your Height Only is another film featuring fighting freaks. I discovered it on the cheapo shelves at a video store in Orlando, Florida. The package gave very little information, and even the photographs on the sleeve were of entirely different people to those actually in the film. My guess is that it was made in the Philippines sometime in the early 1980s. As the title suggests, it's a spoof of the Bond films, taking the Roger Moore period as its target. Agent 007 is recreated here by a tiny man billed as Weng Weng, Agent 003½. He really was tiny, and his lack of height is accentuated by the ludicrous flared white suit he wore in the part. Like Bond, Weng Weng was a super cool secret agent, and for a zero-budget quickie, the film actually parodied the Bond series rather well. Weng Weng reports to his superior for his assignment, involving a drug ring and lots of pretty girls, before going to see the Filippino equivalent of Q. Here Weng Weng gets kitted out with the requisite Bond-style gadgets, including a remote controlled flying hat with a razor sharp brim! Most of the jokes in the film concern Weng Weng's height – he runs through villains' legs in fight scenes and hides in small holes etc. before leaping out and laying waste to the bad guys. The coolest scene by far is the one which he parachutes to safety from the top of a block of flats using an umbrella.

Weng Weng takes advantage of his comparative lightness and parachutes to safety with an umbrella.

Weng Weng and his lethal hat.

Mention has already been made of Chesty Morgan, whose 73-inch bust must be considered an aberration of nature, and although the films she appeared in were really sexploitation, there was nothing sexy about her at all. Other abnormal (or should that be super-normal?) performers include Long Dong Silver and John Holmes, both owners of very, very long penises that kept them busy at the seamier end of the film biz. It's even rumoured that someone, somewhere even made a hard-core sex film starring Siamese twins, but I'm very glad to say that I've had no luck in tracking it down.

Unlike sex on film, of which it seems the public can't get enough, freak films have all but died out. Most freak films are not very good. The performers can rarely act, and inevitable side- effects of their low-budget origins are shoddy scripts and poor direction. But the inclusion of such strange and exceptional human beings often gives them an enduring quality that only the finest screen actors in the very best make-up – John Hurt as Merrick in *The Elephant Man* (1980), for example – can emulate.

I'd like to think that the demise of freak films occurred because people no longer feel comfortable gawking at those who are different. But it may just be that with the extraordinary make-up effects we take for granted today, mother nature just can't compete.

This, then, is the current state of play in what was once the rich world of exploitation films – they just don't make 'em like they used to. Nowadays sex and drugs and perhaps even new kinds of (special effect) freaks have gone mainstream and the days of shady operators, working with tiny crews and next to no money on cut-price shockers is long gone. Quite simply, exploitation films died out because they were too successful. Everyone wanted to see what they offered, and the public always gets what it wants.

7 Totally Deranged Movie

Maniac

One of the many great things about exploitation movies is that you can, if you so choose, actually learn something from them. As a rather simple but effective ruse to avoid censorship and get away with showing the kind of titillating gratuitous sex and violence that we take so much for granted these days, early smut peddlers were obliged to give their movies a veneer of respectability. Most often they claimed to be exposing one or another of the more exciting social evils floating around: drug abuse, teenage crime, the diseases that back then were an inevitable by-product of promiscuity. But few dared risk such a tenuous reason to exhibit female nudity, violent murder, illicit drug-use, corpse-snatching and ferocious fighting females as Dwain Esper's 1934 masterpiece, *Maniac*. For this film, ostensibly, was about that hidden plague on modern life as it appeared in its many varied forms: madness.

Maniac has a fine pedigree. Producer/director Dwain Esper and his screenwriter wife Hildegarde Stadie were the dynamic duo behind many other adult-only exploitation cheapies including *Marijuana, Weed with Roots in Hell* and the superbly titled *How to Undress in Front of Your Husband*. The Espers were not only responsible for making these films, but for showing them as well. In the tradition of other early exploitation film-makers, they would travel the country with their wares, scaring up trade with the promise of salaciousness not available elsewhere, combined with a message 'too important and shocking' for any right-thinking adult to miss. Most of these films dealt with the fairly obvious but perenially attractive topics of sex and drugs. What gave *Maniac* that extra special something was that it dealt with madness in all its many and cinematically pleasing forms.

Maniac - probably the finest film to include pure adrenalin, cat fights, ham acting, eyeball eating and bare breasts.

Maniac is rather like a book on film. You spend almost as much time reading the dialogue cards on screen as you do watching events unfold. The movie even begins with one:

> The brain, in and of its physical self, does not think, any more than a musical instrument can give forth melody without the touch of the musician's hand. The brain is indeed the instrument of thinking, but the mind is the skilful player that makes it give forth the beautiful harmony of thought . . . It is because of the disastrous results of fear thought not only on the individual but on the nation that it becomes the duty of every sane man and woman to establish quarantine against fear. Fear is a psychic disease which is highly contagious and extraordinarily infectious. Fear thought is most dangerous when it masquerades as Forethought. Combat fear by replacing it with faith. Resist worry with confidence.
>
> *Wm. S. Sadler, MD, FACS*
> *Director of the Chicago Institute of Research*
> *and Diagnosis*

The dialogue then goes on to claim that the Chicago crime commission made a survey of 10,000 convicted criminals and found them *all* to be suffering from some kind of mental disease.

The first scene introduces us to Dr Meirshultz, played with arm-waving, eye-popping intensity by Horace Carpenter. We also meet his assistant, Maxwell, played with even greater and more over the top arm-waving and shouting by Bill Woods. You can immediately tell by Dr Meirshultz's hair that he is (a) a genius, and (b) a mad one. He has a huge white Afro complemented by a ridiculous Santa Claus beard.

Maniac has one of the greatest first lines in any film. Ever. Dr Meirshultz, holding a syringe of cartoon proportions in the air turns to his assistant and proclaims in a cod German accent, 'Tonight, my dear Maxwell, I'm ready to try my experiment on a human.'

Maxwell is coerced, after some protest, to steal a suicide victim from the morgue. Maxwell fears he might get caught, but Meirshultz suggests he try one of his famed impersonations. (Coveniently, Maxwell is a vaudeville performer.)

The maniac himself.

I say suggest, but virtually all of the dialogue in *Maniac* is delivered at full blast, the highest volume possible, accompanied by much wringing of hands and eye popping glares. Even the whispers are loud enough to wake the hams playing the corpses.

Sneaking into the morgue together, with Maxwell disguised as the coroner, they manage to revive a dead, and quite beautiful, young woman. Meirshultz, however, is not satisfied with his achievement. What he wants now, he shouts, is a body with a shattered heart, so he can revive it with a living heart. 'De end vill justify de means!'

Maxwell pops out for another trip to the morgue, but is frightened away by a rather violent fight between a cat and a dog. Meirshultz doesn't take the news well. His voice reaches even greater levels of volume as he wanders around his lab, alternately screaming and laughing wildly. The sight of the living heart he had prepared for the experiment spurs him on. With much screaming and laughing, he hands Maxwell a revolver. 'I haff it! You know my powers! You haff seen my work. You have faith in me! Nya Ha Ha Ha! My beating heart will live again in your body! Nya Ha Ha Ha Ha! Kill yourself and you will live again!' Maxwell takes the gun, but shoots Meirshultz instead of himself. Fade out, and time to read another lesson in madness.

> *Dementia Praecox*. This is the most important of the psychoses, both because it constitutes the highest percentage of mental diseases and because recovery is so extremely rare. *Dementia Praecox* patients show blunting of the emotions, serious defects of judgement, development of fantastic ideas, belief that they are being forced to do things or are being interfered with.

Maxwell barely has time to register horror at what he's done before the doorbell sounds. A woman needs Dr Meirshultz to help her husband, a man hallucinating so terribly he believes he is the 'Orang-Utan murderer'. It's about this time in the film you realise that Mrs Esper may well have borrowed one or two of her concepts from Edgar Allan Poe. The woman rushes off to fetch her deluded husband, Mr Buckley, and

Maxwell decides to impersonate the dead doc, using his vaudeville make-up box. Another dialogue screen fills the audience in on Paresis, the general paralysis of the insane, and then back to the action.

The woman has returned with Maxwell's first customer. 'I'll give you a shot,' Maxwell says in his best stage actor's shout. Rummaging through the surgery for something suitable, he dismisses 'super-adrenalin' and settles on water. But whatdyaknow? He clumsily picks up the syringe full of the super-adrenalin. Not suprisingly, poor Mr Buckley gets a little excited. 'Agony! Agony! I can't stand it!' he screams. 'What was in that hypo?' asks his wife.

Screaming and gibbering like an ape, Buckley pushes his wife into the surgery, where she discovers the dead Dr Meirshultz. Meanwhile, monkey boy finds the revived female corpse from the morgue and runs off with her into the woods, pausing only to pull her top down and show her breasts to the audience. Purely for educational reasons, of course – after all, he *is* mad.

Mrs Buckley agrees to keep shtoom about the discovery if Maxwell, whom she now knows is not Meirshultz, kills then revives her husband, giving her the power to control him. Seems like she's leaping to conclusions there, but that's madness.

Warming to their theme, Satan the cat drags the still-beating heart out of its jar and eats it. With the crucial experimental organ gone, and no hope of reviving the dead Dr Meirshultz, Maxwell drags his body down to the basement, and, in another direct steal from Poe, bricks it up behind a wall.

Growing gradually more insane, Maxwell believes he can see 'the gleam' in the cat's eye. 'Stand between me and salvation, will you?' he mutters loudly before catching the poor cat, squeezing its eyeball out of its socket and swallowing it. Yes, you read it correctly. He eats the cat's eye. Is this a cool film or what?

Another dialogue card informs us as to the joys of Paranoia, fixed suspicions and persecutory delusions being top of the list.

Paranoiac. So now you know.

PARANOIAC
This is an extremely rare but very serious disease. Characteristics of it are fixed suspicions, persecutory delusions. The paranoiac is often particularly dangerous because of the difficulty of detecting his disease.

Maxwell, now as barmy as a fruit-cake, starts seeing things. Incredible, monstrous visions. Fire-breathing dragons, scenes of purgatory and the devil. Scenes, in fact, far beyond the budget of a low-rent little shocker like *Maniac*. What he is actually seeing are little clips from two bizarre silent movies, *Witchcraft Through The Ages* and *Siegfried*. Distracted by such high quality footage, he doesn't notice the one-eyed cat hiding behind the wall where he's stashed Dr Meirshultz's body.

Now Maxwell's wife appears on the scene. A down-on-her-luck show girl, she has read in the paper that Maxwell has inherited a fortune from a dead Australian relative. She visits Meirshultz and, completely fooled by the disguise, confides in him about the inheritance. She's told to come back later, because it's time for another lesson in insanity! Manic Depressive Psychoses are the subject this time, and we are told that, 'Such patients are often able to commit sex offences.'

Maxwell believes he saw 'the gleam' in his wife's eyes when she told him about the inheritance. He must kill her! He enlists the aid of Mrs Buckley to try to dispose of his wife, giving her a hypo to jab Mrs Maxwell with. Seeing the opportunity to dispose of two problems at once, he also arms his wife with a hypo, telling her that Mrs Buckley is mad. Locking them both in the cellar, Maxwell stomps around upstairs laughing like the crazy man he is, while down below the two women just about manage to rip each other's clothes off while scrambling around for the hypos.

The police arrive just as Mrs Buckley smashes a huge plant pot on Mrs Maxwell's head. 'What kind of a place is this?' asks a shaken police officer. 'Those women, they had the gleam,' shouts Maxwell. Breaking up the fight, they hear a cat cry. Smashing down the wall, they discover Meirshultz's body.

Cue the final card of the film:

> Manias are created by inability to adjust to the world as it is. Insanity is our defence against a world which is not of our making or to our liking. The normal persona can make such an adjustment. It is not always easy, but it is being done constantly. The person of inferior mental capacity cannot do this. He therefore creates a world in his mind which is his own idea of the world of his choice. He retreats to this world when ever the real world becomes unbearable. This explains the periods of rationalism that all mental cases have. The periods of rationalism depend upon the unbearableness of the real world.
>
> There are many people of sound mind who find one particular thing unbearable. When this is the case, he is said to be the victim of such a complex.

The movie ends with Maxwell behind bars, still shouting. 'The gleam. They drove me to it. I only wanted to amuse, to entertain. But I showed them, Dr Meirshultz. A brilliant impersonation! My supreme creation!'

Never before or since has so much ham acting been combined with an eyeball eating scene for the purpose of teaching the world about madness. At all costs, seek this one out.

8 Ed Wood Junior

The legendary Ed Wood Jnr.

In 1941, thousands of young American Marines invaded the beaches of the Pacific islands to do battle with the occupying Japanese forces. One of those Marines was Ed Wood Junior. Writer, director, raconteur, one of Wood's favourite stories was to tell of how he was dressed for that invasion. He claims that, under his uniform, he wore a pink bra and ladies' pants. Ed Wood Jnr is still, to this day, the most famous, if not the *only* famous, transvestite film director, and the story of his life is almost as strange as his films.

In recent years Wood's name has become synonymous with 'bad' films, thanks largely to the American film critics the Medved Brothers. The Medveds aroused much interest in otherwise neglected pictures with their 'humorous' Golden Turkey awards. One of Ed Wood's films, *Plan 9 From Outer Space* even earned the dubious honour of Worst Picture ever made.

His first film was released in 1953, and is best known as *Glen or Glenda*. But it has had many titles: *Glen or Glenda, Which is it?*, *I Changed My Sex*, *He or She* and even *Transvestite*, which should leave audiences in very little doubt as to its subject matter. In many ways it was Wood's most personal and important film, a story which he obviously needed to tell. He was also probably the only person qualified to make it. Costing just $29,000, he wrote, directed and starred in it.

Even today, the film is unlike any other I've seen. It featured two narrators – one, an off-screen voice, calmly asking the audience to accept the strange reality of transvestism as one of nature's little mistakes; the other, a barely explained on-screen appearance by Bela Lugosi, cast as a kind of all knowing spirit, or even the Devil. Lugosi had of course shot to fame during the 1930s in the stage and then film version of Bram Stoker's *Dracula*. By the time he came to make *Glen or Glenda*, he was on the verge of the chronic alcoholism and

Flesh Gordon – one of the last sex-ploitation flicks.

This page, left: *Supervixens* – bigger than *Vixens* in every way.

Below: *Mondo Topless* – not Russ Meyer's cleverest film, but one of his most successful.

Facing page: *Emmanuelle* – one of the last great soft-porn hits, which inspired countless rip-offs.

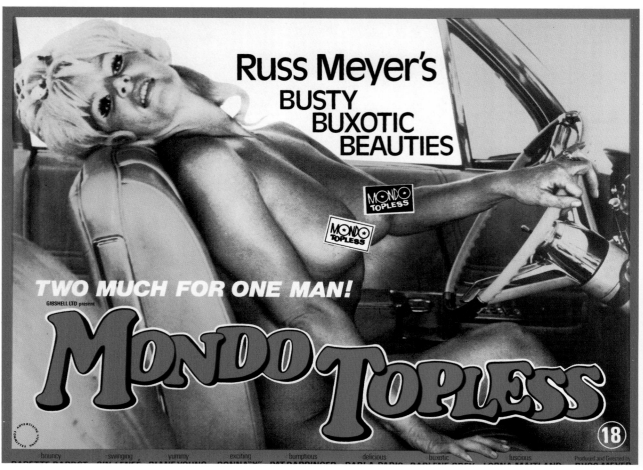

SF DISTRIBUTORS present

a JUST JAECKIN film

ALAIN CUNY
SYLVIA KRISTEL
MARIKA GREEN

Emmanuelle x

DANIEL SARKY · JEANNE COLLETIN · CHRISTINE BOISSON · SAMANTHA music PIERRE BACHELET

PHOTOPLAY

THE WORLD'S TOP FILM MAGAZINE

1'3

SIX TOP POP
SINGERS IN
FULL COLOUR

Mamie Van Doren. Miss Classy Chassis herself!

morphine addiction that was to kill him, and Wood was virtually the only director to use him in his final years. Despite the near incomprehensibility of Lugosi's role and dialogue in *Glen or Glenda*, it was a curiously affecting appearance. Wood's relationship with Lugosi was to last until the death of the once-great actor in 1956. So close did they become that Lugosi even went along on one of Wood's later honeymoons.

Glen or Glenda actually contained two linked but separate stories. The first dealt with a transvestite, coming to terms with and coming out about his transvestism. The second was inspired by the current story that was sweeping the nation at the time – a man who had become a woman through surgery, Cristina Jorgenson. Although both topics were a pretty obvious choice for an exploitation film-maker like Wood, they contained greater intensity than might be expected. Wood, playing both Glen *and* Glenda under an assumed name, Daniel Davies, revealed his need to wear soft, feminine clothing, and the film dwelt on how he came to terms with it and finally broke the surprising news to his fiancée, played in the movie by Dolores Fuller. In a curious but, for Wood, rather typical twist, Fuller was his real life fiancée, but had absolutely no knowledge of his transvestism. In fact, the first she heard about it was when it came to the scene in which Glen tells all, and asks to borrow her softest angora sweater. (They never married, although according to Fuller, Wood's transvestism was not the reason for their eventual break-up. When I interviewed her in 1988, she remembered him fondly, and described quite lovingly how he would beg to borrow her softest angora sweater, the wearing of which he claimed inspired him to produce his best work.)

Glen or Glenda was followed by *Jailbait* (1954), an impressively competent film by Wood's standard. A criminal involved in the murder of a cinema night-watchman forces a plastic surgeon, the father of his partner, to give him a 'new' face in order to avoid capture. The plastic surgeon, however, discovers that the crook has already killed his son, so gives him the one face that will ensure he can't get away – that of the murdered man.

Raising the money for projects had always been a problem for Wood, and his experiences during the making of his next film, *The Bride of the Monster* (1955), were to become all too familiar. Wood began filming in 1953, but time and again was delayed as he ran out of money. Finally he offered the role of the hero to the son of a wealthy Arizona farmer in return for the finances necessary to complete the film.

The Bride of the Monster starred one of Ed Wood's greatest discoveries, Tor Johnson, a 400-pound Swedish wrestler who was to attract a loyal and fond following despite his lack of acting ability. Another Ed Wood regular who made his debut appearance in the film was Paul Marco, in the role of Kelton the cop. Finally, the film featured Bela Lugosi in his last ever speaking role.

Tor Johnson, 'The Swedish Angel', in action in *Plan Nine*.

Lugosi as Dr Vornoff was on a quest to create a new race of atomic people who would conquer the world. He transformed normal people into 'super-beings' by strapping them onto a table and sending electricity through their bodies from a lampshade strapped to their heads. Tor Johnson was one of his more successful subjects, and Lugosi had him christened Lobo. In the end Lugosi himself was given the treatment, and battled with Lobo before falling into a pit containing a giant killer octopus.

Lugosi, aged 73 at the time, apparently needed regular shots of hard drugs (including formaldehyde, according to Paul Marco) to make it through the more arduous scenes. Wood wrote one particular speech for Lugosi that seemed to say as much about the reality of his life as it did about his character in the film:

> Home. I have no home. Hunted, despised, living like an animal. The jungle is my home. For 20 years I have lived in this jungle hell. I was classed as a madman, a charlatan, outlawed in the world of science which had previously hailed me as a genius. Now, here in this jungle hell, I have proved that I was right.

Lugosi was so fond of the speech that when out walking with Wood he would suddenly lapse into it, delivering it loud enough to confuse passers-by on Hollywood Boulevard.

Lugosi was to star in the next of Wood's pictures, *Plan 9 From Outer Space* (1956), but he passed away just a few days into filming. Most film-makers might have considered the death of their star too great a blow to continue. Not Ed Wood. He wrote in a line of dialogue and bunged in some sound effects to convince the audience that Lugosi was run over, then had him re-incarnated in the form of his wife's chiropractor. Nor did the fact that the chiropractor was a foot taller and looked nothing like Lugosi hold Wood back. He simply had the new actor hold his cape in front of his face. It wasn't even the same cape, for in a fitting tribute to the greatest role in his career, Lugosi was buried wearing his.

As always, Wood had trouble making budgetary ends meet, and as always he had a novel way of solving the

The one and only
Vampira.

problem. At the time his landlord was a Baptist by the name of Reynolds. Wood befriended Reynolds and began to show a great interest in his work, becoming a regular at his Sunday sermons. Before long, Reynolds became Executive Producer of *Plan 9*. In return, Wood and his entourage, including the huge, bald Tor Johnson agreed to let Reynolds baptise them in the apartment's swimming pool.

Plan 9 concerned a bunch of extra-terrestrials who, worried about Earth's rapidly increasing nuclear capabilities, decided to execute their famous Plan no. 9 and resurrect the Earth's dead, who would then march on the nation's capital. Curious folk in the cast included Criswell, a minor league celebrity mindreader and fortune teller, and Vampira (a.k.a. Maila Nurmi), a Los Angeles late night horror TV host.

Highlights of the film included a liberal use of stock footage, an airline cockpit constructed from a sheet of plywood and a shower curtain, and flying saucers made out of paper plates. I've always disliked the way this film has been held up as an example of 'bad' film-making. Sure, it's shoddy, but I'd much rather sit through an incredibly cheap but incredibly strange movie like this than an expensive, overblown and unforgiveably dull one.

Wood followed *Plan 9* with *Revenge of the Dead*, also known as *The Night of the Ghouls* (1958). Skeletons at a phony seance, floating instruments and the eventual appearance of real ghouls seeking revenge formed the plot, and Criswell, Tor Johnson and Paul Marco were in the cast.

Before *The Night of the Ghouls* came *The Bride and the Beast* (1958), which was written but not actually directed by Wood. Nonetheless, his screenplay was so distinctive and peculiar, not even the most individual of directors could have made a difference. It was about a beautiful young girl who married an animal trainer, but discovered on her wedding night that she was far more attracted to the gorilla he kept locked up in his basement. Understandably confused, she went to see a psychiatrist who discovered, using hypnosis, that she was a gorilla in a past life, explaining not only her obsession with the ape in the basement, but also her deep-rooted love of angora sweaters.

Wood directed one more film, *The Sinister Urge*, in 1960. A slightly more adult piece than his horror and fantasy flicks, it exploited the theme of a young man driven to rape by a pornographic movie. It featured a cop in drag, and one can't help but wonder if Wood wasn't talking about himself when he had the porno movie director in the film protest that he used to make good films. Unable to raise money for his own projects he wrote scripts for others, including *Orgy of the Dead* (1966). Mostly, he survived by writing pornographic novels, like *Killer in High Heels*, usually with a transvestite theme.

Ed Wood Jnr died of a heart attack a few days after being evicted from his small Hollywood flat in 1978. He was an alcoholic and completely broke. His death went unnoticed by all but a handful of friends.

Despite the critics then and now, Wood's films must have had something other than just a laughable campness to justify the following they have today. Film marathons, constant video re-releases, Tor Johnson masks, comic books and even a *Plan 9* stage musical have appeared. As I write this, director Tim Burton is planning a film about Wood, to star Johnny Depp in the lead role, probably costing more than all of Wood's films put together. Somewhere, I hope, Ed Wood is sitting in his favourite angora sweater, and smiling.

The Bride and the Beast. But you didn't need me to tell you that.

ED WOOD JUNIOR FILMOGRAPHY

These are the only full length, completed films directed by Ed Wood. All were also written by him. Aside from these features, Wood was responsible for a handful of unfinished and short films, including some Westerns, a melodrama and a few TV pilots. Wood also wrote many screenplays that were filmed by others, including *One Million AC/DC* and *Take It Out In Trade*.

GLEN OR GLENDA (1953)
JAILBAIT (1954)
BRIDE OF THE MONSTER (1955)
PLAN 9 FROM OUTER SPACE (1956)

THE BRIDE AND THE BEAST (1958)
NIGHT OF THE GHOULS (1958)
THE SINISTER URGE (1960)

Plan Nine From Outer Space. Absolutely not the worst film ever made!

9 Totally Deranged Movie
Glen or Glenda

Glen or Glenda, I Led Two Lives (1953) sounds as much like a strange confession as it does a movie title, which is fitting. Working within the narrow, sensationalistic confines of the low budget exploitation market, Ed Wood Junior cobbled together an intensely personal film, which both exploits and genuinely attempts to promote understanding for transvestism and sex-changes.

With lush, romantic title music that could have been written by Mantovani, the credits tell much of the tale. After the legend – original story written and directed by Edward D Wood Junior – comes the following mouth-watering introduction:

> In the making of this film, which deals with a strange and curious subject, no punches have been pulled . . . no easy way out has been taken. Many of the smaller parts are portrayed by persons who actually are, in real life, the character they portray on the screen. This is a picture of stark realism taking no sides . . . but giving you the facts . . . All the facts as they are today . . . *you are society . . . Judge ye not.*

The music changes dramatically, a dark foreboding chord, and a familiar face fills the screen. It is Bela Lugosi, in a room full of rather cheap looking props – some masks, a skeleton hanging from the wall, a few skulls. The camera pulls back, and, looking up from the huge, dust covered book on his lap, in his deep Hungarian accent, he begins his bizarre narration: 'Man's constant groping of things unknown – drawing from the endless reaches of time, brings to light many startling things. Hah! Startling? Because they seem new, sudden. But most are not new. The science of the ages!'

105

On his last word, we see a dramatic shot of lightning – presumably representing the awesome but unpredictable power of nature. Lugosi is now in his laboratory, mixing chemicals into a bubbling, smoking liquid. 'Life has begun! Haha haha hah!' He continues with his odd monologue for a few more minutes over footage of a baby being born and an ambulance pulling up outside a house. 'A new life is begun. A life is . . . ended.'

The life that has ended is a suicide, dressed in a rather fetching two-piece suit and cloche hat. The note he's left behind reveals him to be a transvestite who has been arrested and jailed four times already for wearing women's clothing, but cannot face life without it.

The policeman who arrives on the scene seeks the help of a doctor. He needs advice. Maybe future suicides can be prevented if the police understand the case, and the compulsion of transvestism. The doctor prepares to describe two entirely different cases, one of a man who sought to become a woman, the other of a man who just needs to dress like one. But lightning strikes again, and we cut back to Bela Lugosi.

'The story is begun!' he intones, as more lightning crashes in the background. We see Ed Wood for the first time, wearing a pencil skirt, tight clasp belt, white fluffy angora sweater and matching white hat.

Over footage that is still, admittedly, quite unusual today, a totally different, reassuringly deep-voiced narration begins: 'Nature makes mistakes, it's proven every day. This man is a transvestite, a man more comfortable when he's wearing girl's clothes. Give this man satin undies, a dress, a sweater, a skirt or even the lounging outfit he has on. He can think better, work better, play better, and he can be more of a credit to his government and his community.'

The crash-course in transvestism continues. We see close-ups of men's clothing. The narrator tells us it's not just uncomfortable, it's downright dangerous! Men's hats are so tight they cut off the blood flow, bringing about baldness! Women's clothes, on the other hand, are soft and comforting and relaxing, even though they are mostly designed by men. The narrator also explains the difference between homo-

Ed Wood Jnr and Bela Lugosi. If ever two people were made for each other . . .

sexuals and transvestites, and shows how everyday folk, like the construction worker and the milkman, might be wearing their wife's briefs under their work clothes or borrow her sweater when at home.

We see Ed Wood as Glen shopping for clothes. Then, over stray shots of female clothing, we hear conversations from Glen's past – his father scolding him for wearing his sister's dress to a Halloween party (even though he won first prize); his sister asking a friend at the water cooler in her office, 'Just how does one go about introducing your friends to your brother when he's wearing your best sweater, and skirt, and make-up to boot?' How indeed.

The big problem in Glen's life is revealed. He's about to get married, and he must tell his fiancée. She's begun to notice things, like the length of his nails, his eyes when he looks into a ladies store window, the time he pawed at her fluffy, white angora sweater. Soon she would realise. But how and when should he tell her? Before the wedding or after? 'My mind's in a muddle, like in a big fog,' he laments. 'I can't make sense to myself sometimes. I thought I could stop wearing these things. I tried, honestly I tried. Then I couldn't stand it any more. I had to put them on or go out of my mind. I'm afraid I'll lose her.'

He seeks the advice of a transvestite friend who advises him to tell her now, before it's too late. He is speaking from experience. His own marriage had ended in divorce when 'the little woman' came home an hour early to find him sitting in her silk dressing gown with a caribou trim.

In the most remarkable scene in the film, Glen, dressed as Glenda, returns home and, to the sound of crashing thunder, falls to the floor. Bela Lugosi pops up again to warn him to look out for 'the big green dragon that sits on the steps and eats little boys!' In a melodramatic montage, Glenda tells his fiancée. She falls to the ground, and then is trapped under huge, heavy logs! Glenda cannot free her, but Glen reappears and manages to lift the wood. They embrace. They get married. A devil-like figure stands next to the priest, grinning evilly.

Lugosi reappears. 'Tell me, tell me. Do you eat little boys?' he sneers. 'Puppy dogs' tails and snails?' We see Ed Wood, obviously wrestling with his tortured desires. He imagines a man beating a woman with his belt as she writhes on a couch. Women dancing with sensuous abandon, then ripping off their dresses to reveal their under-garments. A woman with a gag in her mouth being released from bondage by another gagged woman. All of these scenes are accompanied by a most inappropriate polka soundtrack, and intercut with shots of Ed Wood in torment, and Bela Lugosi glowering in that cute Hungarian way of his.

Finally, we see Wood sitting alone in a room on a stool, haunted by voices and images from his past, including a little girl's voice repeating, 'I'm a girl, I'm a girl, everything nice, not puppy dogs' tails!' The devil figure from the wedding reappears and leads a gang of people toward Glen, all pointing accusing fingers. They obscure him, and when they back away we see he is finally happy – transformed into Glenda! The deranged fantasy sequence continues. Glen's fiancée appears and signals him to embrace her, but she turns into the devil. She pulls away and fondles her silky blouse laughing at Glen in his feminine clothing. Glen imagines other faces, all laughing at him, tormenting him, and then he collapses.

Not to fear, however. The calm reassuring voice of the narrator returns to explain: 'Glen–Glenda has made the decision. Glen has decided to tell Barbara of his dual personality. To tell her of the nighties, the négligés, the sweaters and skirts, the robes and dresses, the stockings and the high-heeled shoes. The wig and the make-up. All that goes into making Glen into Glenda. He tells Barbara he cannot cheat her of the knowledge that she, as his fiancée, should possess. All the facts. He tells her softly, hurriedly at first, then slowly as he becomes more technical. His hands move to

Ed Wood Jnr re-enacting a persecutory delusion in his best film, *Glen or Glenda*.

caress the smooth material of her angora sweater which he has so long and so desperately wanted to put on his own body. He tells this to her, and she looks from the sweater to his hands. Then, when it is all over, and that much of the story that he knows is told, Barbara is unsure of her own thoughts.

How will Barbara react? She looks at him and says reassuringly, 'Glen, I don't fully understand this. But maybe together we can work it out.' She then rises and, in one of the finest moments in motion picture history, unbuttons her angora sweater and hands it to Ed. Not a dry eye in the house.

The film is far from over. We return to the suicide scene and the kindly but curious policeman and the sympathetic doctor. The doc explains that Glen's case was entirely of his mind, brought on by the environment of his youth. He explains that Glenda was a character invented by Glen to receive the love he never got during his youth. But other cases are not so simple. For example 'Alan' (played by 'Tommy' Haynes) was a little boy born to parents who wanted a girl. At school, he was rejected by boys and girls alike. At home, his mother would encourage him in 'girly' pursuits. We see him dusting and cleaning up. The voice-over informs us that he is 'becoming a woman'. We follow him into the army, where we discover that he had a suitcase hidden in a nearby town, full of the soft items he loved to wear.

The day of battle arrives, and Alan is one of the soldiers taking part in the war. He comes home, honourably discharged, but while in army hospital he had learned that foreign doctors had begun experimenting with sex-change operations. He decides to become a woman.

Accompanied by discreet footage of a surgeon at work, the narrator informs us of the sex-change process, of the repeated sessions under the surgeon's knife and the hormone shots, which will continue for as long as Alan lives. To tie this section of the movie into the far more personal first half, Alan is also seen at the feet of Bela Lugosi, who magically transforms him into a far curvier Anne.

We follow Anne's adjustment to life as a woman. Make-up, deportment, even her psychology must be dealt with, as she is 'A woman born at the age of 24, in a world that for 24 years she had seen as a man.'

Finally, the doctor explains that, although 'a sex-change was a success for Alan, it would never work for Glen. Alan had been a pseudo-hermaphrodite, whereas Glen's body is that of a male. The doctor explains that if Glen can transfer his love to Barbara, the love he was denied by his mother and father as child, he may not need to dress as a woman. But nothing is certain.

'The end is only the beginning,' the narrator tells us. 'Thanks to Barbara's love and understanding, Glenda disappears forever from Glen. Glen has found his mother, his little sister and his wife in Barbara.'

A happy ending. 'But what of the hundreds of less fortunate Glens the world over?' asks the cop.

Bela Lugosi has the answer: 'Yes. What of the other, less fortunate Glens, the world over? Ah, snips and snails and puppy dogs' tails.'

And so ends *Glen or Glenda*, a film that has survived many of its contemporaries. Its almost surreally bad acting, remarkably inconsistent style and ludicrous over-use of stock footage are coupled with a rather poignant truth – the story of Glen or Glenda being almost exactly that of Ed Wood Jnr. In reality, Wood did find a woman to marry and love. But unlike Glen, he never stopped wearing the sweaters.

10 Blaxploitation

From time to time a certain type of film will score with such popularity that a whole wave of imitations and sequels will be spawned, leaving film historians with a genuine genre to look back upon. If the 1950s are remembered for teen movies and the constant threat to Planet Earth from Bug-eyed Monsters, and the 1960s are remembered for swinging sex comedies and drugs on film, then one of the finest products of the 1970s must be the black action picture.

Of course, there had been successful black actors working in cinema before the Seventies, and even films with black themes and all-black casts. Most experts point, probably with some embarrassment, to the 1905 picture *The Wooing and Wedding of a Coon* as the first genuine black film. But just like the far more enjoyable films that were to follow it – musicals such as *Hallelujah!* and *Cabin in the Sky* – it ruthlessly exploited black themes and talents, rather then accurately reflecting or benefiting from a black perspective. Even as recently as the 1960s, more often than not Hollywood featured black actors either for comic relief or to make some kind of lame point about prejudice. One notable exception was George Romero's *Night of the Living Dead* (1969) which featured a problem-solving black hero, without making an issue out of his blackness. Quite tellingly, the film was produced on a tiny budget by Romero and a bunch of fellow mavericks in Baltimore, just about as far as you could get from Hollywood, both literally and figuratively.

In retrospect, it's easy to see how the image of blacks portrayed by mainstream movies would remain clichéd. Those with any power over the films that were made in the industry were white males. But within the studios, there were producers and directors working in the low-budget end of the market who were adept at spotting trends. The growth of the civil rights and Black Pride movements in the Sixties and

Seventies was to provide them with an ideal new tag upon which to hang their low-budget exploitative fare. Blaxploitation was born.

The way was paved by a handful of interesting oddities. *Uptight* (1968) was a Paramount picture that focussed on a gang of black radical separatists in Cleveland immediately after the assassination of Dr Martin Luther King. It bombed at the box office, but superficially at least it predicted the wave of black thrillers to come. *The Learning Tree* (1969), a gentle autobiographical tale, earns a mention if only because it was the first major American film to have a black director, Gordon Parks. *Putney Swope* (1969) speculated as to what would happen if a 'token' black employee in an advertising firm were to become the Chairman of the Board. He changed the agency's name to Truth and Soul, Inc. and replaced his fellow board members, dour faced old 'honkys' to a man, with hip young black dudes with Afros.

Although these films were ostensibly about black issues, they mostly came from a white perspective, satirising some aspects of the black–white relationship and tensions, as well as mocking the myths and stereotypes of the black super-athletic stud. Ultimately, however, the black characters were seen as being as weak and flawed as the whites, perpetuating the myth of blacks as 'lazy, good for nothing niggers'. They were not yet portrayed as heroes in the straight-forwardly mindless way of, say, James Bond.

Cotton Comes to Harlem (1970) was the first black action thriller to really hit home with audiences. With a black director (Ossie Davies) at the helm, it freewheeled along, taking one of Chester Himes's better Harlem based cops'n'robbers tales and transposing it to modern-day New York. It was an important feature, because it proved that there was an audience for black heroes. But these heroes were still stereotyped and slightly foolish, more realistically 'black' then before, but still manageably safe for a white audience not to feel threatened. Would crowds turn up to see a tough black taking on whitey and winning? The answer was yes, and his name was Shaft.

'Who's the black private dick that's a sex machine to all the chicks? Shaft!' Who else. *Shaft* (1971) was the first of the really fine blaxploitation pics of the Seventies. It had a neat little plot, based on a novel by Ernest Tidyman; one of the best soundtracks ever, courtesy of the brilliant Isaak Hayes; and Shaft himself, a fast-talking, super-tough hero with a jiveass name, convincingly and winningly played by former fashion model Richard Roundtree. The ingredients added up to the perfect Saturday night feel-good movie that audiences were looking for in 1971. Costing just over one and a half million dollars to make, the film took in over $7 million in the United States alone, with the soundtrack album going to Number One, and staying in the charts for over a year.

When reviewing the *Shaft* films many critics, both at the time of its release and more recently, made special reference to Shaft's success with the many foxy ladies whom he bumped into over the course of each 90-minute outing.

Richard Roundtree, dressed head to toe in black leather, as the one and only Shaft

Phrases like 'black sexual athlete' were bandied about, as if the films were somehow perpetuating the myth of the black man as super-stud. But Shaft's success rate owed more to the James Bond tradition of incredible, immediate sex appeal than it did to any racial or racist stereotyping; he bedded a lot of women because that's what male heroes, of any colour, did back in the early Seventies. I don't remember any of the critics looking at the early Sean Connery Bond movies prattling on about those films perpetuating the myth of white Scottish men as super-studs.

The success of *Shaft* persuaded MGM to produce two sequels, the above average *Shaft's Big Score* (1972) and the appalling *Shaft in Africa* (1973). Although successful, neither did as well as the original. In part this was due to them lacking the spark of *Shaft*, but more than anything the sequels were victims of their parent film's success. By the time they were released, they were competing with a plethora of funky, hip black action movies, inspired by *Shaft*, each with their own tough-as-nails hero and groovy soundtrack. In the space of just two years, the once revolutionary Shaft seemed, well, kind of old-fashioned. The diminishing financial returns on the two sequels (the last cost more to make than it earned at the box office) meant an end to Shaft's cinematic adventures. He did reappear briefly, as the star of his own television series, but that too suffered from being less exciting and less fresh than the kind of brutal, violent and sexy action films that audiences wanted to see. The show folded after only eight episodes.

In many ways, Shaft was too obvious a hero for the Seventies. His blackness was really the only thing that distinguished him from most other fictional detectives. The cinema audience of the early Seventies seemed to feel that a right thinking detective with a strong moral code was nowhere near as exciting as the new kind of anti-hero inspired by the two other ground-breaking black action films, *Sweet Sweetback's Baadasssss Song* (1971) and *Superfly* (1972).

Sweet Sweetback's Baadasssss Song was perhaps the first genuinely anti-establishment picture in this field. Writer/director/composer/star Melvin Van Peebles gambled a lot of his own money to complete this ground-breaking and distinctly personal movie. It was shot over 19 days for around $500,000, using a cast of newcomers, many with little or no acting experience.

It was Van Peebles's third movie. His first was the low budget, autobiographical *The Story of a Three Day Pass* (1967), made in France, where Van Peebles had moved largely because he found it impossible to get a break in the American film industry. The film was shown at various American festivals, and attracted enough favourable attention to interest a studio in Van Peebles. Columbia Pictures offered him the job of directing *The Watermelon Man* (1970), a pleasant enough satirical swipe at the firmly entrenched racial prejudices of even the most liberal American. A man wakes up to find himself transformed overnight from white to black. (He discovers this in the toilet, providing the film with one of its cheapest laughs.) He soon discovers that life for a black American is a very different experience. His wife goes off him, neighbours make threatening anonymous phone calls, and he is slowly eased out of his responsible job, demoted to the level of janitor. The only plus to his colour switch is the sudden interest shown in him by the office's token Dutch nymphomaniac, but he soon realises that, like everyone else in the movie, she can't see past his colour. The movie ends with the once mild man joining a black power group, preparing for the 'inevitable' revolution.

Although it ended on a militant note, *The Watermelon Man* barely hinted at the uncompromising style and message that Van Peebles was to unleash with *Sweet Sweetback's Baadasssss Song*. The film began with a message from Van Peebles to the audience: 'This film is dedicated to all the Brothers and Sisters who have had enough of the Man.' It opened with a shot of the hero as a teenager enjoying himself unreservedly with a young woman, and demonstrating considerable prowess in the process. It then cut to present day Los Angeles, where Sweetback, played by Van Peebles, is all grown up and mixing business with pleasure. Accompanying two white cops downtown for questioning, he witnesses them administer a brutal and completely unnecessary beating to a young black brother. Sweetback snaps and, surprising even himself, beats the cops to death. The frustration and anger he has felt after years of repression and obeying 'the man' finally come to the surface. The rest of the movie follows the now fugitive Sweetback staying one step ahead of the law and avoiding arrest until he escapes to Mexico. The movie ends as it began, with a message: 'Watch out. A bad ass nigger is coming back to collect some dues.'

Sweet Sweetback's nearly didn't reach any audience, after the all-white jury of the Motion Picture Association of America awarded it an X Rating, reserved for porn. But after a low key release in just two cinemas, word of mouth spread, and before long there were queues around the block. It went on to gross over $4,000,000 in domestic rentals alone and to set the tone for the wave of imitations that was to follow.

Van Peebles never really repeated his early success. Although he continued to work in the cinema, he also successfully branched out into the theatre and television, and earned the distinction in the 1980s of being the first black trader on the floor of the New York Stock Exchange. Rather fittingly, one of his sons is following in his father's footsteps, and looks set to do even better. In 1992, Mario Van Peebles wrote, directed and starred in the enjoyably fast moving and violent *New Jack City*, a very Nineties version of the kind of films his old man helped to kick off.

Superfly (1972) was the other original that helped to shape the derivative (but wonderful) deluge that was to follow. Key to its success was the incredible Curtis Mayfield soundtrack, which certainly equalled if not surpassed Isaak Hayes's *Shaft* score. Playing the hippest pusher in Harlem, Ron O'Neal as Superfly slugs, loves, needles and philosophises his way through an obviously low-budget but above standard action fest, creating the template for a new cinematic cliché, the pusher with a heart of gold. Although Superfly is governed by the rules of the streets that he works, he yearns for a different life. The film builds to him pulling off one big drug scam, earning enough cash to get away forever. He also manages to turn the tables on the white mobsters and corrupt

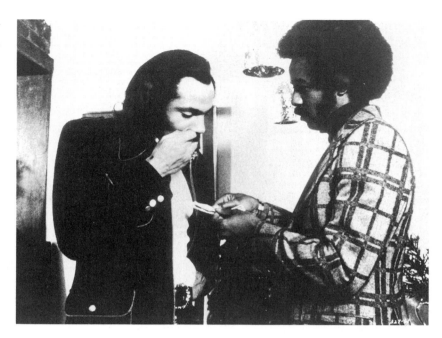

Superfly. The junkie-hero checks his stuff.

police that have dogged him. True to what was rapidly becoming the form, the black anti-hero not only gets away with whatever illegality he specialises in, but makes whitey look stupid in the process.

Ron O'Neal in the title role is a sublime casting decision. He not only looks cool and tough enough to run a strong-arm drugs operation, swaggering perfectly in the pimp's uniform of wide-brimmed hat, ankle length coat and big-collared silk shirt (open to reveal extra-large crucifix), he also manages to persuade the audience that there is more depth to him than the flashy exterior suggests. Superfly is a man who has it all, but finds out it isn't enough. The ultimate success of his plan at the end of the picture left audiences begging for a sequel. The super-cool character has pulled it off, he can now leave the streets and the lifestyle that made him and would have destroyed him. Where would he go? What would he do?

Sadly, the answers to those questions are Rome and *Superfly TNT* (1973). Most of the elements that made the first film so hot and cool were missing from the sequel. The soundtrack sucked, the direction (this time by Ron O'Neal

himself) was dull and uninspired, the script and plot pointless and slow, and even the clothes, usually the last saving
grace of even the trashiest black action film, looked terribly
camp and out of place when transported from Harlem to
Rome. Most of the film's 87 minutes running time is filled
with shots of the once superbad Superfly sitting on his arse,
playing poker and ruminating as to what to do with his life,
now that he has enough money to sit on his arse playing
poker all day. Eventually he drifts into gun-running, helping
a small group of oppressed Africans to rise up against the
French. He really shouldn't have bothered. The film deserved
to fail as spectacularly as it did, and should be avoided at all
costs.

Despite the diminishing returns that the sequels to *Shaft*
and *Superfly* received, the popularity of the blaxploitation pic

Ron O'Neal prepares
to satisfy yet another
chick in *Superfly*.

was slowly growing. *Black Caesar* or *The Godfather of Harlem* (1972) was an exciting contemporary re-working of the old Edward G Robinson gangster movie *Little Caesar*. Despite the customary low-budget, director Larry Cohen filled the film with well-paced action and stylishly captured the energy and rhythm of the streets. The black action/gangster film was the most common and *Across 110th Street* (1972), *Detroit 9,000* (1973) and *Hell Up in Harlem* (1973) all provided audiences with the chance to see black dudes in action. To compensate for the audience's familiarity with the conventions of the black hero/anti-hero on the rampage, the movies became gradually more violent. When *Detroit 9,000* was released in the UK it had a full nine minutes of excessive gore trimmed out. *The Candy Tangerine Man* (1975) is one of the more mindlessly enjoyable, and excessively violent, pimp movies. The hero, when he isn't beating up corrupt white cops, dealing with his 'bitches' or winning women at pool, swans around town in a candy coloured Rolls Royce!

With the success of the many black male heroes, it must have seemed appropriate to jump on the feminist bandwagon, only just gathering speed in the early Seventies. Black superchick films, starring tough, no-nonsense female leads, formed a genre all their own. The biggest star to emerge from these pictures was the beautiful Pam Grier, starting with American International Pictures's production, *Coffy* (1973). Legend has it that Grier was working as a receptionist at AIP, one of the bigger exploitation companies, when they entered the blaxploitation fray. Their first little epic, *Slaughter* (1972), starred Jim Brown and did well enough to prompt the inevitable sequel, *Slaughter's Big Rip-off* (1973). Spotting a fine-looking black woman at their front desk, the story goes, they unplugged the switchboard and thrust her out in a starring role. The story is complete nonsense, of course. Grier had already starred in a number of exploitation films, including *The Big Bird Cage* (1971) and *Women in Cages* (1972).

Coffy differed from most of the male action pics in that the lead was given a reason for her violent actions, over and above greed, as in the pimp movies, or employment, à la *Shaft*. Coffy is a nurse, on a campaign of revenge for her

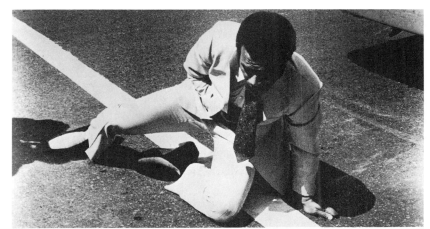

Right: The Godfather of Harlem dies in style.

Below: One of the better blaxploitation flics - *The Godfather of Harlem.*

KENNETH RIVE and BEN FISZ present for INTERNATIONAL FILMS THEATRE LTD.

starring

GODFATHER OF HARLEM (x) FRED WILLIAMSON

Written, Produced & Directed by LARRY COHEN • AMERICAN INTERNATIONAL PICTURES- Distributed by Gala FILMS

11-year-old sister, turned into a helpless, mindless addict thanks to the local pushers. In violent scene after violent scene, she cons or seduces her way into the apartments and businesses of the guilty parties, proceeding to blow their heads off with a shotgun, forcing them to overdose on the drugs they push and even, in one memorable scene, disposing of a thug using just a handful of sharp needles. A decent soundtrack by jazz-funk musician Roy Ayers and frequent scenes of Ms Grier half-naked helped turn the film into a hit.

Imitations were plentiful, including *Foxy Brown* (1974), which was rather like an unofficial sequel to *Coffy*. It had the same director, Jack Hill, and also starred Pam Grier. The name had changed but she was still a nurse and, although her motive was slightly less interesting (her lover was an undercover narcotics cop whose cover was blown by an informer and got killed), Grier as Foxy did almost exactly what Grier as Coffy did to her enemies, only more so. In this outing the thugs were burned to death, had their throats slashed and, in a grand finale, one of them was castrated, allowing Foxy to deliver his pickled private parts to his girlfriend, the leader of the murdering drug and vice ring.

For the next three years, Grier ruled the roost as the queen of blaxploitation, starring in a string of pictures including *Black Mama, White Mama* (1973) and *Sheba Baby* (1975) in which she played the same no-nonsense kind of woman, although this time working as a private eye. Grier took the title role in *Friday Foster* (1975), based on a newspaper cartoon strip about a glamourous fashion photographer who spent more time solving murders than she did shooting clothes. Although it was a brave attempt by Grier to put a little distance between herself and the increasingly derivative all-out action pictures with which she had made her name, audiences obviously preferred those films in which Grier showed a little less of her acting range and a little more of her body. Its failure at the box office led Grier to reconsider her career, and she resurfaced some years later in less exploitative movies like the Richard Pryor vehicle, *Greased Lightning* (1977). I believe that she was last spotted in a couple of episodes of 'Miami Vice' on television.

Pam Grier was the best, but there were other black super-chicks out there, and the statuesque Tamara Dobson as *Cleopatra Jones* (1973) was one of the better ones. Cleopatra Jones was the female version of Shaft, only more so. Tall (6' 2"), tough (martial arts, anyone?) and cool, she also fought on the side of good, as a CIA-affiliated narcotics agent. In this fun movie, she was pitted against an evil drug baron, ludicrously but enjoyably hammed up by Shelley Winters. Cleopatra Jones came on like a super-cool black Jane Bond, smashing her way into rooms, karate-chopping anyone fool-ish enough to get in her way, then leaving the destruction behind her as she roared off in her customised black Corvette (licence plate: CLEO). The sequel, *Cleopatra Jones and the Casino of Gold* (1975), took her right to the heart of the drug trade, teaming her up with a female private eye, Mi Ling, in Hong Kong. Apart from the change of scenery, it was more of the same fast paced, silly but enjoyable stuff. In a noble attempt to offer the audience a little bit extra, Cleopatra spent a lot of the movie lounging around in a series of ever more camp and bizarre 'fashion' statements.

A very watchable film that was disappointing only because the first was so good, it was unfortunately released a little too late. By 1975, the excitement that had once been generated simply by having a black hero in a movie, had faded. But hang cool. There are a few more films to rap about. My favourites, in fact: the black horror films.

Seeing as the majority of blaxploitation films were aimed at the less discerning cinema-goers, it was only a matter of time before someone tried to incorporate a funky black theme with that other staple of junk cinema, the horror film. Sadly, it was only a short-lived trend, but all the more reason to treasure and cherish those films that were made.

The first was also the best: a black vampire film that essen-tially took the Dracula legend, gave it an Afro-American spin and released it to the world as *Blacula* (1972).

It opens in Transylvania, 1790. William Marshall, playing the African Prince Mamuwalde, is visiting Count Dracula, hoping that cinema's most famous vampire will help him fight the slave trade. True to form, the Count couldn't care

Eat, Blacula, Eat!

less about that. Instead, he has his eye on Prince Mamuwalde's wife Luva, played by Vonette McGee. He steals her
from him, locking her in a handy mausoleum, and then
inflicts his curse upon the helpless prince: 'You will starve for
an eternity! You shall be Blacula, a living fiend doomed never to know that sweet blood which will become your only
desire.'

Next stop, Los Angeles, 1972. Two gay antique dealers are
excited by the arrival of their latest find, an ornate, centuries-
old coffin from Transylvania. Out pops Blacula, claiming his
first victims. The rest of the movie stays firmly within the
clichéd boundaries of cinematic vampirism. Blacula takes
many more victims, while pursuing Tina, whom he believes
to be the reincarnation of his love Luva. Seeing as she's

played by the same actress, that's understandable. His nemesis is a lone doctor, struggling to persuade the authorities that (a) vampires exist, and (b) there's a black one loose in modern day LA. He finally convinces the police, and they attack the vampire in an abandoned warehouse that is his lair. Tina, now a vampire herself, is staked, and Blacula dies when he walks out onto the roof of the building into the sunlight.

Judged purely as a vampire film, *Blacula* is derivative and unexciting. But the fun is to be found in the setting. William Marshall, a successful Shakespearian actor, plays the tormented prince with the right combination of tragic self-pity and superiority, especially when encountering the modern day black citizens in the standard movie costume of wild flares, stacks, garish jackets and the occasional fedora. The black vampire, decked out in black evening wear and a cool cape looks like the sharpest dude on the block.

The following year, Marshall reprised his role, and Blacula lived again in *Scream, Blacula, Scream* (1973). It had the potential to be a far better film than it actually was, by combining

Nice fangs.

One of Blacula's
many followers gets
on the wrong side of
the L.A.P.D.

the basic vampire theme with the more interesting one of
voodoo. Pam Grier appeared in a surprisingly passive role as
the young voodoo priestess who finally killed off the Undead
Prince. One of the film's better moments was when Blacula
complained about not being able to see his reflection. 'I don't
mind being a vampire, but this isn't hip. A man's got to see
his face.' Blacula's death in *Scream, Blacula, Scream* was
brought about by a stake through a voodoo doll's heart; this
method of vampire-disposal proving more effective than
most, as he never reappeared.

Blacula's brief appearance in the movie theatres, however,
inspired others. The lamest and funniest of all the black
horror pics has got to be *Black Frankenstein* (1973), also known
as *Blackenstein*.

From the very first shot you know that you're in for a treat.
A prone body on a surgeon's lab. Weird machinery crackling
and humming all around. Bolts of electricity filling the air.

A slightly sinister looking scientist pottering around. And then, cut to a private jet landing in Los Angeles as the soul soundtrack kicks into gear.

Meet Vietnam veteran Eddie Turner, his arms and legs blown off by a landmine. His girlfriend, Winifred is, conveniently, the assistant to Nobel Prize-winning genetic scientist Dr Stein, who is currently experimenting on the reconstruction of missing limbs. In a remarkably unpredictable plot twist, Eddie agrees to become the subject for Dr Stein's experiments. All is proceeding well, until the doctor's assistant, lusting after Winifred and jealous of her love for Eddie, deliberately fouls up the experiment in its final stages. His limbs restored, Eddie has been turned into a raging, super-strong maniac. He kills Dr Stein and smashes up his lab before running amok.

It's hard to describe just *how* inept and lame this movie really is. Compared to *Blacula*, the acting is so poor, it is almost surreal, and the special effects and sets look as though they were left over from a cheap 1930s production. In fact, they were produced by Kenneth McStrickfadden, who designed the sets for the original *Frankenstein* in 1931, but presumably with age and a much larger budget on his side. One of the more worrying side effects of Dr Stein's experiments was what they did to your hair. When Eddie first set forth as Blackenstein, seeking revenge on a fat white orderly who had tormented him when still limbless, his hair appeared to have grown into a flat-topped Afro, echoing Frankenstein's famous misshapen head, but in a far hipper way.

Once you've seen and enjoyed Blackenstein's haircut, there's little else to recommend the film for. The movie ends with Blackenstein, having survived beatings and bullets, being ripped apart by crazed Rottweilers. The movie's failure to attract an audience bigger than it deserved meant that, thank heavens, there was never going to be a *Scream, Blackenstein, Scream*, but despite the poverty of ideas it displayed, I still have an enormous fondness for this piece of junk.

The Exorcist was given the blaxploitation treatment in *Abby* (1974), although apparently the film's producers, American International Pictures, considered calling the film *The Blackorcist*. Carol Speed played the unfortunate Abby, and William Marshall appeared as the exorcist attempting to rid her of the evil African spirit of Eshu. *Abby* was complete hokum, but likeable, sticking fairly closely to the structure of the original that it ripped off.

Slightly less derivative, but also far less successful, was *Dr Black and Mr Hyde* (1976). Appearing after the boom in black movies had died, it put quite an interesting spin on the Robert Louis Stevenson classic. Dr Pride, working at a free clinic in the ghetto, discovers a serum that will turn black skin white. He experiments first on a prostitute and then on himself. The effects not only alter his personality, turning him predictably nastier, but also his social standing. With each transformation he becomes more white and more violent, his spree of terror ending only when the police team, consisting of one white and one black lieutenant, trap him on top of the Watts tower. Slowly dying from multiple bullet wounds, he topples to his death.

What could have been an interesting commercial movie that also made a few salient points about society and skin colour was instead a rather tawdry if enjoyable horror rip-off. Although well directed, by William Crain the director of *Blacula*, and well acted, its lack of success was the final nail in the coffin of black exploitation horror films. And just in time, too. The next project planned by AIP was to be a black version of *The Mummy*, to be called, what else? *The Blummy*.

Part Three

Teenage and Drive-In Movies

11 Teenage Movies

The 1950s was a rich decade for offbeat movies. The social and economic change in the post-war years inevitably affected what could be committed to film. Along with a relaxing of moral standards came the rise of the teenager as a self-contained and newly affluent group. In previous years there was no real middle-ground between family films, which were safe, wholesome entertainment, and adult movies. But as Mom and Pop chose to spend more and more time indoors watching television, the shrewder low-budget film-makers saw a golden opportunity. The success of *The Wild One* in 1954 and *Rebel Without a Cause* in 1955, adult films that happened to tap into teenage angst successfully, paved the way for a slew of cheap imitations, which in turn spawned a whole genre of crazy but cool, hilarious but hip moving pictures.

Part of the reason for the emergence of the teenager as such an easily identifiable group lay in the new styles and music that appeared in the Fifties. Teenagers had bought records for as long as they'd been making them, but rock'n'roll was the first sound that seemed not only to appeal just to them, but to scare the dickens out of their parents. Looking back at Bill Haley and the Comets performing the title song in the first rock'n'roll movie, *Rock Around the Clock*, it's a bit hard to see why the first 'official' teenagers got so worked up about it. But they did, and soon the words Rock and Teenage became synonymous with a certain type of society-threatening behaviour.

Film-makers responded in two ways. Either they capitalised on the fear that juvenile delinquency engendered, or they made movies in which teenagers were shown to be not just neat and cool, but really, really nice kids as well. Before long, you couldn't move for movies with the word Teenage in the title. Horror, crime, science fiction, romance – every type of film was given the teenage workover. First up for us: the JD movies.

One American critic, Jim Morton, suggested that the juvenile delinquent movies of the Fifties were the direct descendants of the gritty, bleak *film noir* of the Thirties and Forties, but made far more quickly and cheaply. Hence, he dubbed them 'sleaze-noir'. The lead players in the teenage market were American International Pictures. Formed by Samuel Arkoff and Jim Nicholson, AIP led the way through the Fifties and Sixties with their popular and cheap brand of exploitation. Some films they made themselves, others they brought in from abroad or via young new producers who didn't have a distributor.

AIP's attitude toward the teenage market was revolutionary. Their films featured genuinely young actors, as opposed to Hollywood pictures, where actresses like Joan Crawford could still be found playing 19-year-olds as they staggered toward middle age. Furthermore, unlike the Mickey Rooney and Hardy films, where teenagers were portrayed as mischievous but ultimately well-meaning and sweet kids, AIP made films where the teenagers were really in trouble. *Reform School Girl* (1957) was one of their better pictures, featuring all the right ingredients: hot rods, sexy, gum-chewing teenage tramps, and a good-looking boy (Ed 'Kookie' Burns!) framed for killing a pedestrian while joy-riding in a stolen car. *The Cool and the Crazy* (1958) had similar ingredients, but this time the action centred around a high school dope racket, with a villainous teenage pusher named Eddie luring otherwise decent teenagers astray. Other distinguishing features in JD movies were switchblades, hotrods, DA haircuts and games of 'Chicken', all popularised by James Dean in *Rebel Without a Cause*.

In 1957, Robert Altman's first movie, *The Delinquents*, more than matched AIP's offerings with a fight at a drive-in, a teen kidnapping and, again, a wrongly accused teenager. *Flaming Teenage* (1957), *Teenage Thunder* (1958), *Teenage Bad Girl* (from England in 1957) and *Teenage Doll* (1957) also cashed in on the post-pubescent boom, scorching the screen with 'tales of today's immoral youth!' One particularly notable teenage crime film was *The Cry Baby Killer* (1958), featuring Jack Nicholson in his first film as the villain of the title.

For those who preferred to watch teenagers having a good time in slightly less violent ways, there were the straightforward rock'n'roll movies of the Fifties. Early screenings of *Rock Around the Clock* (1956) had incited some impressionable audiences to riot. In some cities, projectionists were warned to keep the house lights up and the volume down for fear of similar scenes when showing any rock'n'roll pictures. But the appeal of rock music on film was great enough to attract full houses, so theatre owners were willing to take the risk. *Don't Knock the Rock* (1956) was the sequel to the original *Rock Around the Clock* and an even bigger hit. In addition to Bill Haley and his Comets, the film featured Dave Appell and his Applejacks, The Treniers and a fabulous performance from Little Richard.

Apart from the historical value of the musical performances in these films, they were pretty lame. Most suffered from bad acting and weak repetitive plots – example: good teenager gets mixed up with bad teenager, is framed for something he didn't do, the Platters sing a couple of numbers and the bad guys get caught. But the success of the rock 'n'roll films was such that even the bigger film companies jumped on the bandwagon. 20th Century Fox contributed with *The Girl Can't Help It* (1956), starring the bountiful Jayne Mansfield and further enhanced by Gene Vincent, Little Richard, Eddie Cochran, Fats Domino and The Platters. The very promise of some 'devil's music' gave a movie a better than average chance of making some moola, which would explain why films such as *Bop Girl Goes Calypso* (1957) and *Carnival Rock* (1957) promised to tell 'The whole tempestuous story of today's rock'n'rollers, the way they want it told!', even though they had nothing to do with rock'n'roll.

The best remembered rock'n'roll films must be those that helped turn Elvis Presley into the international star that he was when he was alive, and the butt of thousands of fat jokes now that he's dead. Thanks to Elvis's natural charisma, screen presence and of course incredible performances, *Love Me Tender* (1956), *Jailhouse Rock* (1957) and *King Creole* (1958) are still enjoyable watching today.

After the boom comes the bust, and by the early 1960s the promise of a few songs and guest appearances by greasy-haired singers no longer had the appeal needed to rescue otherwise lamentable pictures. Even teenagers stayed away, despite being offered such delectable fare as *Twist Craze*. It wasn't really until the advent of the Mersey sound and the international success of the Beatles that genuine teenagers could be tempted back to cinemas with the promise of hip'n'happening music.

A third type of teen movie also happens to be my favourite. Committing rock'n'roll to celluloid was fairly predictable. After all, Bing Crosby and Frank Sinatra had both enjoyed acting careers directly as a result of their popularity as singers, and both had epitomised a new style of music. Likewise, the production of teenage crime films was not unexpected. As far back as 1921, in the film *As The World Rolls On*, youthful criminals had appealed to film-makers as an interesting subject. But what was new and interesting in the late Fifties was the combination of teenage angst with those other great drive-in favourites: atomic-age, horror and science fiction.

I was a Teenage Werewolf (1957) was the first off the blocks, courtesy once again of AIP. Despite an irredeemably camp but memorable title, the film was very good. Michael Landon, later to star in both 'Bonanza' and 'Little House on the Prairie', played a young high school student transformed via hypnosis into a snarling, hairy teenage werewolf. Cleverly avoiding the traditional, lunar, causes of lycanthropy, Landon is transformed by far more modern means – anything that startles him, in fact, could trigger his conversion, including the ringing of the school bell. It was like a low-budget, black-and-white remake of *Rebel Without a Cause*, with fangs, brawls and dancing to rock'n'roll.

I was a Teenage Werewolf was one of AIP's most successful pictures of the year, so they quickly followed it with *I Was a Teenage Frankenstein*. More ridiculous, but no less enjoyable, it

Michael Landon contemplating his future in that little house on the prairie.

Whit Bissell sneers knowingly at the young Michael Landon, who was a teenage werewolf.

co-starred Whit Bissell as a modern-day Dr Frankenstein, who builds his creature with the body parts of dead teenagers, killed in plane and hot-rod crashes. The monster himself, played by Gary Conway, has a horribly mangled face on top of a suitably hunky teenage body. He is even seen weight-lifting in the doctor's cellar! The film was originally released on a double bill with another AIP chiller *Blood of Dracula*, with the posters advertising free first aid and smelling salts for the easily scared.

Realising they were onto something, AIP cannibalised existing footage and re-used the props and costumes from *I Was A Teenage Frankenstein* and *I Was A Teenage Werewolf* to produce *How To Make A Monster* (1958), an incredibly cheap but enjoyable behind-the-scenes story of the horror movie biz. In

Is she ugly, or what? Frankenstein's daughter follows in the old man's footsteps.

the film a make-up artist at American International Studios learns that the studio he has worked for for 25 years is about to discontinue its horror films and concentrate on comedies and musicals instead. For revenge, he transforms actors with a special drugged make-up that makes them his slaves. Under his control, a teenage werewolf and teenage Frankenstein murder various studio executives. The film was released on a double bill with another great teenage movie, *Teenage Caveman*, which saw Robert Vaughan leading a tribe of impeccably neat cave-teens and also starred Darrah Marshall, a former Miss Teen America. Frankenstein reared his teen head once again the following year in *Frankenstein's Daughter*.

Teenagers From Outer Space (1959), an independent film picked up by Warner Brothers, astounded American youths with the sight of a good teenage alien versus a bad teenage alien running amok in suburban America. Possessing a really neat ray-gun, the bad guy gets to melt the flesh off a dog and at least three innocent teens before he is stopped by some metal pellets (or bullets as we Earth dwellers call them). It ends with a thrilling showdown between the good alien and a huge lobster, with the good guy vowing to stay on Earth as our protector.

Like the teenage crime and rock'n'roll movies which had boomed in the mid to late Fifties, teenage horror films had lost much of their appeal by the end of the decade, proof of which could be seen in AIP's decision to release their giant ape film, originally to be called *I Was a Teenage Gorilla*, as *Konga* (1961). But even without the involvement of AIP, teenage movies continued to be made. *Teenage Millionaire* (1961) and the less-upbeat *Teenage Strangler* (1964), neither of which really need to have their plots explained, struggled on with the teen tag, but would probably have done better without it. The last recorded sighting of a bona-fide teenage movie was *Teenage Rebellion* (1967), also titled *Mondo Teeno* to cash in on the incredibly short-lived craze for 'mondo' movies initiated by *Mondo Cane*. In its trailers, the makers promised to show us that: 'In Los Angeles, New York, Rome, London, Tokyo, all over the world there's a teenage rebellion. Mondo Teeno. Yes, teenagers set the pace, for new customs, new fads, new dances. Wheels give them freedom, and sex is a new toy to play with!' But by then, of course, all of the teenagers who might have been interested in seeing what others like them were up to in far flung countries were too busy out doing it to want to sit in a cinema or drive-in and watch pap like this.

Another reason for the decline in teen-orientated movies was that the makers failed to keep up with what was actually hip. With only a handful of exceptions, like the Dick Lester Beatles movies, film-makers attempted to flog rock'n'roll long after the kids had moved on, and failed to capture the more knowing, slightly more cynical tone of the Sixties. The teenager on film didn't die. He just grew up.

Frankenstein's daughter – what a gal!

FRANKENSTEIN'S DAUGHTER X
starring
JOHN ASHLEY
SANDRA KNIGHT

12 The History of the Drive-In

Popular as teen movies were in the Fifties, they never would have existed if there had been nowhere to see them. Most of the large cinema chains turned their figurative noses up at the normally cheap if cheerful rock'n'roll/juvenile delinquency/horror fare, fearing not only that such films might blemish their images, but that they might well have a few slashed seats and beaten up popcorn ladies if they encouraged teenage hoodlums to come to their beloved picture palaces. So, apart from a few lower-rent flea pits, the only place where hepcat teens could be guaranteed the chance to catch the latest teen idol or monster was at the drive-in.

The most completely unnecessary and quintessentially American advance made in the presentation of movies, drive-ins had in fact been around since 1933, when Mr Richard M Hollingshead Jnr opened the Automobile Movie Theater in Camden, New Jersey. The first film to be shown there had been released over a year before: *Wife Beware* starring Adolphe Menjou. But although Hollingshead had taken out a patent on his invention, it proved almost impossible to enforce, and drive-ins sprang up right across America. 'Ozoners', 'Under the stars emporiums' and 'Cow pastures' were just a few of the nicknames they attracted as they grew in popularity.

What soon became apparent was that people were more interested in the experience of going to see a film in their car, than in what was actually being shown. Visiting a drive-in became a family affair, with children's playgrounds, adult bingo and even square dances held during or after the main attraction. As competition heated up, some owners added pony rides, strong men and high-wire acts. Stranger variations included the Multi-Scope, which featured hundreds of small screens, one per car, and, in Iowa, the Fly-In, with space for 500 cars and 25 airplanes, re-routed from the nearby airport!

As America's car culture blossomed in the 1950s, the drive-in came into its own. Typical double-bills might have included *Get Yourself a College Girl* coupled with *Teenage Wolfpack*, *Wild Guitar* supporting *Daddy-O* or maybe *Castle of Blood* with *Hercules in the Haunted World*. Unlike the regular theatres, drive-ins did not initially suffer from the rise of television, as the chance of watching a movie in the open air on a warm summer's evening was of greater appeal than going to a stuffy cinema. What's more, drive-ins were gaining quite a reputation among American teenagers as the cheapest motels in town. So heated were these passion pits that local councils often imposed curfews on drive-ins in attempt to prevent lewd behaviour, and managers would issue guidelines to their staff requesting them to check the back seats, and make sure that heads were visible at all times.

Sex was a problem in another, bigger way. Most drive-in screens could be seen by passing motorists. If the *Sound of Music* was showing, then fine. But if it was a Russ Meyer movie, and a twenty-foot breast suddenly loomed into view on the way over to Grandma's, there may well have been an accident. Drive-in owners were to fight many battles over the showing of adult movies with varying results. Some overcame the problem by building fences around their lots to obscure 'innocent' sightings. Others were shut down.

Drive-ins had a more important effect upon motion pictures than just supplying a novel way to watch them. They provided an outlet for cheaper movies that might not have been picked up for exhibition by the larger chains. Some independent producers, such as Roger Corman and his New World Company, and Samuel Arkoff and AIP, made many films – low-budget horror and teen movies in particular – specifically for drive-in audiences.

But by the 1970s, the drive-in was being seriously threatened. The increase in multi-plex, small screen cinemas meant that cheaper films could now get indoor screenings. Moreover, the bigger studios usually refused to release their first-rate movies to drive-ins until after the indoor theatres had exhausted their appeal, which meant that everyone had already seen them by the time they hit the outdoor screen. For instance, *ET* was not shown at a drive-in for a whole year after its release. In the entire history of the drive-in, only one major movie has had its premiere at one. That film was *True Grit*, and legend has it that the Duke himself turned up to the showing in Texas and stood on the roof of his pickup truck firing a double barrelled shotgun by way of celebration.

The drive-in's appeal as fun for all the family had also waned. The cost of insurance had seen a decline in the number of drive-ins that offered playgrounds for kids, and the trend towards showing adult features meant they were no longer suitable for family outings anyway.

As to the future, the drive-in is still out there, mainly on the West Coast of America where the weather is more consistent. But like the dinosaur, its huge size and inability to move with the times may well see it fade into memory in the near future. Another great dumb chunk of American history lost forever. Shame.

13 Forgotten Star
Mamie Van Doren

For many years one of my most-treasured possessions was a battered, well-read copy of *Playing the Field*, the autobiography of the 'platinum powerhouse', Mamie Van Doren. Despite forever languishing in B-features and drive-in films, this star had far more class than her other nickname, 'the poor man's Marilyn Monroe', might lead you to believe. Her real name was Joan Olander, and she was born in 1933 in South Dakota. When her parents moved to Hollywood in 1948, the pretty 15-year-old who had fallen in love with the movies knew that it was more than just chance. Her time had come.

With her hair dyed platinum, she entered and won the Miss Palm Springs beauty contest, which earned her an offer from Howard Hughes's RKO Pictures. Young Joan was about to find out what Hollywood was really like. An invitation to dine with her boss, Mr Hughes, followed – as did a proposition. The Casting Couch was alive and well, but Joan resisted the odious advances of Hughes, and found herself stuck with tiny roles in equally small pictures. Attempting to leave RKO, she approached 20th Century Fox, only to discover that they had already signed up a curvaceous young blonde named Marilyn Monroe.

Joan slogged on, having as little luck in her personal life as in her career. A brief marriage to a violent alcoholic was followed by affairs with a mobster, an elderly ex-boxer (Jack Dempsey, then in his sixties) and singer Eddie Fisher.

She eventually escaped RKO by signing a seven-year deal with Universal Pictures, who cast her first as a night-club singer in *Forbidden*, and changed her name in the process. The 'Van Doren' part was chosen because apparently they thought she looked Dutch. Her first decent-sized role was in *The All American* (1953). According to her autobiography, she worked days in front of the cameras, and nights rehearsing her lines with the director Jesse Hibbs, while fondling his crotch.

Despite the unusual rehearsal techniques, Van Doren's performance got her noticed, and Universal tried to build her into a star. The company's publicists did a fine job of keeping her new name in the papers. In 1953 an eager American public could follow her appearances as 'Miss Eight-Ball', 'Miss Adopt-a-dog-a-day', the American Corn Growers Association's official sweetheart 'Miss Kernel', an automobile association's 'Miss Classy Chassis', a deep sea divers club's 'Miss Deep Sea Diver' and a local magicians club's 'The Girl they couldn't saw in half'. Let's face it, there weren't many things that Mamie Van Doren wouldn't put her name to.

The majority of films that she graced throughout her peak years (1954–1959) cast her, not surprisingly, as a busty blonde sexpot. In the better roles she was allowed to demonstrate some of her acting ability by getting slapped around before singing. In others, she would play humorously out of character, perhaps as a college professor, before singing. Her biggest successes came when playing slutty bad girls from the wrong side of the track, a role that her cheap looking blonde hair and tight-fitting sweaters meant she was a natural for. *Running Wild* (1955) established her as a B-movie star.

Meanwhile, her fraught private life continued to attract a different type of attention. Van Doren was pregnant, but unmarried, and the sleaziest of all the celebrity gossip mags, *Confidential*, ran a piece accusing her and her mother of being prostitutes. Van Doren married the father of her child, only to be released from her contract by Universal who felt that the reality of her as a young married mother would detract from her success in roles playing wanton bad girls.

Van Doren moved over to United Artists where she appeared in *The Girl in Black Stockings* (1957), a murder mystery where she played one of the suspects, finally winding up as one of the victims. She was described on the posters as 'every inch a teasing, taunting, come-on blonde'. Next came *Untamed Youth* (1957) in which she played a rock'n'roll entertainer who, along with her sister, spent 30

A moving comment
on the human
condition. . . *The Girl
in Black Stockings.*

Mamie Van Doren
boosting morale for
the girls in jail.

days in a women's prison before helping to blow open the scam run by the warden – supplying cheap teenage labour. The two musical numbers sung by Van Doren in *Untamed Youth*, 'Oo Ba La Baby' and 'Salamander', were written for her by Eddie Cochran, who also appeared in the film. Van Doren's attempts to do a female Elvis, wild hip gyrations included, had teenagers leaping in the aisles and got film censors in quite a tizz. Several of her more suggestive thrusts were removed from the picture, and her dance steps were watched more closely in the future.

After a brief spell in Las Vegas, where she dated Elvis Presley, Van Doren burst back onto the screen with *Born Reckless* (1958) playing, of all things, a rodeo rider. The film bombed, deservedly, but it brought her to the attention of Clark Gable, who had her cast as his 'bad' girlfriend (Doris Day being the 'good' one) in *Teacher's Pet* (1958). The film was a worldwide success, but partly due to the invasion of European 'sex-goddesses' like Bardot and Loren, and partly because of Van Doren's inability to choose decent roles, she was never to achieve the kind of lasting stardom she hoped for.

Mamie dancing in *Untamed Youth*.

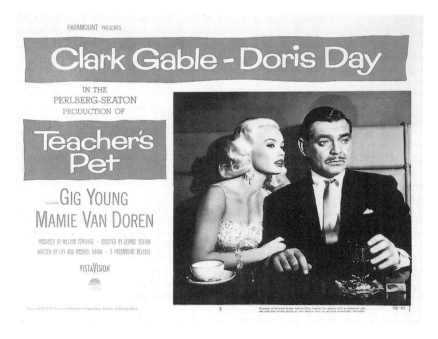

PARAMOUNT PRESENTS

Clark Gable - Doris Day

IN THE
PERLBERG-SEATON
PRODUCTION OF

Teacher's Pet

GIG YOUNG
MAMIE VAN DOREN

VISTAVISION

Mamie Van Doren's most respectable movie.

Van Doren continued to date voraciously, walking out with George Hamilton, Cary Grant and Warren Beatty, among others. Her promiscuous lifestyle and her increasingly bad relationship with the press meant that she would never become America's sweetheart, and her film appearances remained firmly in the realm of the B-movie.

Mamie Van Doren demonstrating her supreme ability to wear a sweater in *High School Confidential*.

High School Confidential (1958), one of the more enjoyable 'teenagers in trouble' movies, was Van Doren's next hit. She played Russ Tamblyn's near-nymphomaniacal Aunt Gwen, and got to purr suggestively while rolling around on his bed wearing the tightest outfits even she had ever seen. The film's success marked the beginning of her partnership with producer Albert Zugsmith, which led to her starring in *Beat Generation*, *The Big Operator* and *Girl's Town* (all 1959). All were salacious, but *Beat Generation* in particular caused considerable upset in its portrayal of a wealthy young beatnik-rapist known as the 'aspirin kid'. Van Doren stayed with Zugsmith for *The Private Lives of Adam and Eve* (1960), co-starring Mickey Rooney as the devil. Condemnation from the Catholic Church further established her as the cinema's number one bad girl.

Having once scaled the heights to co-star with Gable, Van Doren must have felt rather sad to find herself sharing the bill with a chimpanzee named Chim and a robot called Thinko in *Sex Kittens Go To College* (1960). As the parts on offer to her got smaller and smaller, she developed her nightclub act, returning to films in a series of dreadful, inept comedies, the worst of which was *Three Nuts in Search of a Bolt* (1964).

Mamie Van Doren may never have achieved the fame or popularity of Marilyn Monroe or her other main rival, Jayne Mansfield, but she had a sexually provocative style all her own. She also outlived them both, which might cause one to stop and consider the price of fame. I'll take Mamie any day.

Below, right: Jane Mansfield – America the Beautiful.

Below, left: The platinum powerhouse.

MAMIE VAN DOREN FILMOGRAPHY

THE ALL AMERICAN (1953)
FORBIDDEN (1954)
YANKEE PASHA (1954)
AIN'T MISBEHAVIN' (1955)
THE SECOND GREATEST SEX
    (1955)
RUNNING WILD (1955)
STAR IN THE DUST (1956)
THE GIRL IN BLACK STOCKINGS
    (1957)
UNTAMED YOUTH (1957)
HIGH SCHOOL CONFIDENTIAL
    (1958)
TEACHER'S PET (1958)
BORN RECKLESS (1958)
GUNS, GIRLS AND GANGSTERS
    (1959)

THE BEAT GENERATION (1959)
THE BIG OPERATOR (1959)
GIRL'S TOWN (1959)
VICE RAID (1959)
SEX KITTENS GO TO COLLEGE
    (1960)
THE PRIVATE LIVES OF ADAM
    AND EVE (1960)
COLLEGE CONFIDENTIAL (1960)
THE CANDIDATE (1964)
VOYAGE TO THE PLANET OF
    THE PREHISTORIC WOMEN
    (1966)
THE NAVY vs THE NIGHT
    MONSTERS (1966)
LAS VEGAS HILLBILLYS (1966)
YOU'VE GOT TO BE SMART (1967)

14 Drive-In Double Bill

Girl on a Chain Gang and
Teenage Mother

Although drive-ins showed every type of film, from family to adventure to horror to sex, they specialised in low-budget sleaze like *Girl on a Chain Gang* and *Teenage Mother*, a genuine double bill that played during the late 1960s. Both films came from the shameless Jerry Gross, a roadshow operator who was more than happy to spice up his cheap and nasty fare with extraordinary 'educational' footage if it would help attract a crowd.

Girl on a Chain Gang (1966) was produced, written and directed by Gross. Drunk Southern cops, canoodling with a local 'bad-girl', spot some Yankees speeding. The chase is on! The car is pulled over, and the passengers – two smartly dressed men, one white, one black, and a woman – are verbally abused ('integrated scum!'), accused of being beatniks and leered at.

Taken to the police station, they find that just about all the cops in this part of the world, including the sheriff, swig whisky while on duty. They're charged with speeding, reckless driving, no directional signals working, driving on worn-out treads, talking back to an officer, and corrupting local morals. The sheriff, Sonnie Lou, who has the anti-social habit of beating prisoners to death with his fists, discovers that they are involved with the civil rights movement, and soon has them framed for prostitution and living off immoral earnings as well.

Deliberately leaving their cell door unlocked, the sheriff and his men shoot the black man as he escapes, and track the white chap into the woods, where they wound him and leave him for a poisonous snake to finish off. After swigging more whisky, the sheriff then forces himself on the woman, Jean

149

(played by Julie Ange), and coerces the local doctor into examining her and faking evidence to prove that she was a prostitute. This includes creating a slide showing the sperm of both the dead young men supposedly taken from Jean and two 'God forsaken high-spenders'.

After a local trial, in which Gross's cast of semi-pro actors get to over-do both their Southern accents and their ludicrous fake beards and hairpieces, the judge decides that Jean isn't just a prostitute, she's a nymphomaniac as well. She's found guilty and sentenced to 90 days on the local chain gang.

The sadistic drunken sheriff is replaced by a sadistic drunken chain-gang boss with a bull whip he calls 'Baby'. His first words to Jean are, 'I want you, woman. I'm gonna wear you down. Before long I'm gonna bend you to my way of thinking.' Soon, she's wearing a prison uniform several sizes too small and is chained to an all-black chain gang. The man she's chained to is planning an escape – and he carries it through regardless of the wishes of his new partner. Sheriff Sonnie Lou is called. With a gang of deputies and hounds, he pursues the escapees into the swamps, full of snakes and 'gators.

Using a rock, the man smashes the chain that holds him to Jean and persuades her to run off, leaving him to make his stand. He beats Sonnie Lou to the ground before he is shot dead by the deputies, but not before he has the satisfaction of seeing poisonous swamp snakes despatch the sheriff. Escaping from the sheriff's jurisdiction, Jean reaches safety – and spills her story to the decent, honest sheriff of the neighbouring town. Justice will be done.

As the cool bongo drum theme music plays, there's just enough time to visit the concessions stand, where, the intermission adverts promise, 'You'll be greeted with fast, friendly service. You'll find hot dogs, juicy hamburgers and mouthwatering delicious pizza. There are refreshing hot and cold beverages, ice-cold cola, and orange drink – goes great with an order of crispy french fries. Then there's a wide selection of favourite candies and other delicious snacks. And there's always a fresh batch of hot buttered popcorn to add to your enjoyment of the show.'

You settle back down into the front seat with your treats, catch the previews of coming attractions, and then the second half of your double bill begins. It's another fine Jerry Gross production, *Teenage Mother* (1968). Obviously moving up in the world, Gross has shot this one in colour!

Opening shots of a drag-racing event help establish the hip teenage setting, as well as providing good crowd shots at no cost to Gross. The story unfolds with the arrival from Sweden of Miss Petersen, the new health instructor for the local high school. It soon becomes clear that Miss Petersen (played by Julie Ange, fresh from her chain gang experiences) has extremely modern ideas about what kind of health she should teach the local kids – we're talking Sex, of course. Miss Petersen has a hard time persuading the local PTA that 'anatomical biology' is a worthwhile subject. They seem particularly opposed to her showing a 'birth film' at the end of her course. The school librarian refuses to order what she considers to be 'indecent' books for Miss Petersen's students, and one of the girls in her class, Arlene, thinks that teach is trying to woo her boyfriend when she keeps him after school one night. Upset and hurt, Arlene falls in with bad company, high school hood Duke, a small-time pusher who also deals in pornographic pictures. She causes a local scandal when she claims to be pregnant, hoping to force her boyfriend into marriage, but it provides reactionary townfolk with the evidence they need to try to get rid of the 'immoral' Miss Petersen.

Still fighting her battle to bring Sex Education to small-town America, Miss Petersen is not helped in the slightest by an attempt by Duke to frame her using his own pornographic pictures. The movie culminates in a showdown between Miss Petersen and the town elders, in which she finally shows the much talked about 'birth film'. We get to see it, too.

The film is five or six minutes of genuine medical footage showing the Universal Obstetrical Forceps used to deliver, in graphic close up and vivid colour, a baby boy. Even on my modern home television the footage was a little gruesome, but on a drive-in screen it must have knocked their socks off. The townfolk are initially unimpressed. 'What will the children learn from seeing this film?' shouts one. Miss Petersen's reply: 'They would have seen the beauty and purity of the reproductive system. These films were not intended for the lodge meeting or stag show.' Nor, you might add, the drive-in. But that's where they wound up.

I always find it fun to watch films in which the sleazy creators are forced to attempt to justify their inclusion of some shocking footage. Jerry Gross has never let me down yet. Who amongst us (as we carefully un-hook the speaker from the open window of our car, and prepare to drive home), would not feel that they had got more than their money's worth from *Girl on a Chain Gang* and *Teenage Mother*?

15 Forgotten Star:
Jack Nicholson

You might think that the stars of these teenage epics, the pre-adult Werewolves and Frankensteins and hot-rodding juvenile delinquent rock'n'rollers have a pretty raw deal. To be preserved forever on film in that difficult phase, when you blushed too much and felt like you'd never fit in, a nervous, twitching, neurotic nerd. Imagine what it must be like to be forever associated with a screen version of yourself, captured in cinematic amber at a time in your life when you're least able to control your emotions and most likely to break out in a horrible, unfair skin complaint. However, in reality the pros outweigh the cons – you get to seem cool at the one time in your life when it actually means something to you, and for the handful that died young enough, James Dean being the single finest example, at least you didn't have the chance to make any major career mistakes or get old and fat.

No, stars of teenage movies get off lightly. You should save your sympathy for kiddie actors. With the exception of maybe Shirley Temple, you show me a child phenomenon and I'll show you a dysfunctional unemployed adult. Look at little Drew Barrymore – a household name at age seven, snorting cocaine six years later. And who knows what will happen to that 'cute' child 'actor' Macauley Culkin when his voice breaks and totally un-cute hair sprouts on that teenage top-lip.

Teen stars know they're in the clear. They've already gone through all those messy bodily changes. In fact, some of them even manage to give the illusion that being a teen is fun, in a totally irresponsible gun-toting, break-all-the-rules kind of way. One of the best at doing that was a forgotten young actor by the name of Jack Nicholson.

153

Arriving in California at the age of 15, young Jack Nicholson started his Hollywood career in the cartoon department of MGM. Attending acting classes in his spare time, it wasn't long before he landed a few small stage and later television parts. He tried out for a number of teenage roles, even getting on the shortlist for *I Was a Teenage Werewolf*, before losing that role to Michael Landon. The producers didn't like his 'sardonic nature'. Undaunted, he continued with his acting classes, where he met the young B-movie producer/director Roger Corman. Corman cast him in his next role, as the lead in *The Cry Baby Killer* (1958). He played a confused young hood who shoots two other JDs and then takes refuge in the storeroom at a drive-in theatre with three hostages. Television crews arrive, and the audience stays to watch more than the movie. Finally, he's forced to give up after the police bombard him with tear gas – hence the title.

Other low-budget movie roles followed, with Nicholson most often cast as a sweet-faced hood. *The Wild Ride* (1960) found him in particularly evil form, as he runs over a couple of motorcycle cops, blackmails his best friend and kills a fellow drag-racer, before getting his just desserts in the exciting high-speed finale. Over the next few years he was to appear in a mixed bag of pictures, but it was for his work with Roger Corman that he is still most fondly remembered. After contributing to the rather lacklustre *Studs Lonigan* (1960), he appeared in Corman's *The Little Shop of Horrors* (shot in 1961 in just two days!) as an over-the-top masochistic dental patient named Wilbur Force who just couldn't get enough pain. The budget for the film was so low that, apparently, Corman only gave him the pages in the script that had his lines on. That way he could save money by giving the rest of the script to someone else! Years later, in a big budget musical re-make of the film, the role was taken by Bill Murray.

Nicholson's potential and range were ably demonstrated in his next movie. Moving away from playing just villains or nutcases, he assumed the role of Rexford, the son of a magician called Bedlo, in Roger Corman's *The Raven* (1963).

Vincent Price with Jack Nicholson in *The Raven*. Where is he now?

Based on the story by Edgar Allan Poe, the film also starred Peter Lorre as Bedlo, Vincent Price and Boris Karloff.

Despite its fabulous cast, the real star of *The Raven* was the incredible gothic castle that had been built to shoot in. Realising that there would be a couple of days to spare at the end of *The Raven*, and hating to see a big, good-looking, expensive set go to waste, Corman set out to shoot another Poe-inspired film over the final weekend. He cobbled together a loose script, called it *The Terror* and started work. Karloff was persuaded to hang around, and Nicholson was cast as a young French army officer. The leading lady was Nicholson's then wife, Sandra Knight, playing a mysterious but beautiful spirit.

Corman was too busy to actually finish filming *The Terror*, so he handed it over to his young assistant, Francis Ford Coppola. Fresh out of film school, Coppola shot a couple of days and handed it over to another student, Dennis Jakob. Jakob completed his short stint before giving way to Monte Hellman. And so it went, with even Nicholson himself taking a stab at directing, until there was enough

Above: Jack Nicholson in *The Terror* – quite a ladies man.

Below: Jack Nicholson. The best was yet to come.

footage to cobble together the movie. During the course of its lengthy shoot, Nicholson's wife got pregnant, and her changing figure is clearly evident in certain scenes of the movie. All in all, the film is a mess. Nicholson is almost completely unbelievable – but at least he had an excuse.

The parts kept coming, and Nicholson kept improving. In 1964 he popped up in *Ensign Pulver* and *Back Door to Hell*, and then appeared in a couple of excellent Westerns, *The Shooting* and *Ride the Whirlwind* (both 1966). But it was in the new wave of movies chronicling the changing fashions and sub-cultures of America's youth that he is best remembered. He appeared in one of the first Biker films that became a staple of the drive-in diet toward the end of the Sixties. *Hell's Angels on Wheels* (1967) cast Nicholson as Poet, a former gas station attendant who joined the Hell's Angels. He does the usual biker things; gets beaten up and then gets revenge; goes to an orgy and makes it with the head Angel's girl – getting into more trouble as a result. There are chase scenes, fight scenes and, of course, lots of free love scenes.

He contributed the script for one of the wilder movies to be directed by Roger Corman, *The Trip* (1967). A film about the delights and dangers of LSD, the posters advertised it as recommended for mature audiences; 'Listen to the sound of love – Feel Purple – Taste Green' and 'Touch the scream that Crawls up the Wall' were two of the less enticing offers they made to prospective audiences. The film starred Peter Fonda and a heavily bearded Bruce Dern, who was to co-star with Nicholson in his next picture, another drug-culture exposé called *Psych-Out*.

Psych-Out (1968) had Nicholson in full hippy mode, even sporting a long pony tail. He played Stoney, the lead guitarist and singer with a band called Mumbling John. The story rather neatly exposed the flower generation in their prime, as Susan Sarandon, playing a deaf runaway, goes in search of her missing brother. Nicholson, along with the other members of his band, helps her to evade the police and finally track down her missing sibling – a deranged Bruce Dern in a white flowing kaftan. Along the way they have a couple of bad trips, including one in which one of the members of the band tries to chop off his hand after hallucinating that it is a rotting stump!

As far as I know, *Psych-Out* was Nicholson's last film, his name only appearing again as the co-screenwriter and co-producer of the 1968 film starring the Monkees, *Head*. The Monkees had finished filming their popular TV series, and presumably *Head* was an attempt by them to reach a more mature crowd. It failed, although the film does have some of the oddest guest stars, including Tor Johnson and Frank Zappa.

Where the charismatic young actor Jack Nicholson disappeared to after that is anyone's guess, but his short career in films was enough to create a cult following for this intense but likeable screen personality. Perhaps he was embarrassed over his imminent hair loss, or maybe he'd just had enough of appearing in hippy and biker films that were never going to reach a wide enough audience to make him into a real star. But whatever the reason, his disappearance after *Head* in 1968 deprived cinema of an actor of great potential. Wherever you are, Jack, good luck.

Part Four

Gimmicks

16 The A to Z of Gimmicks

Let's compare the history of cinema with a long, one-way motorway, stretching from the Hollywood, California, of today back just under 100 years into the past. As roads go, it's not a bad one. At the very least, it's functional, with only the occasionally jarring pothole, like *Ishtar* or *Howard the Duck* to jolt the traveller out of a comfortable and otherwise enjoyable reverie. This view's not bad. Nice realistic colour, but not quite as panoramic as you might like – turn your head too far to either side and it just kind of fades to black. It's a little on the flat side as well, lacking that realistic third dimension we tend to take for granted elsewhere. There are plenty of famous faces travelling this way, and scores of odd little cul-de-sacs to explore. But someone really ought to do something about the litter! It's terrible. Piles of unwanted junk on either side. Not just old movies or dead stars; we're talking rubbish piles consisting solely of new things, hardly used at all! There goes Cinerama, abandoned after just a few cruel years at the top. What about 3-D? How did that wind up dumped when it still had so much life in it? Or Sensurround? There's Percepto, and Emergo and the Fear Flasher and the Horror Horn. Surely someone could find a use for them? What a terrible waste, although there's a heap over there with Smell-O-Vision and Odorama on top, so I suppose there's some justice. Yes, the cinematic highway is made distinct by many such rotting piles, ideas that seemed good at the time, but for any number of reasons failed to click. This is their story.

When films first appeared, they themselves were a gimmick. The promise of lifelike pictures that *moved* was enough to sell them to an eager public. What a concept it must have seemed back in 1895. One minute you were looking at a blank piece of wall, the next, there was a train roaring soundlessly toward you! For years after their introduction as the

With posters like this, wouldn't you want to experience Cinerama?

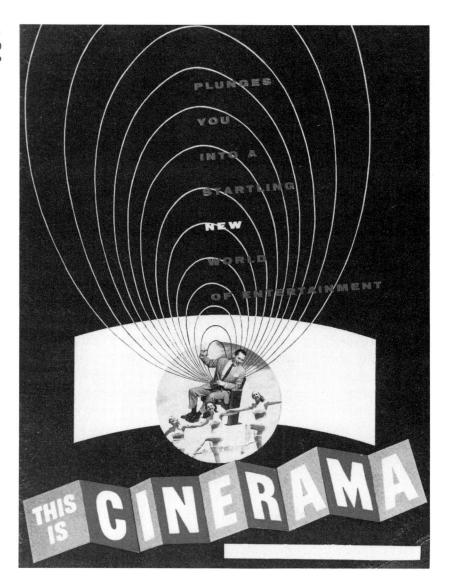

marvel of the age, moving pictures in and of themselves could guarantee a fair sized audience. No embellishment was necessary. No plot, no stars, no close-ups or cut-aways. Just plant your camera down, catch an event on film and wait for the paying customers.

But as with most things, familiarity bred a certain ennui, and both the audiences for these early experiments and the creators of the films themselves wanted more. The move away from the straightforward presentation of events and simple attempts at humour, like *L'Arroseur de la Ciotat*, in which a gardener looks down his hosepipe only to catch a faceful of water, were pioneered by George Melies. More than anyone else, Melies can be credited with realising and developing the potential of cinema as an artistic medium.

Melies was the father of today's modern special effects, allegedly stumbling upon the concept of trick photography when his camera jammed one day. Watching the faulty footage back, Melies discovered that the jam created the illusion of a carriage turning into a hearse. After recreating the effect deliberately for the first time in *L'Ecomptage d'une Dame* (1896), in which he 'transformed' a French woman into a skeleton, he was off and running. He went on to produce over one thousand movies, from the fantastic, like his best known pictures *Voyage dans la Lune* (1902) and *20,000 Lieues Sous les Mers* (1907), both adapted from the novels of Jules Verne, to the more straightforward, like his version of *Hamlet* and a film recreation of *l'affaire Dreyfus*. Melies gave up making films in 1913 after suffering financially through years of plagiarism and outright piracy. An unsuccessful return to the theatre meant that he eventually sold off most of his movies for their worth as celluloid. He died in 1938, living in a hostel for cinema veterans, and only about 50 of his films survive today.

The addition of plots and special effects had broadened the horizons of this new form of entertainment considerably. Then the studio bosses found that audiences were showing a preference not only for certain types of situations and stories, but also for certain performers. The Movie Star was born, God help us all.

The next gimmick was sound. If moving pictures themselves had shocked people with their ability to 'capture' reality, imagine the excitement when these moving images finally learned how to talk. After the success of *The Jazz Singer* in 1927, sound rapidly became a vital part of the cinema package, going, in just a few years, from being a gimmick to a necessity. From the mid-Thirties onwards, silent films would only appear when the lack of sound itself was considered a big enough gimmick, as with Mel Brooks's *Silent Movie*.

Experiments with sound had been taking place since the 1890s, and films with portions in colour appeared about the same time. George Melies and DW Griffith had both used hand-tinting in their films, and coloured sequences were included in the original *The Ten Commandments* (1923), the original *Phantom of the Opera* (1925) and the original *Ben Hur* (1926).

Technicolour emerged as the dominant colour process with the development of a device called the beam-splitter camera. But Technicolour was expensive, adding as much as 50 per cent to the cost of a film, and so other, cheaper methods were employed, like Cinecolor, Ansco Color and, later on, Eastman Colour. As the use of colour as a gimmick wore off, desperate promoters at the more lurid end of the market tried to keep the excitement alive by inventing new, ever more outlandish names for the same old stuff. Of course, only really stupid people were fooled by Exoticolor or Lunacolor, but they both sounded kind of cool.

Colour caused nothing like the sensation that sound had. It wasn't really until the arrival of television that studios, desperate to offer a bigger experience, switched most of their productions from black and white. Television was also the threat that prompted otherwise sane men to throw money after exciting but dumb gimmicks like 3-D and Smell-O-Vision, but we'll come back to that later. In the last decade, with the arrival of the technique known as colorisation, old black and white movies are being given a kind of colour. It's thought that this will make classic black and white films like Frank Capra's *It's a Wonderful Life* and Laurel and Hardy's *Babes in Toyland* more attractive to the video generation. Personally, I think it's like dragging Grandpa down to the nearest shopping mall and kitting him out with a jogging suit, some Hi-Tops and a baseball cap. No one's going to fancy him any more and everyone just feels exhausted.

Sound and colour, both dismissed as gimmicks when they initially appeared, are now an essential part of the cinematic experience. Let us, then, try to forget what we know in hindsight and put ourselves in the shoes of those brave idealists hoping to blaze a trail right through the pages of variety and into the history books. Let's try to give the benefit of the doubt to the hucksters and showmen, the gimmick makers and inventors of ever more exciting, ever more dumb tricks that were all intended to become as indispensable to the movies as sound and colour are now. Here, with one or two unavoidable blank spots, is the A to Z of cinematic quirks, foibles and, of course, gimmicks.

A is for AROMA-RAMA.
This was one of two very different systems tried out in the late Fifties to enhance the viewing pleasure of a cinema audience with smells. I would have thought that having someone work their way through a hot-dog in the seat next to you had pretty much achieved that already. The only film to benefit from the wonders of Aroma-rama was a rather dull documentary about China, *Behind the Great Wall* (1959). It worked by pumping about 72 different smells into the auditorium through the building's air-conditioning unit. Apparently it was successful as far as it went, but having the occasional waft of magnolia in your face was hardly enough to make people queue around the block. Not as fondly remembered or potentially amusing as Smell-O-Vision.

B is for BLACK STAMPS.
Without doubt the most feeble of all movie gifts, black stamps were given away free to the first 10,000 people who went to see the Hammer double bill of *The Curse of the Mummy's Tomb* and *The Gorgon* when it played in the States. The stamps had no redeemable value, nor did they feature in or relate to the films in any way. Lame.

B is also for BLAXPLOITATION.
Not a one-off gimmick in itself, but rather a trashy cash-in genre that made the Seventies worth living. So excited do I

get about this rash of low budget movies starring broad shouldered black studs and foxy chicks with afro hair-dos that idolise pimps and pushers, that I've devoted a whole chapter to the phenomenon.

C is for CINERAMA.

Along with 3-D, the various wide-screen processes experimented with during the Fifties can be directly attributed to the justifiable fear within the film industry over the threat posed by television. Cinerama made use of a huge curved screen and stereophonic sound. Appropriately titled *This is Cinerama*, the first movie to benefit from this breathtaking development premièred at the Broadway Theater in New York on 30 September 1952. After a deliberately dull opening scene, in which a narrator, shot in black and white, gave a brief history of cinema up to Cinerama, curtains on either

The London Casino – Britain's first Cinerama cinema. As you can see, the gimmick was more important than the movie.

side of the conventional size screen pulled back to reveal the huge, curved Cinerama screen, and the audience was engulfed in the sound from six channels instead of the usual one. The first sequence, in which the cameras had been mounted on the front of a roller coaster, literally had people in cinemas screaming and gripping the armrests of their seats! It was just like the first days of cinema.

Despite the hoopla surrounding *This is Cinerama* there had been experiments in wide-screen photography before. At the turn of the century, French Director Abel Gance had shot his epic *Napoleon* using a similar three-strip system called Polyvision. In fact, Cinerama itself had been invented in 1928 and was experimented with as far back as the mid-1930s. It involved filming each sequence simultaneously on three cameras mounted together as one unit. In the specially equipped theatres, three synchronised projectors would then recreate the images on the curved screen that virtually filled the entire field of human vision. Much of the impact of Cinerama on audiences was from the refined, stereophonic sound system, something we pretty much take for granted today, but remember that Cinerama was unveiled some time before stereo records were available to the public.

Promotional photograph for *This is Cinerama* showing a giant woman floating in the air. Don't ask me why!

Initially, Cinerama was seen as an experimental process, and only the one theatre in New York was fully equipped to show it. But when the same film was still packing them in two years after the première, the producers knew they had a gimmick worth running with. *This is Cinerama* was followed with *Cinerama Holiday* and *Seven Wonders of the World* (both 1955). The first real, non-travelogue feature film to utilise the big-screen thrills of Cinerama was *The Wonderful World of the Brothers Grimm* (1962), followed soon after by *How the West Was Won* (1963).

Despite its popularity, Cinerama had serious drawbacks. The first was the technical complexity and expense of the process itself. The use of three cameras and three projectors meant that three projectionists were needed at every cinema where it was shown, a sure way to eat into profits. Also, there was growing dissatisfaction with the actual quality of the projected film, for even in the best equipped and staffed Cinerama theatres, distinct lines could be seen on screen where the three projected images joined. The development of one-camera wide-screen systems (Cinemascope, Todd-AO, Ultra Panavision) capable of creating an equally impressive effect using just one camera, finished Cinerama off.

D is for DUO-VISION.
The split-screen had been a featured gimmick in a number of movies before Duo-Vision trundled along. Rock Hudson and

Wicked, Wicked - the first (and last) movie to be shot in Duo-Vision.

Doris Day had conducted one of cinema's most unlikely romances over the phone in full split-screen glory in *Pillow Talk* (1959), and Brian De Palma had relied on it heavily in *Sisters*, *The Phantom of the Paradise* and *Carrie*.

But Duo-Vision took the split-screen experience to its illogical extreme when producer/director/screenwriter Richard L Bare decided to shoot his 1973 film *Wicked, Wicked* entirely as a split-screen experience. 'See the hunter, see the hunted – both at the same time!' boasted the ads, not realising that most people found it hard enough to follow the plot when there was just one image on screen. Not many people cared for the experience, presumably going home with crossed eyes and a headache. Neither Mr Bare nor Duo-Vision have been seen since.

Wicked, Wicked – Duo-Vision in all its glory.

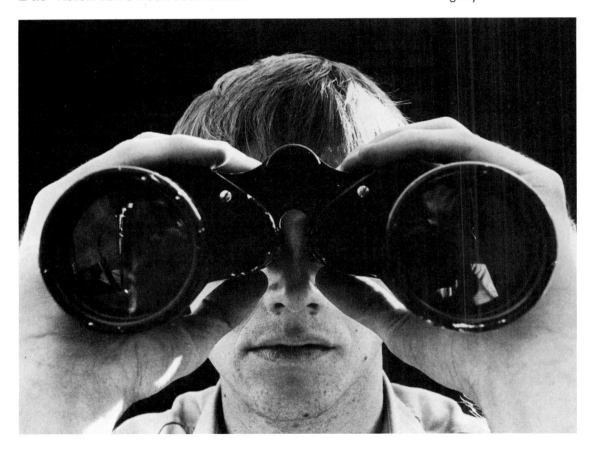

E is for EMERGO.
Genius William Castle cooked up Emergo as the device with which to sell his 1959 movie *The House On Haunted Hill*. At a key moment in the movie a skeleton emerged from a vat of boiling acid. Lucky visitors to any cinema with Emergo installed would have had the thrill of seeing a 12-foot plastic skeleton emerge (sorry, it's as dumb as that) from a box hidden by the side of the screen, cranked out over the audience on a length of fishing wire, In some cinemas kids would come armed with popguns, bows and arrows and catapults, hoping to shoot the varmint down. Emergo probably added little to the actual atmosphere of the movie, but must have been a whole lot of fun. It was never officially used again, but some canny theatre owners held on to their black boxes and lengths of wire to dust off the gag for a film called *The Bat*.

F is for FEAR FLASHER.
Along with the Horror Horn, the Fear Flasher appeared in the Warner Brothers 1966 horror/thriller *Chamber of Horrors*. Originally produced for TV, the film was re-packaged for the cinema because it was considered too shocking for home audiences. The Fear Flasher and the Horror Horn were added as 'fright breaks', alerting the more highly strung viewers to scenes of terror, and giving them the chance to look away. It was reminiscent of William Castle's fright break in *Homicide* (1961), and the warning bell before 'horrific' scenes in *Terror is a Man* (1959), which began with this message:

WARNING

The picture you are about to see has a scene so shocking that it is necessary to forewarn you.

We suggest that the squeamish *close their eyes* at the sound of the bell and reopen them when the bell rings again.

The Management.

G is for GHOST VIEWER.
Thanks again to William Castle for this one. The ghost viewers were souped up 3-D glasses, a vital part of Castle's

Illusion-O process used in *13 Ghosts*. The glasses were donned by the audience when given an on-screen command, signalled also by a pale glow on screen. By looking through the blue lens, they saw nothing, while the red revealed one of Castle's ghastly ghosts. Incidentally, the 13 ghosts of the title were a screaming woman, clutching hands, a floating head, a flaming skeleton, Emilio with cleaver in his hand, his unfaithful wife, her lover, an executioner with a decapitated head, a hanging woman, one lion, one lion tamer (headless) and Dr Zorba. The thirteenth ghost was an unfilled post, indicated in the film by an ectoplasmic question mark.

H is for HALLUCINOGENIC HYPNOVISION.
This was the brand name given to the hokey moment in Ray Dennis Seckler's *The Incredibly Strange Creatures Who Stopped Living and Became Crazy Mixed Up Zombies* (1964), when Estrella the gypsy hypnotizes her victims. A spinning black wheel with a white spiral on it is briefly shown to the audience. Rather lame and unthreatening you might think, but when I showed that clip on a Channel 4 documentary about Steckler, I was told I had to blank out the centre of the wheel in case viewers at home fell under Estrella's control! Other posters claimed that the film was shot in Bloody-Vision.

Hypnovision also alluded to another gimmick, one that had been around for some time, although I'm not sure where it was first introduced. The posters carried this warning: Unlike Anything Before! You Are Surrounded By Monsters! Not 3-D But Real Flesh And Blood Monsters! At a key moment, and only in key theatres, in the scene when monsters broke out of their cages and invaded a carnival, abducting young women, local actors and cinema employees wearing monster masks and carrying cardboard axes would run out from behind the screen and abduct a couple of live victims from the audience. On several occasions fist fights were known to break out between over-zealous monsters and protective boyfriends, after which plants were used.

H is also for HYPNOMAGIC.

'Introducing the amazing new audience thrill – Hypnomagic – it makes *you* a part of the show!' boasted the posters for *The Hypnotic Eye* (1959), a fun little film in which The Great Desmond, played by Jacques Bergerac, specialised in hypnotizing volunteers on stage. He favoured beautiful females, but the plot turned nasty when they got home and, still under his evil influence, disfigured themselves. The Hypnomagic began when Desmond conducted a demonstration near the end of the film. He requested that the house lights be put up, at which time the lights in the cinema would go on as well. Speaking directly into the camera, Desmond then hypnotised his assistant, and presumably some of the more simple folk who payed good cash to get in. Hypnomagic balloons were also given out as an added bonus. What a thrill.

I is for ILLUSION-O.

Illusion-O was the name given by our old friend William Castle to the process he used to enhance the viewing pleasure of *13 Ghosts* (1960). Ghost Viewers (look under G) were handed out to each member of the audience. When the command 'Use Viewer' flashed on the bottom of the screen, patrons could decide whether or not they wanted to see one of the 13 ghosts on offer. Although put to tacky use, it was a simple and effective process. At the end of the film Castle appeared, suggesting that customers might want to keep the viewers for home use. Handy.

K is for KUNG FU.

Not really a gimmick, but well worth a mention, Kung Fu was the generic name given to the rash of martial arts films that caught the imagination of certain jaded cinema-goers in the early 1970s. For the purist, it was almost as insulting as the other great generic term, Chop-Socky, which made up in onomatopoeia what it lacked in accuracy. The first wave of Kung Fu movies were often hilariously over-dubbed and mistranslated, but still found a loyal audience thanks to their exuberance and fast action.

The boom in martial arts movies, mostly imported from Hong Kong studios like the famous Shaw Brothers and Golden Harvest, was one of the more exciting and interesting trends of the early Seventies, even inspiring a popular mainstream TV series starring David Carradine, 'Kung Fu'. The single biggest Kung Fu star to emerge was Bruce Lee, the first and to this date only Chinese action star to make it big in American movies. He was actually born in San Francisco, and achieved his earliest acting successes there, appearing as Kato in the TV series 'The Green Hornet', and making guest appearances in a number of films. It was in the brutal and uncompromising fight films he made in the early Seventies in Hong Kong that he established his reputation. *The Big Boss, The Chinese Connection, Fist Of Fury* and *Way Of The Dragon* paved the way for his first and only American hit movie, the legendary *Enter The Dragon*. In 1973 he died under mysterious circumstances while making his next movie, *The Game Of Death*, and the Hong Kong movie industry rushed to fill the gap with a handful of piss-poor Bruce Lee clones. Bruce Lei, Bruce Li, Bruce Le, Tiger Lee, Dragon Lee, and Bronson Lee all appeared in films designed to cash in on his popularity. Sadly, Bruce Lee's son, Brandon Lee, died in 1993 (aged 28) under equally mysterious circumstances, on the set of the martial arts movie *The Crow*.

Despite there being many other great action stars in the Hong Kong industry – Sonny Chiba, Samo Hung, Jimmy Wang Yu, Yuen Baio, Angela Mao Ying and Alexander Fu Sheng are just a few of the names I'll confuse you with – major international stardom has eluded them all. One of the biggest and most talented stars of the Nineties is the actor and director Jackie Chan, who has almost achieved Bruce Lee's breakthrough on a number of occasions. Chan has almost singlehandedly dragged the martial arts movie out of the overdubbed cliché-ridden rut that Lee's death left it in. His films, such as *Armor of God* and *Police Story*, deserve a far bigger audience than they get, as does the whole range of Hong Kong fantasy, horror and action. Unfortunately, the rise and dominance of low-budget western versions of these movies has brought stardom for lesser talents like Chuck

Norris, Steven Seagal, Jean Claude Van Damme and Dolph Lundgren, and now the chance of a genuine breakthrough for Chan or any of the other superb Hong Kong action stars looks unlikely.

L is for lots of letters in the alphabet that don't have a cinematic gimmick to call their own.

M is for more of the above.

N is for NATURAMA.
One of the many gimmicky names given to one of the many versions of wide-screen photography inspired by the success of Cinerama. The only film that benefited from Naturama was *Juvenile Jungle*, made in 1958. I doubt if it helped much.

O is for ODORAMA.
Not to be confused with Aroma-rama or Smell-O-Vision, Odorama was a deliberately trashy gimmick used by the super-cool John Waters in his movie *Polyester* (1981). Unlike the other two smell-based treats, Odorama did not involve free-floating smells pumped around the room. Instead, each

John Water's *Polyester* featured a romance between Tab Hunter and Divine, and gave the world Odorama!

customer was given a scratch and sniff card. The numbers on the card corresponded with numbers flashed on the screen, and the audience helped create the right ambience by furiously scratching, then sniffing, the correct patch of the card at the right time. Alarmingly accurate, especially in the fart scene.

P is for PSYCHORAMA.
Psychorama was used to tart up *Terror in the Haunted House* (1958). It would probably be illegal today, as it flashed scary words like DEATH and BLOOD, and pictures of things like spiders and snakes on to the screen for one-fiftieth of a second to add an extra subliminal shudder to the proceedings. Sadly, they forgot to flash messages like COME AGAIN or TELL YOUR FRIENDS, so the film and Psychorama both flopped. The process was used a year later in another movie from the same producer, William S Edwards, *A Date With Death*, but the results were pretty much the same.

Q is for quite a lot of nice things, but no gimmicks.

R is for relatively few outlandish ideas to lure people into cinemas.

S is for SMELL-O-VISION.
Appearing at about the same time as Aroma-rama, Smell-O-Vision was another attempt to encourage audience members to use their noses while at the movies. It dated back to 1953, but was not utilised in a feature film until the release of *Scent of Mystery* in 1960. Starring the late Peter Lorre, the late Diana Dors and the late Denholm Elliott, the film attempted to excite viewers with over 30 aromas, including garlic, pipe tobacco, gunsmoke, perfume, seafood, bananas and peppermint. The smells were contained in vials, racked in a rotating drum, and triggered by a signal from the 'smell track' on the film itself. They were then piped right up to the expectant nose via plastic tubes attached to every seat.

The biggest drawback with this method of olfactory interaction was that it was one thing getting the smells into the cinema, but quite another getting them out. The Smell-O-Vision system was meant to extract the scented air once it had been sniffed, but didn't always quite achieve the extraction. Hence the main reason why it failed, apart from its inherent dumbness, was that people were leaving the cinema in a state of advanced nausea. It was also a complete flop with people suffering from heavy colds. The movie was later re-released, minus its smelly clues, under the title *Holiday in Spain*.

Only a handful of cinemas in New York, Los Angeles and Chicago went along with the gimmick, but the mind boggles over what might have been. What if it had been a big enough hit, and all of today's films were shot in Smell-O-Vision? I can imagine thoroughly enjoying *Scent of a Woman* and *Delicatessen*, but would probably pass on *A Fish Called Wanda* and *A Man Called Horse*.

S could just as reasonably stand for SENSURROUND.
This gimmick, developed to enhance the thrills in Universal's *Earthquake* (1974), and used again in *Midway* (1976) and *Rollercoaster* (1976), used special de-coders in selected cinemas to add air vibrations to the soundtrack of the film during the dubbing process. It was intended to create the illusion of movement, as if the audience were actually participating in the on-screen disasters. In reality, it was like watching a movie in a cinema that was too close to a tube station. Apparently some cinemas suffered falling plasterwork as an unwanted side-effect of the sub-audible bass. Must have made that earthquake feel even more real.

U is for UNDERWATER.
In his definitive study and appreciation of cinematic gimmicks, *Beyond Ballyhoo*, author Mark Thomas McGee reported on the première for Howard Hughes's otherwise dull 1955 movie *Underwater*. He held the première (where else?) under water. The audience wore aqua-lungs and diving masks that presumably had some kind of sound system installed in them. The event received huge press coverage thanks to the 211 journalists Hughes invited along. But a

turkey is a turkey, even when it's wet, and an otherwise fine gimmick failed to attract the crowds.

V is very nearly at the end of this A to Z.

W is for WIDE-SCREEN.
Following the success of Cinerama and its legitimate offsprings, Super Cinerama, Todd-AO, and Cinemascope, came a whole orphanage full of imitative little bastards. Wonderama, Thrillerama, Dimension 150, Superscope, Techniscope, Actionscope, Dynavision, Hi-Fi Scope, Megascope, Naturama and Vistascope were just some of the exciting names used to describe mostly bog-standard wide-screen photography. Some, like the Aquascope promised with the movie *The Mermaids Of Tiburon*, probably weren't even that, just a cool sounding name to put on the poster.

Z is for ZOMBIE EYES.
What else? Zombie eyes were given out to lucky females waiting in line to see the Hammer films *Dracula Prince of Darkness* and *Plague of Zombies* when they were released by 20th Century Fox in America in 1966. Lucky males got Dracula fangs.

17 William Castle

The Abominable Showman

I can appreciate a good, well-made movie along with the next guy. A film doesn't have to have been produced on a shoe-string, written by depraved, profit hungry maniacs or acted out by talentless amateurs who only got the job because of their willingness to strip buck naked at the drop of the hat for me to like it. But, to be honest (and this really isn't something that I'm overly proud of), those are the kind of films I like best. Even the most refined cineaste must surely admit that there's something attractive about low-budget shockers, movies that often only succeeded because of a brilliant advertising campaign or the willingness of the producers to risk prosecution by showing just a little bit more than was permitted, be it nudity or violence or any other juicy little titbit they could sneak in.

Elsewhere in this book I sing the praises of Russ Meyer, the auteur who almost single-handedly opened the door for nudity on American movie screens; Herschell Gordon Lewis who, along with his partner, Dave Friedman, helped pave the way for the ultra-gory crap that the mainstream studios churn out today; and the daddy of them all, Kroger Babb, the roadshow promoter and founder of Hallmark Productions, a company that might never have had a good film to show, but never let that get in the way of drumming up trade. The alternative history of the cinema is full of such characters, men driven by personal passion or the over-riding desire to make a fast buck, but who somehow managed to remain charming and endearing figures despite it. William Castle was one such man.

In his autobiography, *Step Right Up! I Want to Scare the Pants Off America*, Castle wrote that his life-long ambition to scare the pants off folks began when he was 13 years old. Watching the stage performance of Bela Lugosi in the hit play *Dracula*, the young Castle was obviously affected by the sound of an audience screaming in terror. After serving a stint as assistant stage manager on the play when it toured, he broke into showbiz properly by persuading the equally youthful Orson Welles to let him take over the running of his theatre. The difference between Orson Welles and William Castle is a small but telling one. Welles cared about the work he did. Castle only cared about selling it. He dabbled as an actor and dialogue coach, but his apprenticeship with Harry Cohn at Columbia Pictures honed Castle's real talent, his precocious skill as a huckster and salesman.

The first picture Castle directed was *The Chance of a Lifetime*. When it appeared in 1942 it was reviewed by *Variety* as 'probably the worst directed picture in the history of motion pictures'. Harry Cohn gave Castle another chance, at the age of 29, to direct a thriller, *The Whistler*. Its commercial success, and the respect Castle earned as the film's director enabled him to pursue a successful career. He directed literally dozens of films – thrillers, westerns, historical dramas, even comedies – all moderately successful but largely forgettable. (*The Return of Rusty* ring any bells? How about *Serpent of the Nile*?)

Castle really came into his own in the late Fifties, when he set himself up as an independent producer and director. From 1958 until his death in 1977 he was involved with the production, direction and, most importantly, the exploitation of perhaps the tricksiest, most gimmick-laden movies ever made.

Macabre (1958), Castle's debut as a producer, got the ball rolling. Castle had no luck in persuading any of the studios he had previously worked for as a director to stump up the cash for the movie, so he mortgaged his house – at least that's what he claims in his autobiography. However, in an interview given to the American horror film mag, *Fangoria*, Robb White, who wrote the *Macabre* screenplay for Castle, claimed that Castle asked him to put up half of the $86,000 needed to make the film. According to White, Castle never quite got around to finding his half, so he financed the entire picture! White also described Castle as 'absolutely the coldest, most ruthless conman I've ever known'.

Macabre was shot in just nine days, but Castle wasn't satisfied. After all, it was his house on the line (maybe!). After many sleepless nights, he realised that what he, and the film, needed was a gimmick. And he came up with a doozy.

Castle decided that he would take out life insurance for the entire world. That way, if anyone were to drop dead from fright during *Macabre*, they would be covered. The chances of that happening were of course incredibly remote if not non-existant, but it gave Castle a terrific angle on which to sell the film. In one of the funnier chapters in his autobiography, Castle recalled his meeting with Lloyd's of London:

> 'How many people do you think will actually expire during the exhibition of your motion picture, *Macabre*?' I hestitated before answering and the American quickly picked up the cue. 'Would you say that twenty-five people might drop dead?' 'Nobody's going to drop dead,' I predicted. 'It's just a publicity stunt.' 'But somebody has to drop dead, otherwise it won't work.' The four of us sat for hours bargaining on people's lives. The British went to twenty, I grudgingly gave them two; the American brought the death rate down to ten. I threw in an extra death, making mine three. We finally arrived at five lucky people who would not live through *Macabre*.

At a premium of $5000, Castle had dreamed up and paid for one of the best publicity stunts ever. Offering the finished movie, gimmick and all, to the various studios in town, he turned down a meagre offer from Warner Brothers, but was horrified several weeks later to discover that Warner had just opened a horror film of their own, using his insurance gimmick. With the threat of a court case hanging over them, Warner offered to buy *Macabre* from Castle for the $90,000 it cost to make. Castle declined, but accepted Warner's offer to stop using his gimmick. Eventually, he took the movie to Allied Artists, an aggressive little firm that specialised in low-budget items like *Macabre*.

The film opened in Boston, with eager punters queueing around the block. Before entering the auditorium, they were given a copy of the life insurance form to sign. Setting a style that he was to use again and again, the movie began with a kind of appetiser, designed to grab the audience's attention and work on their nerves before they'd seen a thing. A clock was projected on the screen, and William Castle's own voice was heard:

> Ladies and Gentlemen, when the clock reaches sixty seconds, you will be insured by Lloyd's of London for one thousand dollars against death by fright during *Macabre*. Lloyd's of London sincerely hopes that none of you will collect . . . But just in case, isn't it comforting to know that your loved ones are protected? You are now insured against death by fright!

The insurance scam featured prominently in newspaper adverts, and in some towns a huge, blown up copy of the policy was hung outside the cinema.

Once on a roll, Castle didn't stop. To keep the excitement going he pulled additional scams, like turning up to the cinema inside a black coffin on a horse-pulled hearse. In some towns, he even managed to persuade local cinema owners to hire nurses to attend the screenings, ready to administer instant first aid to anyone who found the movie too much to bear, and there were ambulances parked outside, just in case. The movie that had cost just $90,000 went on to earn over $5 million, and more of that was probably earned on the strength of the gimmick, than on the actual film, which was a moderately thrilling melodrama.

Flushed with the success of his first independent feature, Castle moved on to his next project. With Robb White he concocted the story of *The House on Haunted Hill*, a modern variation on the old haunted house story. In Castle and White's screenplay, six people are invited by a millionaire to spend a night in a 'haunted' house with him and his wife. It's actually an elaborate plot by him to kill her with a 'believable' alibi. To make matters more interesting, the millionaire's wife also sees this as the ideal opportunity to dispose of her troublesome husband.

The success of *Macabre* prompted Allied Artists to provide Castle with a decent budget up front, enabling Castle to put together a far stronger cast. Quality actors like Carolyn Craig, Elisha Cook and Richard Long played alongside Vincent Price in the lead role, beginning a sucessful partnership with Castle. At the end of the shoot they had an above average movie for the money, but no gimmick. Castle racked his brains, and the idea he came up with was wild even by his

The French poster for *The House on Haunted Hill* makes great play of the plastic skeleton.

standards. When it was released in 1959, *The House On Haunted Hill* was the first, and as far as I know, still the only movie to be shown using Emergo.

Emergo was not about a new photographic method, but rather, as the name suggests, involved an object emerging from the screen. Castle had looked at the movie and decided that the most dramatic part was near the end, when what appeared to be the skeleton of Vincent Price emerged from the vat of acid his loving wife has shoved him into. In fact it was a puppet, manipulated by Price, in an attempt to scare his wife to death. Castle's idea was to have the skeleton puppet keep moving, over the woman's head, out of the cinema screen itself, above the terrified audience and then back into the screen. To accomplish this extraordinary feat, hundreds of plastic skeletons, 12 feet tall, were shipped off to cinemas with a large black box and a length of fishing wire. At the key moment, the projectionist had to open the box and crank the skeleton out.

Like all great technological advances, Emergo had its faults. At the first couple of performances the weight of the skeleton proved too much for the fishing wire, and a few unlucky audience members found themselves with a larger than life prop in their laps. But once the bugs were ironed out, and some decent fishing wire purchased, Emergo came into its own. By the second day of the film's release, the Golden Gate Theater in San Francisco was completely sold out, with a line of kids and teenagers six blocks long. William Castle had become the King of Gimmicks.

It was almost unthinkable that Castle could now release a film without some kind of trashy, tacky, but curiously satisfying gimmick attached, and for the next few years he did everything he could to avoid letting his fans down. After Emergo came Percepto, used in conjunction with my favourite of all his films, *The Tingler* (1959).

So sublime was *The Tingler* that I've singled it out for discussion as a deranged movie in its own right but, briefly, it featured Vincent Price as a doctor who makes the shocking discovery that a large creature grows on the spinal cords of people in great fear. The only indication of its existence is a tingling on the spine, and the only way to kill it is by screaming; otherwise it would snap your spine. For Percepto, Castle ensured that certain seats in certain cinemas were wired with a mild buzzing device so that when Vincent Price, on screen, warned people to scream if they felt anything tingling on their spine, cinema employees could buzz the hell out of the audience. On a few occasions, entrepreneurial cinema owners, bitten by the Castle bug, were known to turn on the lights, stop the movie, and have a 'dead' customer carried out! Castle claims that he must have buzzed around 20,000,000 people in the backside, but I suspect that his figures, like his gimmicks, should be take with a pinch of salt.

The Tingler and Percepto were followed by a less physical but perhaps more dramatic device. In a very blatant steal from that year's biggest hit, *Psycho*, Castle and Robb White

The Tingler strikes!
Scream! Scream!

worked on a script in which the transvestite 'gimmick' at the end of Hitchcock's picture was extended throughout the whole film. After a strenuous search, Castle eventually cast a woman by the name of Joan Marshall in the dual lead roles of Emily and her husband Warren in *Homicidal* (1961).

Changing Marshall's name to the more ambiguous Jean Arless, Castle went ahead and shot the film. Bizarre is far too tame a word to describe *Homicidal*. It was insane. Deranged. Fabulous. It begins with Emily arriving at a seedy motel and, having booked in under her sister's name, Miriam, persuading a musclebound bellboy to marry her that evening in return for $2,000. The marriage would be anulled the next day. He agrees, and that evening they are married in a run-down chapel by a lecherous Justice of the Peace. At the end of the ceremony, the JP leans over to kiss the bride, only to have her repeatedly stab him in the abdomen. Barmy Emily escapes to her family's estate (in Denmark!), where she informs Miriam that she has married their step-brother, Warren. She proceeds to terrorise her sister, decapitating an old woman in the process. Finally, in scene shamelessly lifted from *Psycho*, Emily is prevented from killing Miriam at the last minute by Miriam's husband. Loose ends are deftly if unbelievably cleared up by the revelation that Emily was brought up as a boy by her loony mother so they wouldn't lose the family inheritance, only to be given to male heirs.

Crazy as the film was, and despite a good, solid and almost convincing dual-performance from Arless, Castle still craved that extra something to get audiences queueing. Hitchcock was again to provide the inspiration. *Psycho* had been released with the warning that, once the picture had begun, no one would be allowed to enter the cinema after the first five minutes. This was partly because of the surprise death of Janet Leigh so early in the picture, and partly because even Hitchcock wasn't too big for a good clean gimmick. Castle went one better. Five minutes before the end of the film, just before the dénouement, the audience was given a Fright Break. Castle's voice would cut into the soundtrack, saying something like, 'Ladies and Gentlemen, if you're too frightened to see the last two minutes of *Homicidal*, please go

William Castle keeps them guessing with *Homicidal*.

to the box office and get your full admission price refunded. You must leave immediately. You have only 60 seconds to get your money back.'

Castle was gambling that no one in their right mind would walk out of a movie as deranged and impossible to explain as *Homicidal* before they'd seen some kind of explanation for what had gone on. The film's financers, Columbia Pictures, thought Castle had finally gone nuts, and that everyone would leap at the chance of a 100 per cent refund, but they offered him a test screening in Youngstown, Ohio anyway.

The place was sold out. Castle and the top brass from Columbia all flew in. They agreed that the first performance would not be a fair test. People might be so curious to see whether they really would get their money back, that they'd leave early just for the hell of it. So Castle and his bosses waited until the second screening at 8.30.

The Fright Break arrived. Miriam and her husband are just about to enter the family home for the climactic confrontation when suddenly Castle's voice is heard throughout the cinema:

> This is the Fright Break! You hear that sound? The sound of a heartbeat! Is it beating faster than your heart? Or slower? This heart is going to beat for another 65 seconds to allow anyone to leave the theatre who is too frightened to see the end of the picture, and get your full admission refunded. Ten seconds more and we go into the house. It's now or never! Five! Four! You're a brave audience! Two! One!

There was a pause. Castle breathed easy. And then, almost as one, thousands of people leapt from their seats and raced to the box office for refunds! Castle was, to say the least, a little upset. He was on the verge of admitting defeat when the owner of the theatre informed him that most of the audience for the 8.30 show had already seen the ending. They'd stayed in their seats from the 6.30 performance!

The introduction of colour coded tickets for each performance overcame that little scam, and *Homicidal* and the Fright Break became the hits they deserved to be. After a couple of weeks, Castle spiced it up even more, by adding an element of humiliation. Anyone too scared to sit through to the end and wishing a refund had to follow a yellow streak painted on the floor in the cinema leading out to the foyer where they would have to stand in Coward's Corner. Nearby would be a uniformed nurse, with equipment used to take the coward's blood pressure! In some cinemas, Coward's Corner was bathed in a yellow light, and a recorded voice repeated, 'These cowards are too frightened to see the end of *Homicidal*. Watch them shiver in Coward's Corner! Coward . . . Coward . . . Coward . . .'

Although Castle was to continue making movies up until his death in 1977, his next two pictures, *13 Ghosts* (1960) and *Mr Sardonicus* (1961) marked the end of his greatest gimmicks. For *13 Ghosts* Castle performed his most generous stunt. He purchased a haunted house in France and had 20 million keys made up. Only one matched the house, and the lucky cinema-goer who received that key would also get the house. That dealt with the publicity side of life, now for an onscreen gimmick. Castle claims that it was at a trip to the opticians that he stumbled on the idea behind Illusion-O. Audiences would be given cardboard glasses, rather like those used to watch 3-D movies. These glasses would reveal the 13 ghosts of the title. Without the glasses, you would see nothing.

Mr Sardonicus relied a little more heavily on audience participation. The title character is an unpleasant chap with a horrible, rictus grin on his face. He got this way after digging up his dead father to retrieve a winning lottery ticket the corpse held in his hand! For the rest of the movie, the now wealthy but disfigured Sardonicus seeks a cure for his affliction. A combination of shock, after being reacquainted with his dead father in a dark room, and a supposedly 'fatal' dose of serum achieve the desired result. His face loses the grin and looks normal. But there is a twist. His face has now become immobile; he cannot eat! The doctor responsible for the cure reveals that in fact the 'serum' he administered was nothing but water; the affliction and its cure are all in Sardonicus's mind. Enter William Castle. It is time for the Punishment Poll! His by now familiar figure fills the screen and he offers the audience the chance to decide the fate of Sardonicus: 'Have you ever envied the thrill-hungry Roman crowds in the Circus Maximus who, with a wave of the thumb, could make life or death decisions that sealed the fate of many a gladiator? The fate of that ghoulish character Sardonicus is in your tender little hands.'

Arriving at the theatre, the audience had been given a card with a hand imprinted on it. When held upright the thumb pointed up and the word 'Mercy' could be seen. When turned over the thumb pointed down, and the card now read 'No Mercy'. On screen, Castle asked the audience to vote, and then he began to count the vote! Invariably, the audience voted for no mercy, but Castle had shot two endings, just in case.

The success of Castle's movies, and the gimmicks that he used to sell them, won him a huge fan following. For a few years, he was probably the best known director in America, after Alfred Hitchcock. Kids formed William Castle fan clubs, and ghost viewers, *Macabre* insurance policies and even the occasional 12-foot skeleton changed hands among fans for inflated prices. But the constant search for new gimmicks had taken their toll. Castle felt the urge to pass on the mantle of the King of Gimmicks to someone else. Castle was to have perhaps his greatest success as a producer, working with Roman Polanski on *Rosemary's Baby* (1968). At the time of his death he was working on a mediocre film called *Bug* (1975), about giant, fire-breathing, meat-eating, intelligent but angry cockroaches. But it was for those five films produced between 1958 and 1961 that he will always be most fondly remembered. Long live the King.

18 Totally Deranged Movie
The Tingler

The Tingler starts with legendary producer/director/show-man William Castle himself striding out on screen. He addresses the audience directly.

> I'm William Castle, the director of the motion picture you're about to see. I feel obligated to warn you that some of the sensations, some of the physical reactions which the actors on the screen will feel, will also be experienced for the first time in motion picture history by certain members of the audience.
>
> I say 'certain members' because some people are more sensitive to these mysterious electronic impulses than others. These unfortunate, sensitive people will at times feel a strange, tingling sensation. Others will feel it less strongly. Don't be alarmed! You can protect yourself. At any time you are conscious of a tingling sensation, you may obtain immediate relief by screaming. Don't be embarrassed about opening your mouth and letting rip with everything you've got. Because the person in the seat right next to you will probably be screaming too. And remember this: a scream at the right time may save your life.

The screen fades to black and we hear ear-piercing screams as disembodied heads, presumably those of fearful audience members, float toward the camera. Cut to a man, snivelling in his death-row cell. Over the credits and suitably spooky music, he is dragged from his cell, screaming all the way, to the electric chair. We are spared the sight of his actual execution. The next thing we see is Vincent Price, preparing to perform an autopsy on the corpse.

The autopsy is watched by the dead man's brother-in-law, Ollie, and reveals that the dead man's spine has been snapped in two. Price speculates that this phenomenon, one he has seen many times before, is a result of fear. But no fear could be so great that it physically snaps your spine. Could it?

Price offers Ollie a ride home, and discovers that he runs a cinema with his wife, who is a deaf mute. When Price meets her, he accidentally cuts his hand on a broken cup, and she grows rigid and faints in terror at the sight of his blood. Price, ever ready with a loopy theory, surmises that she grew stiff because she was unable to scream and release her 'fear tension'.

Determined to investigate further, Price decides to experiment on his wife. She is a no-good scheming witch, so we don't feel too bad when he threatens her with a pistol and shoots her with a blank cartridge. She faints in fear, and Price takes an X-ray of her spine. The X-ray reveals, for the very first time, the Tingler!

The Tingler, he postulates, draws its strength from human fear, and grows in size accordingly. To learn more, Price somehow needs to catch one alive. The only way to do that would be to take a Tingler from the dead body of someone who could stand whatever pain or terror they were subjected to and die without screaming.

Driven on, in true movie mad-scientist style, Price needs to experience the fear that calls the Tingler into existence for himself. Locking himself in his lab, Price commits a movie first. He injects himself with 100 micro-milligrams of LSD. Price, who presumably had never even seen anyone under the influence of acid, much less experienced it himself, plays the scene as he would a frightened drunk. Despite his best efforts, he cannot keep himself from screaming, the pain and the fear are so great. Only someone who really could not possibly, physically scream would be able to produce a Tingler. A deaf mute, for example.

Price, now completely obsessed with proving his theory, visits Ollie's mute wife, who is still jittery after having seen his blood. He offers to give her a shot of barbituates to calm her down. The audience is left guessing. Has he done as he said, or did he inject her with LSD?

How to scare your deaf mute wife to death, as demonstrated in *The Tingler*.

Alone in her darkened bedroom, the mute woman begins to hallucinate. Windows open, door handles turn. A hideously deformed man brandishing a knife appears from under the bed covers, chasing her out of the room. Lights flicker on and off. A large, hairy arm peeps around a door and throws an axe, barely missing her. She hides in the bathroom, where the taps begin to run on their own. But it isn't water that comes out, it's blood. Horrifically red blood in a film that is otherwise completely shot in black and white. (The first time I saw this

The Tingler ◆ 193

The hand in the bath full of blood is the only thing in full blood red colour in an otherwise black and white movie.

film, aged about 13, the red blood almost had me screaming!) From out of the blood-filled bath rises a ghastly clawed hand. The woman, unable to scream, doubles over in pain, clutching at her back. A sign appears on a cupboard door – it is her Death Certificate. Cause of death: Fright!

Ollie, thinking his wife might still be alive brings her to Price. He delivers his verdict: she is dead. Scared to death. Meanwhile the woman's corpse sits up under her shroud. Price checks her again; she is dead. Ollie agrees, rather readily, to an autopsy, and Price is beside himself with excitement. Watching the shadow of Price cutting the poor woman open, we see him remove a large, wriggling creature from her back. The Tingler! It attacks Price, but he screams and it falls unconscious to the ground. Price imprisons it in a glass case.

Scared by his ugly, dangerous discovery, Price decides he must keep it a secret. He hopes that by replacing the Tingler in the body of its creator, it will return to its tiny, helpless state. Ollie, however, is planning to escape. It turns out that he had engineered his wife's death to get at their money. While Price confronts Ollie in the cinema, the Tingler escapes, crawling through a loose board into the theatre below. A woman screams and faints as it tries to crawl up her leg, and Price turns off the cinema's lights, announcing that there is nothing to worry about, a young lady has fainted and will be carried out. Please remain seated. The Tingler makes its way into the projection booth, stopping the film. Vincent Price's voice is heard again. 'Ladies and Gentlemen, please do not panic. The Tingler is loose in the cinema. Scream, scream for your life!'

With a cinema full of panicky screamers, the Tingler is rendered harmless. Price and Ollie collect the weird beast, and return it to the body of Ollie's wife. Price is going to call the police on Ollie, but before he can do so, Ollie imagines his wife has returned from the dead. She rises, staring at him and he collapses, dead, paralysed with fear and unable to scream. Vincent Price, of course, has the last word.

> Ladies and Gentleman, just a word of warning. If any of you are not convinced that you have a Tingler of your own, the next time you're alone in the dark – don't scream.

I love this film. OK, so maybe the Tingler does look like a badly stuffed lobster. Maybe the plot does crank along in a rather predictable way. But it's one of those pictures where all the slightly less than satisfactory elements gel perfectly. To see Vincent Price on a scary acid trip is alone worth the price of admission! Imagine what it must have been like to see this film in one of the specially equipped cinemas, with hidden buzzers in selected chairs. During the blackouts in the cinema, not only were a handful of audience members buzzed, but occasionally young women (plants, of course), were carried out as if in a faint. Frankly, I yearn for these experiences, but even without them *The Tingler* is a great ride.

19 Three–D

– Comin' Right At Ya!

The first movie to be shot using the anaglyphic process we recognise as 3-D was a dodgy jungle B-movie called *Bwana Devil* (1952). The movie got the lousy reviews it deserved, but it did phenomenal business, and at a time when Hollywood was running scared from television, which had caused a worryingly large slump in income, that made people sit up and notice.

Bwana Devil was shot in Natural Vision, a 3-D process perfected by Milton L Gunzberg. It was not an especially new idea. There had been experiments in 3-D filming as far back as the 1920s, and the first full length feature using a 3-D process was made in Italy in 1937. Even before *Bwana Devil* burst triumphantly onto the scene, over 200 different patents for 3-D type processes had been filed!

But none of those early experimental movies ever caught on as *Bwana Devil* did. It precipitated a virtual avalanche of movies that were as deep as their wide-screen cousins were wide. *House of Wax* and *It Came From out of Space* (both 1953) were two huge successes, not only because they appeared while the novelty of 3-D was still fresh, but because they both had been crafted to ensure that the 3-D was integral to many scenes. *Life* magazine compared the coming of 3-D with the birth of the talkies, which must have heartened both Milton L Gunzberg, who had landed an exclusive deal with Polaroid to manufacture 3-D glasses, and the many theatre-owners who had spent small fortunes in upgrading their cinemas with the necessary equipment.

When used properly, 3-D could provide breathtaking cinema. *The Creature from the Black Lagoon* (1954) contained some of the most fabulous underwater shots I've ever seen, enhanced beautifully by the process. But there were of course

The Creature from the Black Lagoon – one of the very best 3-D pictures.

some 3-D films that were so cheap and shoddy that nothing could help them. *Robot Monster* (1953), featuring a monster that resembled a gorilla in a deep sea diver's helmet, has entered the movie history books as the one of the lamest creations ever. *Cat Women of the Moon* (1954) and *Taza, Son of Cohise* were also a couple of real stinkers.

The 3-D boom began to die out around the end of 1954. Contrary to popular belief, it was not solely due to the increasingly poor quality of the movies. The ratio of good films to bad was about the same as it ever had been. Nor could it be argued that the public got bored with the novelty. When 3-D resurfaced in the Seventies it did just as well as it had back in the Fifties. The greatest single factor in the demise of 3-D as a viable technique was cost. It was more expensive to make than regular movies, and more expensive to exhibit properly – both costs that were ultimately borne by the theatre-owners. Furthermore, there were the hundreds of cardboard glasses to be given away at each screening. Although 3-D features always drew a larger than average crowd, ultimately the profit margin was reduced.

Many theatre-owners were reluctant to equip their cinemas with the proper equipment. Why lay out more for a silver nitrate screen, stereophonic sound system, special projectors (they needed two in each cinema to properly project films shot using the anaglyphic method), when there was always a non 3-D version of the same movie available? What if you laid out all that cash only to find that the studios stopped making 3-D movies altogether? Every week there seemed to be a new gimmick with special requirements. Who was to know which ones would really catch on and survive?

The theatre-owners' uncertainty was aggravated by the mixed messages they received from the big studios as to which new methods were being adopted. As a result, many just played it safe, either ignoring 3-D or, worse still, show-ing 3-D movies on the wrong equipment. The majority of complaints received about the quality of 3-D can be traced back to cinemas that failed to upgrade their equipment. Negative feedback, the prohibitive cost and the feeling that its lifespan as a novelty was nearing its natural end, resulted in most producers and exhibitors plumping for one of the many wide-screen processes available. Cinemascope, Vistavision and Todd-AO among others were to become the accepted visual 'extra'.

Although production of films in 3-D rapidly declined in the mid-Fifties, it did not stop altogether. The follow up to *The Creature from the Black Lagoon*, *Revenge of the Creature* snuck out in 1955. In 1961 a Canadian film, *The Mask*, included a few 3-D scenes and did very well out of it, and one of Francis Ford Coppola's early efforts, a skin-flick called *Bellboy and the Playgirls* (1961) also had a handful of three-dimensional action. (Curiously, this film is never included in Coppola's official filmography. Wonder why?)

Arch Oboler, who had started the whole thing off with *Bwana Devil* attempted to re-kindle the excitement for 3-D with the release of *The Bubble* in 1966. Calling his new process Spacevision didn't fool anyone, and audiences stayed at home rather than pay to see a floating, three-dimensional beer mug, one of the film's highlights. Throughout the rest of the Sixties, 3-D in America was effectively a dead cause, although it enjoyed wider use in some parts of Europe, as well as in the Soviet Union.

The process enjoyed a second coming in the early Seventies, kicked off by its use in an extremely tacky soft-core porn movie, *The Stewardesses* (1972). The success of this movie surprised everyone, including those responsible for it. It knocked Russ Meyer off the top spot by earning enough to become the largest grossing independent feature to date. A flurry of activity among the sleazier operators saw yet another rash of poor quality imitative movies produced and released. The titles alone – *The Chamber Maids, Ecstasy '72, Prison Girls, Three Dimensions of Greta* and *The Playmates* – all give you a pretty fair idea of what was being served up.

But amongst all the dreck, there were a couple of productions that are worth seeking out today. Andy Warhol's *Flesh for Frankenstein* (1974), a very sick and surprisingly funny film, turned a handsome profit on a small budget, and made original and effective use of the 3-D process, spoofing the kind of genre picture that 3-D seemed best suited for. I lied about my age back in 1974 when this film first did the rounds, and remember enjoying some of the more tasteless effects, like the one in which Frankenstein's newly stitched-together bride has a slight mishap, her guts flowing in magnificent 3-D all over the audience. The ending was a cracker too, with Dr Frankenstein impaled on a spear, his heart hanging off the end, appearing to dangle right into the audience's laps!

A handful of hard-core sex movies benefited from 3-D: *Wildcat Women* and *The Lollipop Girls in Hard Candy* are two that I would dearly love to see. There was even a gay hard-core film in 3-D, *Manhole* (1977). Kung Fu fans needn't feel left out either, as *Revenge of the Shogun Women* and *Dynasty*, in super 3-D and stereophonic sound, both escaped into cinemas around 1980. The dribble of releases continued through the later part of the Seventies. There was enough to confirm that there was still life in the process, but not to justify any claims that audiences actively preferred films with this extra dimension.

The Eighties saw a few suprise hits. The spaghetti western, *Coming at Ya!* (1981) was an impressive hit, but would have been much bigger if there had been enough 3-D glasses to go around. *Parasite* (1982) was another low-budgeter that did pretty well, featuring scenes of a parisitical alien life-form bursting forth from its victims' guts. The big studios were

A late entry in the dodgy 3-D stakes – *Parasite.*

still prepared to fool around with this gimmick from time to time. Paramount released *Friday the 13th, Part Three* as 'Part 3-D'. *Treasure of the Four Crowns* (1983), from the people who produced *Coming at Ya!*, was an exciting, almost dialogue-free adventure romp, and later that year Columbia brought out their *Spacehunter: Adventures in the Forbidden Zone*. Universal followed suit with *Jaws 3-D*, which was possibly the worst shark movie made since *Jaws Two*, but a huge success nonetheless. A science-fiction 'epic' *Metalstorm* and *Amityville 3-D* were among the last bigish budget releases of the Eighties, both bringing in so-so business and not so coincidentally bringing the second 3-D boom to an end.

Theatrically at least, that's where the saga ends. But alone among all the visual gimmicks, 3-D continues to work. The success and popularity of the excellent 3-D featurettes *Captain EO* and *The Muppets 3-D* at Disney World and the Disney MGM Studios prove without doubt that a well-made movie that uses the 3-D process in a clever and entertaining way will always find an audience.

20 Forgotten Star
Rondo Hatton

There are certain moments in your youth that are so power-ful and distinctive and electric that they remain with you always. For Wordsworth it was apparently a chilly night-time excursion marked by a huge and powerful bolt of lightning, impressing upon him the raw power and majesty of nature. For me it was a Tuesday afternoon playing truant from school and watching the matinee movie on TV while eating Marmite on toast. The film was *The Pearl of Death*, a pleasant little Sherlock Holmes thriller starring Basil Rathbone. Throughout the film, a shadowy menacing figure was alluded to, hinted at, feared: the Creeper. When he finally appeared, it not only caused me to drop a Marmite finger in my mug of tea, it also started me on a quest to find out all I could about this most remarkable looking of performers. It's not a pretty story, but then he wasn't a very pretty man.

If ever there was an example of the casual cruelty of Hollywood in its treatment of people, then the Rondo Hatton story is surely it. Universal Studios is today one of the more successful surviving studios, and as any visitor to the Universal Studios theme parks in LA and Florida can testify, they're not slow in letting you know just how successful they've been. You can get frightened all over again by *Jaws* (1975), visit the Bates Motel, as featured in *Psycho* (1960), and enjoy the fun of being trapped on a bus during an *Earthquake* (1974). Even *The Phantom of the Opera* and *Frankenstein* have been stripped of their cinematic dignity and made to mingle with the tourists. But nowhere amongst all this profitable celebration of former glories is there the slightest mention of one of the strangest tales of near-stardom ever to lurk in someone's back catalogue – the tale of Rondo Hatton.

If you are one of the few who have not only heard of Rondo Hatton but cherish the memory, then it's likely you'll associate his name with his most famous and successful creation, the Creeper. The Creeper was far less of a 'monster' than earlier Universal creations. He was essentially a clichéd creation, a huge and powerful brute, simple and easy to manipulate, but capable of snapping a man's back with ease. Accordingly, he was never to achieve the popularity of either Frankenstein or Dracula. But due to Hatton's unique and unforgettable physiognomy, the Creeper was popular enough to be reincarnated three times, in *The Pearl of Death, The House of Horrors* and *The Brute Man*.

It was standard practice for the Universal publicity department to invent catchy nicknames for their stars. For example, Lon Chaney Junior was the 'Master of Menace', and Boris Karloff, the 'Titan of Terror'. But unlike either of his horror-star contemporaries, Rondo Hatton's terrifying appearances on screen had nothing to do with the skill of Universal's make up artists. Whoever was in charge of the publicity department really earned his cash the day he came up with this one. Rondo Hatton was to be promoted with the most incredible, remarkable, almost unfeasible lack of sensitivity as, 'The Monster Who Needed No Make-Up'. This is his story.

Rondo Hatton was born on 22 April 1894, in Hagerstown, Maryland. His family moved to Tampa, Florida in 1912, and young Rondo attended the local Hillsborough High School, where his popularity was assured by his sporting prowess. He excelled in most track and field events, and figured prominently in the school's football and baseball teams.

After Hillsborough High, Hatton spent a short time at the University of Florida, but returned to Tampa and joined the National Guard, Tampa Rifles, Company H. He served with them in the Mexican Border War, and was subsequently transferred to France under the command of Captain Sumter L Lowery, a former classmate.

While fighting near Paris, Hatton was on the receiving end of one of those fine new inventions that wars always bring about: poison gas. He breathed in an unsubstantiated amount of the German gas, and was hospitalized with damaged lungs. Many young men exposed to the toxic gases failed to survive, but Hatton was lucky. Sort of. He lived, but was to suffer from a side effect of the gas for the rest of his life, until it eventually killed him in February 1946: Acromegaly.

According to Black's Medical Dictionary, Acromegaly is, 'A disorder caused by the increased secretion of growth hormone by an adenoma of the anterior pituitary gland. It results in excessive body growth of both the skeletal and the soft tissues. If it occurs in adolescence before the bony epiphyses have fused, the result is gigantism.' Hatton was presumably out of the adolescent phase by this time, so the disorder's effects on him were more likely to be as follows: 'If it occurs in adult life, the skeletal overgrowth is confined to the hands, feet, cranial sinuses and jaw. Most of the features are due to overgrowth of the cartilage of the nose and ear and the soft tissues which increase the thickness of the skin and lips. The overgrowth of the soft tissues occurs so gradually that the patient and spouse are often unaware of the change. It is only relatives who have not seen the patient for many months or years who are aware of the striking change in physical appearance.'

In layman's terms, the end result is not unlike a slowly melting candle. The features are still recognisable, but extended, drooping, thickened, leaving the victim with a face that only a wife, a mother or a B-movie producer could love.

Hatton was discharged from the army with a monthly disability allowance of $106.26. He embarked on a new career in journalism, writing for the *Tampa Tribune* and the *Tampa Daily Times*. His screen career began when he went on assignment to cover the filming of the first all-talking pictures to be shot in Florida, the United Artists movie, *Hell Harbor* (1930). Spotted by the film's director Henry King, Hatton was offered a small part on the basis of his distinctive, brutish features. He appeared as the owner of a dock-side bar. He's kept very much in the background, although he does have a few lines of rather awful dialogue, like his remark after seeing a peg-legged sailor crushed under a chandelier: 'He's done for.'

Although *Hell Harbor* did reasonably well for the studio, it was one of the more forgettable movies made during the Thirties. But it was King's insistence that Hatton could make a decent living by playing interesting background characters that was to inspire him to move to Hollywood a few years later, in 1936.

Upon arrival Rondo immediately contacted Henry King, who was as good as his word and cast him in his next picture, *In Old Chicago*. He appears way down in the credits as Rondo, and played the right-hand thug to the film's other heavy, Brian Donlevy. Most of Hatton's screen appearances over the next few years were of the same type, mainly non-speaking roles in forgettable B-pictures, playing a thug or saloon owner or convict. The practice for studios back then was to hire out contract players to other studios, and it's likely that Hatton appeared in similar background roles in hundreds of movies throughout the early 1940s.

His brief appearance in the RKO production of *The Hunchback of Notre Dame* (1939) was a sad indication of what the future held for him. He was cast in the annual 'Festival of Fools', taking part in the 'ugly man' competition. He sticks his head through a hole in the wall to the cheers and jeers of the audience. He also appeared uncredited in a number of other pictures, including *The Big Guy* (1939), *Moon Over Burma* (1940) and *The Cyclone Kid* (1942).

The turning point in his career came in 1944 when he was offered the part of the Creeper in *The Pearl of Death*, the sixth in Universal's very successful series of Sherlock Holmes films which began in 1942 with *Sherlock Holmes and the Voice of Terror*. The film begins with Holmes rescuing the famous Borgia Pearl from a vamp called Naomi Drake, who works for the notorious master criminal, Conover. The pearl, worth £50,000, is delivered by Holmes to the Royal Museum for safekeeping. Holmes demonstrates to the museum's curator that the pearl is not as safe as he thinks, and in the process unwittingly helps that very same master criminal, Conover, to steal it. Conover is arrested, but the pearl cannot be found, and he is released for lack of evidence.

Meanwhile, a series of distinctive murders begins, in which the victims are found with their backs broken. Holmes is convinced that Conover is behind them, knowing that his right-hand man is the nefarious Hoxton Creeper, who specialises in spine snapping. He surmises that the pearl is hidden in one of six plaster busts of Napoleon that were in the shop where Conover took refuge after fleeing the museum. Conover and the Creeper are methodically tracking down and murdering the poor sods who bought the busts in order to find the pearl. Holmes and Conover discover the identity of the owner of the final bust at the same time. Rushing to the address, Conover and the Creeper find that Holmes has beaten them to it, and is waiting for them disguised as a physician. They struggle, and Conover gains the upper hand. Holding Holmes at gunpoint, he commands the Creeper to search the house for the bust and, of course, the Borgia Pearl. Holmes finally outwits Conover by telling him, in a voice loud enough to be overheard by the Creeper, that Naomi has been arrested and will be hanged. The Creeper, infatuated with the luscious Naomi, is understandably distressed by this news and goes on a mad rampage, killing Conover. Holmes kills the Creeper, smashes open the last bust and finds the pearl. Another job well done.

The films in the Holmes series, starring Basil Rathbone as the immortal detective, were consistent crowd pleasers, and Universal freed their best talent to work on them. Consequently, *The Pearl of Death* is the finest film that Hatton appeared in, and it's generally regarded as his best work as well. In his first incarnation, the Creeper is mute, a ploy that makes best use of Hatton's presence without spoiling the effect with his negligible acting ability.

The build-up given the character was particularly impressive. He's not seen clearly until about half-way through the picture, but his handiwork, the crushed and strangled bodies of his victims, gives Holmes a clue as to his identity. His menacing presence is felt throughout by such cinematic devices as a large shadow cast on curtains, or just his large strong hands creeping into frame. Interestingly, Hatton's facial appearance is never mentioned, adding a further shock when he is finally seen. On viewing the film again recently I was surprised to find that you only actually see him for about five minutes at the end of the picture. The impression he makes, of course, lasts much longer.

Hatton next appeared in all 13 episodes of the Universal series *Royal Mounted Rides Again* (1945). Playing Moose, a villainous henchman, he sits on guard outside his boss's office. In the final episode he gets to draw his derringer, but is shot before he can use it, never even making it out of his chair.

His next proper movie appearance was in the role of yet another homicidal henchman, this time with the unlikely name of Moloch. The film was *The Jungle Captive* (1945), the third and final movie in Universal's rather lacklustre Ape Woman series. *Variety* breathlessly reviewed the film thus:

> Universal didn't pull any punches in trying to build this chiller into one of the starkest mellers of the year. Pic was made on an obviously low budget, but has a mad, sadistic theme. Yarn deals with the delving of bio-chemist Otto Kruger into experiments resulting in returning life to an ape woman. With the aid of gruesome Rondo Hatton in the role of his assistant, Kruger uses the blood of a gal lab technician who works in his office. The assistant, in order to aid the chemist in his experiments, thinks nothing of killing a couple of people to achieve his objective. In the end, the ape-woman is killed, but not before she has turned on the chemist. Acting by all the members of the cast is just average, Kruger's suave performance standing out. Setting and camerawork as well as direction and screenplay endeavour to keep viewers in the thrilling mood upon which the story is based, and rather sucessfully too.

I beg to differ. They threw everything into this one. As well as Hatton, it features a mad doctor, a Jekyll and Hyde-type transformation, an ape woman brought back from the dead, a tough young hero and a swooning damsel in distress. The screenplay, by Dwight V Babcock and M Coates Webster, from an 'original' story by Babcock, is nowhere near as interesting as their names, sounding at times as though they've just copied the dialogue from some third rate comic books. In one incredibly bad scene, Kruger as the mad doctor attempts a brain transplant for the first time. He works from instructions typewritten on a single file card, thoughtfully stolen for him by Moloch. The card includes such helpful tips as : 'A light mallet should be employed, and the chisel should be held with the point directed to the nose, so that a slip would not enter into either the eye or the brain.' So now you know.

As the lumbering Moloch, Hatton actually gets given a few lines. Bad idea. If you think Chuck Norris is unconvincing, then you should hear Hatton mangle dialogue. The impression of both brute power and simple sadness that the mute Hatton brought to *The Pearl of Death* is immediately blown when he opens his mouth and speaks in *The Jungle Captive*. In their review, the *Los Angeles Times* wrote: 'Rondo Hatton drew only giggles from the audience of kids.' Anyone who sees his performance will feel more sorry for the poor soul than anything else, something of a drawback if you're being sold to the public as a menacing brute.

The exploitation of Hatton reached an unfortunate low in this film. As the Creeper, no mention is made of his face or features. He plays a role in the script that could easily have been filled by any number of the craggier character actors of the day. But in *The Jungle Captive*, dialogue is constantly aimed at Moloch's appearance.

Rondo was paid a flat fee of $1,250 for his work on *The Jungle Captive*, a marked improvement over the $408.35 he received for *The Pearl of Death* and a good indication that Universal was grooming him for star status, if only at B-movie level. He had been shot three times by Sherlock Holmes at the end of *Pearl of Death*, but, in true Hollywood fashion, Universal wasn't going to let a little thing like that stand in the way of them making a few bucks. The appeal of Rondo Hatton as the Creeper was enough to warrant a case of selective amnesia, allowing him to appear twice more.

In *The House of Horrors* (1946), nothing about the film or Hatton's character should come as a great surprise. A talented

The one and only
Rondo Hatton.

but out of luck sculptor, Marcel Kosleck, contemplates suicide after receiving a particularly savage battering from some unnecessarily vicious art critics. While he sits on the deserted docks, he comes upon the Creeper, crawling from the murky waters. 'The perfect Neanderthal man!' rejoices the artist, and takes him home to dry him off and begin work on his masterpiece, a sculpture of Rondo Hatton.

The Creeper returns his hospitality by sitting pretty and still for him. So enamoured of his new model is the artist that he doesn't even blink when he realises he has none other than the notorious spine-snapping criminal the Creeper in the house.

Making small-talk over a snack one night, the tormented artist gets onto one of his favourite subjects; his least favourite people, the churlish art critics. The Creeper, who has grown quite fond of his new patron, listens attentively, and before long critics are turning up with snapped spines all over the shop. A snoopy society dame/art critic (surely the least appetizing combination ever) stumbles upon one of Marcel's sketches of the Creeper and puts two and two snugly together. The Creeper is despatched to deal with her, but gets the wrong gal. Returning to the studio he finds Marcel in a heated argument with the snoopy socialite, and realises that once he's served his use for the artist he'll be disowned. He strangles Marcel and destroys his 'masterpiece'. Stalking the socialite, he is seconds from finishing her off when, in true B-movie fashion, the police arrive and shoot, but only wound, the Creeper.

The House of Horrors contains some of the worst dialogue of all of Hatton's flicks. He gets to show off his admittedly limited talents with lines like, 'You're my friend, shake' and, 'You're going to tell the police about me, huh?' The finest line in the movie must be that uttered by the policeman assigned to the case: 'I have often wondered why a man would want to snap a woman's spine.' But despite such clunkers, the film works well. It's moodily shot, with some nice sets, like the interior of Marcel's studio, eerily lit by candles with grotesque sculptures lurking all around.

Hatton's final appearance as the Creeper was also to be his last appearance on film. Shot over 13 days in 1946, *The Brute Man* is a scant 58 minutes long, but somehow manages to feel like three times that. Although the ending of *The House of Horrors* left the way open for a sequel, *The Brute Man* appears to take place before the events in that film. It contains all the trademarks we've grown to expect from a Rondo Hatton picture: poor dialogue, wooden acting, dreary third rate clichéd plot, all dressed around the strangest leading man in cinema history.

The Brute Man is far more interesting than Hatton's earlier efforts. For the first time, we are shown an explanation for his terrible appearance, one which cruelly echoes reality. In flash back, Hatton is shown to be a handsome young student and football star at Hampton University. An accident in the college lab exposes him to a mix of potent chemical fumes that bring about his disfigurement. In the film, he then goes on to strangle all those he holds responsible as well as any-one unlucky enough to get in the way. He also gets involved with a blind pianist, the only person in the movie shown not to be repulsed by his appearance.

The rest of the third rate plot revolves around Hatton's efforts to further elude the comically helpless police while trying to gather the necessary cash for the operation that would restore the pianist's sight. Eventually, of course, the Creeper is caught.

The only part of the film that is even remotely interesting or suspensful is in the opening few minutes, after Rondo has menacingly loomed over the titles. He is shown walking through the quiet grounds of Hampton University, pausing briefly to look in through the window of the Collegiate Cafe, where young students are jiving and talking. Gradually, they all stop and stare with a mixture of horror and curiosity at the deformed lumbering man outside. A rather uneasy, unintentionally honest statement about the film-makers and their intended audience, perhaps.

Rondo Hatton was never to see either of his last two movies released. He died a couple of months after the filming of *The Brute Man* ended. The cause was coronary thrombosis, brought about by chrono myocarditis, a direct result of his acromegaly. His body was returned to Tampa, Florida, where he rests today.

Hatton's legacy is suitably a minor one. A handful of B-movie nuts sing his praises as the last of the truly great Universal monsters. The National Sleaze Convention in Wilmington, Delaware adopted him as their Mascot, and rubber likenesses of his face can be bought from a few movie-related memorabilia stores that cater to the more esoteric end of the fan market in Hollywood, on the shelves next to masks of Bela Lugosi and Tor Johnson. More recently, the lead thug in Walt Disney's big-budget family film, *The Rocketeer* (1991), was made up to look just like the Creeper, though that was probably more of an attempt to evoke the feeling and look of the 1940s than to play off any fond memories that audiences might have of Rondo Hatton.

Rondo Hatton's films might not have been very good. He may well have been one of the worst actors ever to command star status, however limited. But his story is worth remembering if only to show that (a) it is possible to make it in the movies by looks alone, and (b) there are no depths to which movie makers will not stoop to make a buck. Which, in my opinion, is not necessarily a bad thing. It just was in this case.

SELECTED RONDO HATTON FILMOGRAPHY

THE BIG GUY (1939)
THE PEARL OF DEATH (1944)
JUNGLE CAPTIVE (1945)
THE SPIDERWOMAN STRIKES
  BACK (March 1946)

HOUSE OF HORRORS (May 1946)
BRUTE MAN (July 1946)

Part Five

Horror and Violence

21 The History of Horror Films

Let's dispense with the definitions first. This chapter is called *The History of Horror Films* rather than *The History of Horror on Film* or *Scary Moments at the Pictures* because it is only about those films which both intend and succeed to be known as horror films. Not films which *happen* to have horrific moments, nor fantasy films or science fiction pictures which might also frighten. No, this chapter is about films which were designed primarily to scare the dickens out of you, whether through subtle lighting and atmosphere or total gross-out blood-and-guts body horror. To further define which films meet my highly developed criteria would take ages, so you just have to trust me. If I say it's a horror film, then it is, got it? For example, *Alien* may well look like a science fiction film to the less sophisticated eye, what with spaceships and androids and things, but it isn't. On close inspection it is a brilliant and scary 'monster-on-the-loose' film – the futuristic trappings are just that, trappings. *Aliens* and *Alien 3* on the other hand, are not horror. They are science fiction/adventure and science fiction/pretentious films, respectively, and both rather good ones at that.

The history of the horror film is, I can't help but feel, rather disappointing. Not in terms of quality, for the films produced today are just as good *and* bad as those produced back in the 'golden days' of the 1930s and 1940s. No, what disappoints me today is the way in which horror films, and the talented people who make the better, more original ones, are denigrated. Horror films are dismissed by all but a handful of more open-minded critics as trash. Cinematic junk-food for the intelligence-impaired. Kiddy-movies that are too violent for their target audience of seven-year-olds, and so find their way into the diet of grown-ups who should know better.

215

Well, it wasn't always this way.

Before the rot set in, horror films were produced by major studios with as much pride as their big-budget melodramas and star vehicles. Of course, there were some particularly lousy, low-budget horror films made back then which were treated with the disdain they deserved. But each film was judged on its own merits, not dismissed because it came dragging a big pile of lumpy genre luggage behind it. Today, unless the film's based on a blockbuster book, like *Silence of the Lambs* or *The Exorcist*, or it has a respectable, 'name' director attached, like Spielberg or Kubrick, it simply is not given a fair shake. Well, my message to all those pencil-necked panty-waisted film critics who can't see the gloriously inventive wood for the admittedly blood-drenched trees is: Shame on you.

Horror films have been around for a long time. The romantic-gothic novels that proved so popular in the

Nosferatu – the first and best screen vampire.

eighteenth and nineteenth centuries, and more importantly the stage adaptations that they inspired, were ideal sources for the early film-makers. Silent shockers included *Nosferatu* (1921) and *Das Cabinet Des Dr Caligari* (1919), but the first ever horror film is believed to be *Le Manoir Du Diable* (1896), from special effects pioneer George Melies. It features a vampire demon, a magic cauldron and a pretty girl – still considered to be the most important ingredients today.

Unlike the horror films of today, these early movies rarely showed acts of violence or horror in the more obvious, bloody sense. Curious, this, for although they were based upon the gentle, 'romantically frightening' gothic plays, they might just have easily drawn inspiration from the Grand Guignol theatre that had been popular in France and many other parts of Europe during the mid-nineteenth century. Grand Guignol specialised in shocking re-creations of violent acts incorporated into contemporary melodrama. For example, a vignette which ended with a duel would actually show the death of one of the duellists with gushes of blood covering the stage much to the delight of the refined audience. Fake beheadings, poisonings, and many other violent displays ensured the popularity of this form of theatre for many years until the novelty finally wore off.

I suspect the omission of such special effects had as much to do with lack of expertise and budget as it did taste or censorship. For example, to get an on-screen decapitation to look realistic takes an awful lot of time and money and skill. Also, the limited bag of tricks used to shock or terrify an audience took many years to be exhausted. There was no need to resort to visceral shocks, so quite simply the film-makers did not.

One of the most noteworthy silent horror films was the very first version of *Frankenstein*, made in 1910. This version was written and directed by J Searle Dawley, who went on to make over 300 one-reelers until he retired from the business in 1921. It was billed as 'a liberal interpretation of Mrs Shelley's tale', which of course is what most subsequent attempts to make a film from her book were, although few had the politeness to mention it.

Dawley was also rather well-mannered in his treatment of the monster's creation, avoiding any mention of grave robbing or the stitching together of different body parts in favour of giving him a chemical birth. In the end, this monster was defeated by the power of love, fading away when confronted by the sight of his creator and his bride to be. A bulky fellow by the name of Charles Ogle was the lucky man to play monster for the first time.

One of the few versions of a one-act Grand Guignol piece on film came out in 1912. *The Lunatics* was a French film based on a short story by Edgar Allan Poe. It was about a visitor to a lunatic asylum who discovers, halfway through a guided tour of the establishment, that the lunatics have taken over. However, the bloodier scenes which had been graphically enacted on stage, involving the gouging out of an eye and the slitting of a throat, took place on film out of sight, with only a flow of blood from under the door to please a voracious audience.

Sadly, several silent horror films have been lost, including *The Vampire* (1913), in which a werewolf made a guest appearance, and *The Werewolf* (also 1913). But another early monster film made a lasting mark. *The Golem* first appeared in Germany in 1913, but it is the 1920 film, directed by and starring the actor Paul Wegener (who had played the Golem originally), that is most famous and can still be seen at film festivals today. Based on the legend of a clay statue that came to life to protect the Jews of Prague from persecution, it is a wonderfully modern piece of work.

The lighting and the design of *The Golem* itself give the film a class which has rarely been matched. In short, the plot has a Rabbi build the Golem from clay to rescue the Jews from tyranny, and with the power of faith gives it life. But his assistant takes control of it and uses its power for less scrupulous ends. The creature rebels against its new master and goes on a violent rampage. In a beautiful and touching scene, the monster's reign of terror is ended by a little girl, who offers him a bite of her apple and, when he bends down, pulls the star of David from his great neck. The unnatural life immediately leaves his body and he is, once again, a statue.

By the time sound was accepted as a vital part of cinema there had already been as many as seven silent versions of *Dr Jekyll and Mr Hyde* (the first in 1920), and a silent version of *The Hunchback of Notre Dame* (1923). A variation on what we now accept as the definitive vampire was provided by the eerie classic *Nosferatu: A Symphony of Horror* (1921) from the German director Friedrich Murnau. Like the earlier German film *The Golem*, it is a masterpiece of moody lighting and design. It was remade by Werner Herzog in 1979, and the more recent Coppola version of Bram Stoker's doomed love story owes more than just a little to this original. Another notable silent horror film was *The Man Who Laughs* (1929), starring Conrad Veidt and directed by Paul Leni. It's a nice looking gothic-horror-romance, but its influence is greater than that. The eponymous character played by Veidt is deliberately disfigured by an evil king so that his mouth is locked forever in a hideous grin. The film was seen by Jerry Robinson, a young comic book artist working on the Batman comic strips in their first few years, and it inspired him to create Batman's greatest villain, the Joker.

Despite the proliferation of silent horror films, it was only after the advent of sound, and two famous productions from Universal Studios, that the horror genre as we know it today really came into its own. The 1930s were the Universal years as far as horror was concerned.

Like most of the big studios, Universal had been in at the very beginning. In 1906 a German emigrant by the name of Carl Laemmle opened a chain of nickelodeons in Chicago. He graduated to producing low-budget movies between 1909 and 1912, when he founded the Universal Film Manufacturing Company. In 1915 Universal City was opened in California, producing and releasing an incredible 150 films that very year. Although, like the other studios, Universal made just about every type of picture, it is for its horror movies that the studio is most fondly remembered. Silent hits included *The Hunchback of Notre Dame* (1923) and *The Phantom of the Opera* (1925), both starring Lon Chaney who was to prove a major asset to the studio until his death in 1933.

Universal coped with the arrival of talkies admirably, and by 1930 almost all of its output was with sound. The studio

The brilliant Lou Chaney Snr in *Phantom of the Opera.*

scored many non-horror hits, most notably with *All Quiet on the Western Front* (1930), which went on to win that year's Oscar for Best Picture. In 1931 Universal was to release two pictures that changed not only the face of the company, but the history of cinema as well. *Dracula*, directed by Tod Browning, and *Frankenstein*, brilliantly directed by James Whale, are still perhaps the best known horror films ever made. Such was their success that Laemmle launched into a series of horror pictures that was to include *The Mummy*, *The Old Dark House*, *The Invisible Man*, *Bride of Frankenstein* and *The Werewolf of London*.

Carl Laemmle faded from the Universal Story in 1936. The studio had been suffering from diminishing profits for several years, although it would be unfair to lay the blame exclusively at the door of Laemmle's office. Like all studios, Universal was hit by the depression of 1929 and then severely damaged by a strike within the motion picture industry that resulted in a studio closure for several months.

But it was Laemmle's blatant nepotism that did him in in the end. Most of the Universal movies released up until 1936 have a few Laemmles hidden somewhere in the credits, with the generous Uncle Carl providing lucrative employment for his son, Carl Laemmle Jnr, his daughter, Carla, and just about any other Laemmle or friend of the Laemmles' who happened to be passing through California. After running at a loss for several quarters, Laemmle finally sought fresh capital, and was eventually manoeuvred out of his own company in 1936.

The failure of *Dracula's Daughter* (1936), which had gone wildly over budget, had led to Universal suspending production of their celebrated horror films and the New Universal, as it was keen to be known, was responsible for foisting Deanna Durbin and Abbot and Costello on the unsuspecting public. But the success of both *Frankenstein* and *Dracula* when re-issued by the New Universal led the studio to embark on a second cycle of horror and drama productions.

Universal had by no means been the only producer of horrific movies in the Thirties. Some excellent films originated elsewhere. *Dr Jekyll and Mr Hyde* (1931) came from Paramount and the remarkable *Freaks* (1932) from Tod Browning crept out of MGM. 1933 was the year that movie-goers got to gasp at the appearance of the greatest true monster of them all, *King Kong*, courtesy of RKO Pictures. But by the end of the decade inspiration seemed to have dried up somewhat on the horror front. It was time for a new player to get involved.

If Universal is best associated with horror in the Thirties, then RKO pretty much carried the quality torch throughout the fabulously frightening Forties. Those films produced by Val Lewton, including *Cat People* (1942), *The Curse of the Cat People* (1944) and *I Walked with a Zombie* (1943), were all low-budget efforts that made up in atmosphere what they lacked in the way of monsters.

In *Cat People*, director Jaques Tourneur allowed the story to build slowly and carefully, only hinting that Simone Simon might actually be descended from a mediaeval tribe of women who turn into raging big cats when their passions are aroused. Scenes in which she deliberately taunts a bird by pawing at its cage, or the way in which she slowly rakes her long fingernails over a velvet couch, gave the audience just enough of a hint that she may well be what she fears. Sadly, Paul Shrader's 1982 remake failed even to come close to the original. The marvellous atmosphere and feeling of uncertainty encouraged in the audience were dashed by the studio's ending, in which a shot of black panther left little doubt as to the Cat Woman's origins. The film's sequel, directed by Robert Wise, suffered from no such interference, and as a result is one of the most delicate and haunting horror films ever made.

Jaques Tourneur's finest hour was to come with *I Walked with a Zombie*, and once again words like haunting, lyrical, and beautiful must be used to describe a film that also manages to provide its fair share of chills. Set on the Island of St Sebastien in the West Indies, Frances Dee plays a nurse summoned there to help care for a woman stricken by a strange mental paralysis. It turns out that she was in fact turned into a zombie by her crazed mother-in-law after her plans to run off with her husband's half-brother became known.

The film's success inspired a series of interesting imitations, including *Revenge of the Zombies* (1943), with John Carradine, and *The Voodoo Man* (1945), both from RKO's rival studio, Monogram. RKO also laid the following fear feasts before the ever hungry crowds: *The Seventh Victim* (1943), *The Body Snatcher* (1945) and the superb *The Spiral Staircase* (1946), about a crazed homicidal maniac who sets himself the task of ridding the world of women who are, by his own loose criteria, somewhat less than perfect. The 1940s also saw its fair share of clunkers, including *Abbott and Costello Meet Frankenstein* (1948), which was scary, but for all the wrong reasons.

A genuine British classic came out in 1945, the anthology film *Dead of Night*, starring Michael Redgrave, which everyone seems to remember for the story about the ventriloquist 'possessed' by his dummy. The film's impact on the cinemagoing public was greatly increased because it marked a return to the production of horror films which had been banned in England during the war.

The Spiral Staircase – a stylish exercise in mood and atmosphere.

A constant stream of familiar faces, including the Mummy, Dr Jekyll and Mr Hyde, the Werewolf, Frankenstein (or at least his ghost) and the son of Dracula, all attempted to scare some life back into the genre, but with little luck. By the end of the 1940s, the appeal of the old-style horror film was definitely on the wane.

The 1950s offered more for the science fiction fan than the horror buff. The combined Cold War fears of atomic destruction and invading foreigners triggered a wave of films aimed at the nuclear xenophobe, in which mankind (for which we can read Americans) withstood atomic-powered onslaughts from bug-eyed invaders. America in this decade gave us some really dumb monsters, or RDMs, as they prefer to be known (see box for more details). On the world stage, Godzilla first stalked the earth in 1953, and in Mexico a series of movies featuring a home-grown monster, the Aztec Mummy, began.

While the Americans were busy working out their future fears, it was up to the British to revive the corpse of the old-style horror film. The advent of Hammer Films, founded in 1948 as a distribution company, with director Terence

Fisher's revolutionary modern versions of, *Dracula* and *Frankenstein*, not only launched the careers of Christopher Lee and Peter Cushing, but also started the trend for sex and violence over moody atmosphere and helped revive British cinema from its post-war torpor. Hammer were later to acquire the rights to Universal's back catalogue, allowing Fisher to perform the same re-vamping of *The Mummy*, *The Werewolf* and finally *The Phantom of the Opera*.

Some horror directors still made do with mood and atmosphere. A fine example was the excellent *Night of the Demon* (1958) from Jaques Tourneur, which scared the bejesus out of me when I was at school. The premise was that anyone who was slipped a piece of parchment containing inscriptions taken from Stonehenge would be killed within four days by a demon. Like most of Tourneur's work, the film was atmospheric and successfully spooky right up until the very end, when a big, clumsy, dumb-looking monster appeared and spoiled it all. That's the Fifties for you, right there.

The Killer Shrews – frightening, but all for the wrong reasons.

REALLY DUMB MONSTERS of the 1950s

Here are some of the best:

The Giant Claw *from the 1957 movie of the same name. It was exactly what it claimed to be, just an oversized, silly looking, flying claw. It had features, but they looked rather unfortunately like it was grinning the whole time, further undermining its ability to scare anyone.*

The Unknown Terror *(1957) sadly didn't remain unknown for too long. The terrors were created out of innocent victims by your obligatory mad-scientist, and looked like people who had been dipped into a foamy bubblebath and not rinsed off properly.*

Attack of the Crab Monsters *(1957). Actually, the Crab Monsters in this Roger Corman horror/science fiction hybrid don't look too bad . . . until you look closely. Then you can see unmistakably human feet poking out from under the foam crab suits.*

Attack of the Giant Leeches *(1959) is even better as dumb monsters go. The leeches are of course played by men in rubber suits, but sadly the suits don't quite cover the air tanks on their backs. By the end of this film's mercifully short 62 minutes I found myself getting quite fond of them.*

The Beast with 1,000,000 Eyes *(1955). OK, so no-one really expected this monster to actually have a million eyes, but to give it just two and then invent a corny excuse for its name – it can see through the eyes of animals – is unforgivably dumb.*

The Killer Shrews *(1959) were no such things. They appear to be a couple of rather ugly little dogs with fake fangs attached that terrorised a group of people in this cheap little film shot in Texas. But with a title like that, you'd be mad not to expect a RDM.*

The new style, technicolour, sexy horror films of the Fifties continued to flourish and grow in the 1960s. The success of the Hammer style when released in America led to Roger Corman's series of bright and enjoyable adaptations of Poe's work, beginning with *House of Usher* (1960). American International Pictures, always quick to spot a trend, supplemented their home grown output by buying in horror films from around the world, the most successful being those directed by Mario Bava and bought in from Italy. Even when badly re-cut and dubbed, Bava's films like *Black Sunday* (1960) found an appreciative audience, and he was later to begin the genre of glossy, stylishly violent horror films known in their native Italy as *gialli*, and generally only known elsewhere by die-hard horror fans. More slavish praise is heaped on Bava later.

Michael Powell's *Peeping Tom* and Alfred Hitchcock's *Psycho* (both 1960) remain two of the most effective and interesting horror films ever made, and both attracted vitriolic criticism, especially in Britain. Without any hint of the supernatural or especially gruesome special effects, the films succeeded, and have spawned countless less innovative imitations in the horror–thriller style.

Noteworthy low-budget films included the wonderful *Carnival of Souls* (1962), and Herschell Gordon Lewis's *Blood Feast* (1963), the first of his many explicitly violent gore films that laid the groundwork for the repetitive splatter movies of the Seventies and Eighties like the *Friday the 13th* series.

Other curios from the gore-geous Sixties included the bizarre *Billy the Kid vs Dracula* (1965) and its sequel, *Jesse James meets Frankenstein's Daughter* (1966). Perhaps the single strangest horror movie ever, but certainly of the Sixties, was *Incubus* (1966), starring Star Trek's William Shatner, and carrying the dubious distinction of being the only film to have its dialogue entirely in Esperanto!

Roman Polanski contributed three of the decade's best films, if all wildly different: the disturbing and low key *Repulsion*, in which Catherine Deneuve slowly loses her mind, the funny but still spooky *Dance of the Vampires* (1967), in which Polanski himself played an inept vampire hunter, and the hugely successful *Rosemary's Baby* (1968).

In France, Jean Rollin carved out a niche for himself with a series of sexy vampire films that pre-empted the Hammer versions of the 1970s, including *Le Viol Du Vampire* which slipped out in 1967.

But Hammer were still producing solid work throughout the Sixties. Oliver Reed appeared in *The Curse of the Werewolf* (1960). *The Phantom of the Opera* (1963) and *The Plague of the Zombies* (1966) also stand out.

One of the more consistent and, of course, underrated directors to work in the field of horror released his first movie in 1969. George Romero's *Night of the Living Dead* was made

Left: Weng Weng – agent 3½ – *For Your Height Only.*

Below: *Shaft* – 'Hotter than Bond, cooler than Bullitt' and quite profitably blacker than both of them.

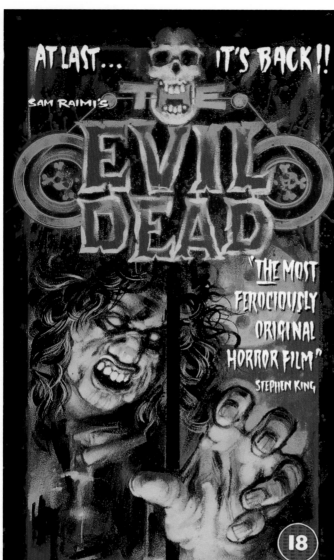

The Evil Dead – one of the films that suffered at the hands of the British censors as a result of the great video nasties scare. Still only available on video with several minutes cut.

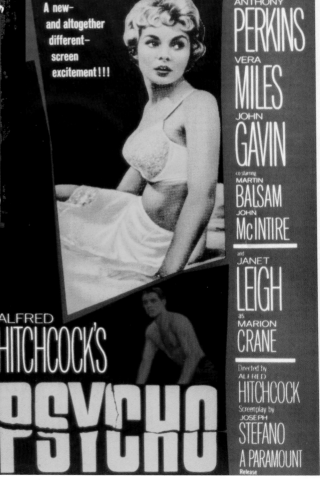

Still one of the greatest horror films ever made – Alfred Hitchcock's *Psycho*.

Won't You Come Into My Parlor?
I Want You To Meet...

The Gruesome Twosome

IN GHASTLY COLOR!

THINK YOU'VE SEEN BLOOD AND GORE?
THINK YOU'VE SEEN WILD, WAY-OUT HUMOR?
THINK YOU'VE SEEN STOMACH-RETCHING MUTILATION?

You Ain't Seen Nothin' Yet!

starring ELIZABETH DAVIS • CHRIS MARTELL • GRETCHEN WELLES • RODNEY BEDELL

Oh, Yes...Our Wigs Are Made from Genuine Human Hair...
And How!

THE SCREEN SEEPS WITH CARNAGE
IN THE MOST BARBARIC HUMOR
SINCE THE GUILLOTINE WENT OUT OF STYLE!

executive producer
FRED M. SANDY

produced and directed by
HERSCHELL GORDON LEWIS

released by
MAYFLOWER PICTURES, INC.

Herschell Gordon Lewis still selling the gore with *The Gruesome Twosome*.

Above: *Suspiria* – Dario Argento at his best.
Below: A surprisingly tasteful poster for Dario Argento's
Tenebres.

on a minuscule budget using a cast of unknowns. Shooting in black and white in and around his native Pittsburgh, Pennsylvania, Romero created a gritty and realistic slice of fear on film, taking many of the more irksome horror film clichés, and deflating them. The movie's success spawned not only two equally impressive sequels, *Dawn of the Dead* and *Day of the Dead*, but also the plethora of cheap'n'nasty Italian zombie and cannibal films that appeared during the Seventies, and now gather dust on the shelves of your local video store.

The Seventies were a seriously scary decade in the history of horror films. It was a time when, briefly, the old-style monsters, rather quaint and inoffensive in their way, coexisted with the far more vicious, disturbing beasts of the future.

Hammer Films had maintained a high international profile throughout the Sixties with several new Dracula movies, but gradually faded from the scene in the Seventies. The finest of all the directors working for Hammer, Terence Fisher, completed his last film in 1973, the seventh Frankenstein feature to come from that company. *Frankenstein Must Be Destroyed* (1973), set entirely within an insane asylum, starred Peter Cushing as the mad doctor, trying one last time to get it right. The resulting monster, created from the body parts of an insane murderer and a mathematical and musical genius is ripped to pieces by the other inmates at the end of the film. Easy come, easy go.

The demise of Hammer did not mean the end of British horror, though. *The Wicker Man* (1976), in which Edward Woodward played a mainland policeman investigating the disappearance of a child on a remote Scottish island, has quite rightly earned its reputation as a genuinely sinister and frightening film, displaying a level of sophistication rarely found in the genre. The fact that Britt Eckland performs a most bizarre folk dance in the nude hasn't hurt its reputation much either.

The 1970s was almost as important a decade in the development of the horror film as the 1930s. Impressed by the success had by independents, the major studios again began to re-invest in horror films, resulting in *The Exorcist* (1973) and

Edward Woodward caught up in some very strange goings on in *The Wicker Man.*

The Omen (1976), amongst others. But once again it was the independent sector that produced the most original and stimulating work. Wes Craven's brutal *Last House on the Left* (1972), Tobe Hooper's infamous *The Texas Chainsaw Massacre* (1974), and David Lynch's unsettling *Eraserhead* (1977) all marked out different territories for their respective creators.

The Seventies also saw the rise of a director whom I genuinely believe to be one of the finest talents working in film today. Following in the stylistic footsteps of that other Italian master, Mario Bava, Dario Argento has also suffered from the inability of most film critics to appreciate or understand horror films. From his first film, *The Bird With The Crystal Plumage* (1970) onward, he has consistently outperformed every other director in the field. Sadly, due to the extremely violent content of his later work, his pictures are rarely seen intact outside Italy, and are often rendered incomprehensible by ruthless editing and intensely bad dubbing.

The work of Brian De Palma began to attract attention during the early 1970s. Having begun his film career with a handful of short 'social comedies', most notable because they starred Robert De Niro in his first film work, he graduated to horror with *Sisters* in 1972. I still think that *Carrie* (1976) was his most original and successful movie. It gave us a shock surprise ending – remember the hand shooting out from the grave? – which was ripped off in countless horror films to follow, becoming almost as much of a cliché as having

Carrie – Don't mess with teenage girls.

someone stalked while taking a shower. De Palma's films have often been compared to those of Alfred Hitchcock, but apart from the breathtaking virtuosity with which he orchestrates his grand, often over-blown, set pieces, in my mind he has none of Hitchcock's originality or the old master's ability to draw decent performances out of actors.

Other promising directors to emerge from the genre include John Carpenter, whose *Halloween* (1978) was another much-copied milestone, and Steven Spielberg, who managed with *Jaws* (1975) to overcome a rather dopey looking rubber shark and scare the pants off everyone.

At the lower end of the budgetary scale, *Driller Killer* (1979), sparked a controversy over violence on film or, more precisely, on video, that the UK still has not recovered from. Directed by and starring Abel Ferrara, it was an unnerving and disturbing film, but curiously for one with such a grisly reputation, not actually that explicit. Only one of the many deaths-by-power-tool that occurred is actually seen in detail. Nonetheless, it was this one film more than any other that started off the 'video nasties' debate in Britain, one of the more controversial and dubious consequences of horror on film.

By the end of the Seventies it would be hard to imagine someone releasing a movie as straightforward as the Hammer films which had kicked the decade off. Now the trend was for bloody serial murders, or extravagant special effects or movies which were psychologically dark and disturbing. The technicolour romance of Christopher Lee as Dracula or even the soft-porn appeal of vampire lesbians was, for at least the next ten years, a thing of the past.

If I were forced to recall anything in particular about the horror film in the 1980s, it would probably be the amount of third rate rubbish that kept coming out due to the popularity of a first feature. It seemed that anything that was even vaguely successful would be considered worth revisiting once or twice or even five or six times if the producers could screw a little more cash out of an idea. *Halloween* (1978) spawned two sequels in 1981 and 1982. The dreadful *Friday the 13th* (1980) came around five more times, *Part Two* in 1981,

Three in 1982, *Part Four: The Final Chapter* (except it wasn't) in 1984, *Part Five: a New Beginning* (damn!) in 1985, and finally *Part Six: Jason Lives* in 1986. Freddie Kreuger proved equally popular, pulling his unpleasant spikey glove back on five more times after the original *Nightmare on Elm Street* in 1984, not to mention the dumb spin-off TV series he inspired. And Leather Face got to wield his power tool of choice twice more after the original *Texas Chainsaw Massacre* in 1974, with the first sequel not appearing until 1986.

But amongst all the uninspired repetition, there were many genuine delights. David Cronenberg gave us exploding heads in *Scanners* (1980), odd flesh fantasies in *Videodrome* (1982), and Christopher Walken as a reluctant psychic in *The Dead Zone* (1983). His biggest hit was to come in 1986 with *The Fly*, a masterful reworking of the 1958 science fiction chiller, made more horrific due to a superb performance from Jeff Goldblum and fine special effects. With *Dead Ringers* (1989), the story of deranged identical twin gynaecologists, Cronenberg established himself as one of the most original and disturbing talents working in film today.

A youngster named Sam Raimi proved that quality low-budget films weren't a thing of the past with his highly

The Evil Dead. One of the dead trying her best to scare you!

inventive and jolting *The Evil Dead* (1982); although when he came to make the more expensive and accomplished sequel *Evil Dead Two*, in 1987, he watered down the shocks with gags. *Re-Animator*, courtesy of Stuart Gordon in 1985, also had its fair share of gags, but still played out its tale of relentless brain eating zombies with a certain original flair. A rare sighting of a British horror film was offered up by Clive Barker, even if *Hellraiser* managed to confuse the locals by having American actors running around North London. The sequels, *Hellraiser Two* and *Three* have failed to live up to the first outing, but with his neat cast of weird looking Cenobites and the carefully conceived universe they inhabit, they are still among the few original modern horror concepts in recent years. The acceptance of gory special effects as pretty much a staple in horror pictures has made for some especially gruesome items, with low-budget film-makers in particular often sacrificing the lion's share of their meagre budgets on gut-churning effects.

The nervous Nineties still have to prove themselves, but as we horror fans look to the future, it is with trepidation. Apart from the ludicrously titled *Francis Ford Coppola's Bram Stoker's Dracula* (1993), in which romance, big-budget special effects, beautiful cinematography and piss-poor acting, joined together to produce a mega-hit, pickings are lean. George Romero added the underrated *Dark Half* (1993) to his back catalogue. Spielberg delivered a horror film for all the family with *Jurassic Park*, but it lacked the bite of *Jaws*. It's too early to tell what the Nineties will be remembered for, but one thing is for sure. Unless the studios and independents invest a little more time and energy into finding new ideas and new talent instead of re-making classics or churning out sequels, then the horror film as a genre will soon be deader than most of its stars.

22 Herschell Gordon Lewis

The Wizard of Gore

The films produced by Herschell Gordon Lewis, initially with David F Friedman and later on his own, are not for the faint-hearted. He created some of the most grisly, gruesome and gory scenes ever committed to celluloid. Unrestrained by censorship, either personal or governmental, his films capitalised on the audience's desire to see death and violence portrayed in a far more explicit and realistic way than ever before. He took horror films to their visceral limit, and the crude but sensational effects have as much impact when viewed today as they did back in the Sixties. It's a fact that his movies, despite now having gathered the kind of cult following that was inevitable, have never been shown in cinemas in Britain.

Although much has been written about the artistry involved, the daring necessary to take that final step in showing such barbarous acts, Lewis's motivation in making these movies was simple: big bucks. Today, he lives in a beautiful house in Fort Lauderdale, Florida, where he is a keen tennis player and a well-liked member of the local country club. As befits his more sedate lifestyle, he no longer makes scary, bloody, horror movies. He does something far more frightening – he travels the world on lecture tours, spreading the word and teaching others how to make a fortune out of direct marketing sales. With his wife he runs a small but fabulously successful company designing (Mrs Lewis) and selling (Mr Lewis), those collectable plates with pictures on that you see advertised in Sunday supplements.

When I first met Lewis I was surprised to find a soft-spoken but confident, intelligent, well-read man. Making the classic mistake of confusing his work with his personality, it took me some time to equate him with the 37 different films

In the Presence of Greatness 2. Herschell Gordon Lewis and me.

he churned out in just ten years. No movie brat, Lewis got into the film business making cheap commercials, business films and government training shorts. Like every good American, he believed in the dream, and, in the hope of making big bucks, he embarked on his own series of features. Teaming up with Dave Friedman, he shot a couple of moderately successful nudie-cuties, before emulating the style of Russ Meyer's *The Immoral Mr Teas* with *The Adventures of Lucky Pierre* (1961). With Lewis as director and cameraman and Friedman as both producer and soundman, the film was completed in just four days, and in theatres about six weeks later. Its great success prompted a follow up, *Boin-n-g!* (1963), a film about the making of a nudie-cutie, with two actors portraying Lewis and Friedman. It was another hit, and the partners continued to produce their own brand of sex and comedy, until the bottom began to droop in that particular market.

Ever the businessmen, Lewis and Friedman knew they needed something extra-special if their films were to survive in the fiercely competitive low-budget world. In early 1963, while they were filming at the cheap but cheerful Suez Motel in north Miami Beach, inspiration finally struck. They made a list of subjects that might be exploited, the kind of things that major companies either couldn't or wouldn't consider. At the time, Lewis was complaining about the lack of realism in the death scenes in most movies, people dying peacefully with a slight smile on their lips and maybe just the teensiest hole in their shirt where the bullet entered. In mid-sentence he stopped, just like Archimedes in the bath-tub. He had it: Gore.

The Suez was just one of many motels at the top end of Miami Beach, trying to catch the eye of weary travellers as they drove past looking for somewhere to spend the night. But the Suez has a gimmick. Out in front, right by the main road, was an enormous, garishly painted model of the Sphinx, flanked on either side by two ridiculous-looking, life-size model camels. It was the sphinx that inspired Lewis on that historic day. Never one to ignore a good, eye-catching and, most importantly, free prop, he wrote a script around the plaster statue. Just nine days later, he had created one of the most important horror films ever made.

Blood Feast had little to recommend it apart from gore. The script was stilted and clichéd and the acting mostly unconvincing and hammy. The plot revolved around a mad Eygptian caterer called Faud Ramses and his attempts to bring the bloodthirsty Egyptian goddess Ishtar back to life with the ancient feast of Ishtar, the Blood Feast. For the feast to work properly, and for Lewis and Friedman to squeeze in the requisite gore, Ramses needed fresh body parts. These he took from various unlucky young women: the legs from one, the brains from another and, in the film's most famous scene, the tongue clean out of the mouth of a third. Ex-Playboy centrefold Connie Mason played the unfortunate tongue donor.

Today, films inspired by *Blood Feast* have access to any number of brilliantly talented special-effects artists, but for the trailblazers Lewis and Friedman, it was a case of making do. To create the illusion of Connie's tongue being ripped from her mouth, they got a lamb's tongue from the butcher, soaked it in strawberry jam for imitation blood and stuffed it into her mouth. The finished scene was almost as shocking for the size of the fleshy, flapping, appendage as for the visceral shock of seeing it yanked free.

The key back then to marketing a low-budget film was the trailer, the 'coming attractions' advert. For *Blood Feast* Lewis took actor Rooney Kerwin looking straight into the camera, annoucing to the audience:

> You are about to witness some scenes from the next attraction to play this theatre. This picture, truly one of the most unusual ever filmed, contains scenes which, under no circumstances should be viewed by anyone with a heart condition or anyone who is easily upset. We urgently recommend that if you are such a person, or the parent of a young or impressionable child now in attendance, that you leave the theatre for the next 90 seconds.

If that didn't get them, nothing would.

Although confident that they were making a new type of film, Lewis and Friedman had no way of knowing whether or not an audience would actually pay to see such gruesome sights. They negotiated an opening for *Blood Feast* at a drive-in cinema in Peoria, Illinois, a small mid-western town. Having vowed not to go near the place, their curiosity got the better of them and just one night after the opening, they drove to see what was going on. About ten miles out of town their car got stuck in a terrible jam which continued all the way to the cinema. It was the film. Never having seen anything like it, the residents of Peoria had gone nuts, and word of mouth was spreading like crazy. To say the film was a success would be a vast understatement. Lewis and Freidman had stumbled onto something big.

That very day, they began working on the script for their next gore feast. *Two Thousand Maniacs* (1964) was a bloody retelling of Brigadoon. One hundred years in the past, a group of Union soldiers passed through a small Southern town, Pleasant Valley, and laid it to waste. A century later, the town reappears, with the ghosts of the dead in place and hoping to have some Herschell Gordon Lewis-style fun with the modern-day Yankees. The Yanks are dismembered and roasted, and one is put in a barrel with spikes inside and rolled down a hill. In the most inventive death, a young woman is laid under a huge rock as part of a fairground

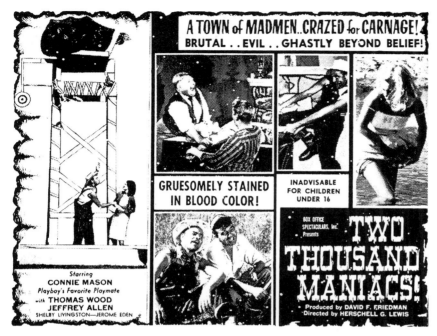

Two Thousand Maniacs – the South will rise again.

attraction. The first customer to hit the target with a softball gets the satisfaction of seeing her squished.

Although it equalled the success of *Blood Feast*, *Two Thousand Maniacs* had a much harder time getting to its audience. When *Blood Feast* first appeared, it took people by surprise. Many local authorities tried to ban it, but how could they? There was no regulation for this kind of picture. It wasn't sexually obscene and it wasn't full of bad language. Moreover, Lewis and Friedman had specifically requested that cinema owners not admit children to the film, so it couldn't be banned on that account either.

By the time *Two Thousand Maniacs* appeared, though, the film police were ready. In between the two films, many states had introduced local legislation prohibiting explicit screen violence. But even with such opposition, *Two Thousand Maniacs* made an incredible amount of money, largely from a drive-in audience hungry for action, blood, and tits and ass.

Without the drive-ins, and their notoriously lax attitude towards the censors' wishes, Lewis and Friedman might have called it a day there and then. As it was, they soldiered on together for one more gore-filled extravaganza, *Color Me Blood Red* (1965).

The story in *Color Me Blood Red*, about a mad egocentric artist consumed with finding the right shade of blood-red paint for his pictures, once again served only as a hook upon which to hang scenes of explicit, graphic and crowd-pleasing gore. However, greater pressure from local censors meant that even fewer cinemas were able to book the film, and rather then face ever diminishing returns, Lewis and Friedman parted company.

Friedman returned to the sexploitation pictures that he had begun his career with, while Lewis tried his hand at a number of different exploitation genres – hillbilly films such as *Moonshine Mountain* (1964), and a handful of swinging Sixties comedies like *The Girl, The Body and The Pill* (1967). He

The poster says it all.

Left: Filling in time, the Herschell Gordon Lewis way, in *The Gruesome Twosome*.

Below: I don't quite know why Herschell Gordon Lewis thought that 'Blinding Colour' would be much of an incentive.

even produced a couple of family films, called *Jimmy The Boy Wonder* (1966) and *The Magic Land Of Mother Goose* (1967).

An unsuccessful attempt to step into the mainstream with a virtually gore-less horror film, *A Taste Of Blood* (1967), led Lewis to return to what he did best. *The Gruesome Twosome* (1967) was one of his goriest and funniest pictures. It's about a mad old woman who runs a wig shop on campus and keeps her demented son, Rodney, locked downstairs. In an effort to cut costs, she enlists his aid in scalping some of the college girl customers to make fresh hairpieces. Even by Lewis's standards it was a weird film. After editing the footage, he found it ten minutes too short to run as a feature. So he went back and shot ten minutes of two wig stands 'talking' to each other to round the film out!

Only a small drop of Lewis's trademark gore found its way into his next film, *She-Devils on Wheels* (1968). The She-Devils of the title get off scot free after decapitating the rival, male, gang leader. They shout their creed defiantly before riding off into the sunset: 'We don't owe nobody nothing, and we don't make no deals. We're swinging chicks on motors and we're man-eaters on wheels.'

By this time living in Chicago, Lewis invested in a small cinema, which he devoted entirely to horror. Suitably named The Blood Shack, it featured Lewis's movies and classic

GUTS AS HARD AS THE STEEL OF THEIR "HOGS"!

SHE-DEVILS ON WHEELS

Starring
BETTY CONNELL
NANCY LEE NOBLE

In Blinding Color!

A MAYFLOWER PICTURES, INC., PRODUCTION

horror films such as *Dracula* and *Frankenstein*. To enhance the audience's experience, the theatre also staged gruesome live shows in the tradition of the French Grand Guignol, in which actors would, for example, slit each other's throats on stage before the main feature began.

Lewis was to make two more films before retiring from the business altogether. Fittingly, they were his bloodiest. *The Wizard of Gore* (1970) starred Montag, a deranged magician whose horrible tricks would actually happen to his witless volunteers an hour or so after the event. One woman had a six-inch nail pounded into her brain through her ears. On stage, it was trick, and she walked away. But later that day she collapsed with blood spouting from her head. Another poor soul got a sword rammed down her throat, and a third was disembowelled with a chainsaw!

The violence in *The Wizard*, though extreme, was actually quite basic by Lewis's standards. In fact, the strangest thing about the film was the script, with the Wizard himself pontificating at great and almost surreal length on such subjects as man's lust for violence and blood, and the big question: What is reality? Although the special effects were quite ordinary, and the fake blood completely unrealistic, the film was nonetheless rather horrible. The sheer insanity behind it makes for a terribly unnerving viewing experience. You'd find yourself asking not only why on Earth you would be watching this stuff, but also who on Earth would be sick enough to film it in the first place.

In Lewis's final film, *The Gore Gore Girls* (1972), the violence that had proved so successful for him was once again ruthlessly exploited, this time to even more absurd and gratuitous extremes. Set in a strip joint, the film is basically one violent episode after another, as the strippers are brutally murdered. If you can suspend your disgust over the concept, many of the ideas are clever and original. One stripper is killed while blowing a bubble-gum bubble, which fills with blood as she dies. Another has her nipples cut off, but instead of blood, milk shoots out, one breast delivering normal, white stuff, the other squirting the chocolate variety. I'm sure all the arguments about the tendency towards violence against women as entertainment not only apply to Lewis's films, but pretty much originated with them. For downright unjustifiable offensiveness, *The Gore Gore Girls* is in a league of its own.

That said, I like Lewis's films. I know that they're unpleasant in many ways, but there is a goofy innocence about them. The awful atrocities committed against young men and women are either so poorly executed or take place in such overblown, unbelievable settings that their horror is defused. They rarely work in the way in which I imagine they were intended. But as gross comedies, they're unbeat-able.

SELECTED HERSCHELL GORDON LEWIS FILMOGRAPHY

THE PRIME TIME (1960)
LIVING VENUS (1960)
*THE ADVENTURES OF LUCKY
    PIERRE (1961)*
DAUGHTERS OF THE SUN (1962)
NATURE'S PLAYMATES (1962)
BOIN-N-G! (1963)
*GOLDILOCKS AND THE THREE
    BARES (1963)*
*BELL, BARE AND BEAUTIFUL
    (1963)*
SCUM OF THE EARTH (1963)
BLOOD FEAST (1963)
*TWO THOUSAND MANIACS
    (1964)*
MOONSHINE MOUNTAIN (1964)

COLOR ME BLOOD RED (1965)
MONSTER A GO-GO (1965)
SIN, SUFFER AND REPENT (1965)
JIMMY, THE BOY WONDER (1966)
ALLEY TRAMP (1966)
*THE MAGIC LAND OF MOTHER
    GOOSE (1967)*
SUBURBAN ROULETTE (1967)
*THE GIRL, THE BODY AND THE
    PILL (1967)*
A TASTE OF BLOOD (1967)
*THE GRUESOME TWOSOME
    (1967)*
SHE-DEVILS ON WHEELS (1968)
THE WIZARD OF GORE (1970)
THE GORE GORE GIRLS (1972)

23 Yellow Fever
Mario Bava and Dario Argento

If you scour the shelves of your local video shop, you'll find a lot of trashy horror films. And amongst that trash you'll find a lot of Italian names. For whatever complex reasons, it's a genre that seems as irresistible to our pasta loving cousins as, erm, pasta. But once you get past the almost shameless dwelling on revolting gore, the love of flashy lighting, and the over the top demonic make-up that seems to provide the spine to these flimsily put-together shockers, there's little left worth talking about. They're trash, it's as simple as that.

There is, of course, an exception to this hideous generalisation, and an important one at that. For amongst the dust-covered dreck you might be lucky enough to stumble upon a film by Dario Argento or Mario Bava, Italians, yes. Directors of horror films, yes. But trash-merchants? Never! For these two are the most spectacular and underrated film-makers ever to set foot on a blood-drenched set.

Their better films tend toward the violent end of the spectrum, and as a result are unlikely to turn up on television, although you can catch some of Mario Bava's less bloody movies from time to time. The failure of the films themselves to attract the attention and audience they deserve has meant that the term *giallo* means little outside Italy. It's a shame, not only because the movies deserve a wider audience, but also because it's one of the few popular cinema styles to actually originate in Italy, where the noble art of ripping off other companies' successful projects has become recognised as the norm.

The term *giallo* itself derives from a series of books featuring the work of crime writers like Edgar Wallace and Frederick Brown, a series identified by their garish yellow (*giallo*, in Italian) covers. Just as the black-covered crime books in the Serie Noir and Fleuve Noir series in France gave birth to the hard-boiled detective thrillers we refer to as *film noir*, so too have the glossy and violent Italian thrillers of the Sixties and Seventies come to be identified with the books that inspired them.

Now, just as not all American thrillers are *noir* films, nor can all Italian horror/thrillers be described as *gialli*. The two most obvious distinguishing characteristics of *gialli* are style and content. Their content differs from their *noir* counterparts in so far as the emphasis is placed as much on the deed of murder itself as in the solving. If *The Silence of the Lambs* had been adapted for the screen by Dario Argento, then we would have had to sit through at least half an hour of gruesomely graphic scenes of murder and disfigurement before we even heard about Clarice.

On the style front, *gialli* are presented in sumptuous, lush colours, as opposed to the gritty black and white of *film noir*. Many critics have dismissed *gialli* as being little more than beautifully lit trash, films that are all style, and violent style at that, with next to no content. To an extent, they're right. But in a field where style is mostly forgotten in the search for the next eye-poppingly visceral scene of gore, they offer a welcome relief from current Yankee fare.

Mario Bava was the man who started it all. Born in San Remo, Italy, in 1914, his first work was as a cinematographer, starting with shorts in the late 1930s, and moving on to features in 1943. He worked with many of the finest directors of the day, including G W Pabst, Roberto Rosselini and Raoul Walsh. His own gradual move into directing came about virtually by default, in a way that I'm sure must be peculiar to the Italian film industry. In 1958, the horror film, *I, Vampiri* was left unfinished after a disagreement between the director, Ricardo Freda and the film's producer. Bava stepped forward and completed it in two days. Bava worked with Freda again in 1959 on *Caltiki, Il Monstre Immortale* and, again, the director was involved in an argument with the producer and decided not to turn up on the set for the first two weeks of shooting. His absence gave Bava another chance to develop his directing skills. After bailing out a few other pictures that suffered from Emotional Italian Directors Syndrome, Bava was given the chance to handle a feature film from start to finish on his own.

Inspired by the international success of Hammer's *Dracula*, Bava decided to adapt another classic tale of terror. He chose *The Viy*, by Gogol, apparently because he had been reading it at bedtime to his children, and they were all scared half to death. By the time it reached the screen it bore little resemblance to the original; *The Viy* had been transformed into a modern horror classic that many fans of Bava still feel is his best work.

Originally titled *La Maschero del Demono* (*The Mask of the Demon*), the film was picked up in Italy by Sam Arkoff of AIP, who brought it back to the States and gave English-speaking audiences their first taste of Mario Bava. Retitled *Black Sunday*, it was far more extreme in its depiction of death and violence than movie audiences of the early Sixties were used to. Consequently, AIP placed a caution on all their advertisements: 'Please note. The producers of *Black Sunday* recommend that it be seen only by those over 12 years of age.'

As for us squeamish Brits, still outraged by what we saw as the excessive gore in the first few Hammer pics, *Black Sunday* underwent the removal of several scenes, including a particularly nasty eye-gouging session, before being allowed onto British cinema screens in 1968. And maybe the censors had a point.

The film begins with Princess Asa, a witch, being branded with 'S' (for Satanist), and then having the metal 'Mask of Satan', complete with spikes, hammered onto her face. For good measure, she is then burned at the stake. You can't keep a bad witch down, though, and exactly 200 years later two scholarly professors stumble upon the site of her ashes. Attacked by an inordinately large bat, one of the professors accidentally smashes the cabinet in which the witch is trapped. The blood from the bat revives her, and she summons her vampire servant.

Bava's history as a lighting cameraman served him well in this picture. The photography and lighting are excellent, creating the mood that gives the film much of its power. The sets are also way above standard, not just for an Italian picture but for horror movies worldwide. The witch's tomb, draped in cobwebs, the baroque castle and the sleepy peasant village, through which thunders a ghostly and frighteningly silent coach – all staple ingredients in a thousand other horror films – have rarely looked as good as they do here.

Bava strayed from the world of horror for his next two pictures, a couple of unremarkable sword and sandal 'epics', *Hercules in the Haunted World* and *Erik the Conqueror* (both 1961). Although understandably hard to verify, he allegedly created the Viking ships seen in the battle scenes from Butoni Pasta. Remarkably, these films did tolerably well at the US box-office, but Bava accepted that he had an affinity with horror films, and it was with them that he would make his name.

The Evil Eye (1962) marked his return to scary stuff. Shot in black and white, it represented a moody and atmospheric mixture of suspense, detective work and violence. In the picture, Nora Drowson, an American tourist in Rome is witness to a brutal murder attempt. Rome is in the grip of terror, inspired by the 'alphabet murderer' whose victims appear to be arbitrarily selected as he works his way through the alphabet. He has already slain three people, taking him up to D. Nora can't shake the feeling that she has forgotten something important about the murder attempt she saw. The more she dwells on it, the stronger her conviction that she will be the next victim, but no one believes her.

Eventually, the husband of the woman she saw being attacked is revealed as the killer. But in a neat twist, Nora finally recalls that what she saw was the 'victim' trying to kill her husband. She is persuaded to forget all about it, and complies to the extent that when she witnesses a jealous husband killing his wife in a cable car, she denies seeing anything. Why get involved?

What!, of course, was not the original Italian title for Bava's next film, but rather the one imposed upon it by its American distributors in 1963. For once it was a rather appropriate new title, as 'What!' is the only reaction any civilised cinemagoer could be expected to have upon first encountering this sumptuous but deranged piece of work. Directed by Bava under the alias of John M Old and originally known as the far more accurate *The Whip and the Flesh*, it had all the trademarks of a classic Bava flick, not least in that it managed both to rip off other films and feel intensely original at the same time.

For *What!* (the title grows on you, doesn't it?), Bava recreated the look and feel of the Hammer vampire films at their best. He also poached their most distinctive leading man, Christopher Lee, putting him to work on a script far more explicit and extreme than any that Hammer would have dared to use. Essentially, Bava made a vampire film without vampires. He gave Lee the fangless role of a whip-wielding sadist, exploiting the menacing but erotic presence he brought to the part of Dracula.

The film begins with a close-up of an ornate dagger in a display case, its point stained with blood. It transpires that the black sheep of the family, Kurt (Lee), is returning home at that very moment. His arrival causes more than just a little upset, as not only is he strongly suspected of murdering a servant girl with the aforementioned dagger, but Nevenka, his former lover, is now married to his brother, who in turn has been bumped up ahead of Kurt in the inheritance stakes.

Kurt arrives home to a moderately frosty reception, and after exchanging many meaningful glances with his ex, bumps into her on the beach and proceeds to flog her ruthlessly with a whip (which she just happens to have on her). Now, if this had been a Hammer production, the camera would no doubt have stayed on Kurt's face as he took his twisted pleasure. But seeing as this is pure unadulterated Bava, the camera lingers on her back for each lash of the whip, waiting for each and every crimson weal to appear.

That night, during a spectacular storm, Kurt is murdered by an unseen assailant, using the very dagger he had killed the servant girl with. He is buried in the family tomb, and that seems to be the end of that, with everyone but Nevenka generally heaving sighs of relief. But in a beautifully lit and shot scene, he reappears to Nevenka – an appearance that could be dismissed as an hallucination if it weren't for the all too real weals he leaves on her back.

The next evening, the ghostly Kurt appears before his father, scaring him to death. His brother gets the bright idea of opening Kurt's tomb to see if he really has been walking around at night. There is a body there, but it is so horribly decayed that it can't be identified. Kurt is seen one final time by Nevenka, this time persuading her to join him, and he stabs her. Kurt's brother and Toster, the lurking handyman, appear to see her stab herself. She has been inflicting pain upon herself to keep their love alive, until finally she kills herself.

What! must be among the first commercial pictures to attempt to deal with the nature of a sado-masochistic relationship. (It beat *9½ Weeks* to the cinema by about 25 years.) Needless to say, it was censored accordingly. In fact, so brutally was it edited and chopped around that it has never been screened intact in its original form. Most if not all of the sado-masochistic sub-plot (known in the trade as 'the good bits') disappeared, leaving audiences with an almost incomprehensible haunted castle flick, and explaining Bava's decision to use a pseudonym in the movie's credits on foreign releases. But even in its chopped around form, the film is enjoyable, mostly for its camerawork and extreme, almost garish lighting which was to become Bava's stylistic trademark.

Black Sabbath (1963), Bava's next movie, was a cinematic trilogy financed in part by AIP. Inspired once again by literary classics – in this case short stories from Chekhov (*The Drop of Water*), F G Snyder (*The Telephone*) and Tolstoy (*The Wurdalak*) – it was very much in the style of the Roger Corman–Poe movies that were then in vogue. Boris Karloff, star of both *The Raven* and *The Terror*, was drafted in to link the three stories together, and to star in the last of the three.

Bava's preference for shooting as much footage as possible indoors, ideally in studios, was fully justified by the spooky atmosphere he conjured up throughout this picture. As horror movies go, the three tales in *Black Sabbath* are as chillingly atmospheric as any of the classic Universal pictures of the Thirties and Forties. In true Bava style, the film was a lighting cameraman's dream, beginning with the opening sequence of Karloff's disembodied head, drifting toward the audience as the lights change from red to green to yellow and back to red again.

'Ladies and gentlemen, How do you do? Come closer, please, I have something to tell you. You are about to see three tales of terror and the supernatural. I so hope you haven't come alone. This is Black Sabbath.'

The Chekhov piece opens with a lovely shot of Karloff, reflected in a luminous pool of liquid as drops of water break the surface. 'The Drop of Water' begins when a nurse is called in to help dress the corpse of a medium. The camera follows her around the vast and wonderful set built to represent the medium's house, and a foreboding atmosphere is created by such strange but apparently meaningless happenings as a creaking lamp descending slowly from the ceiling under its own weight.

Left on her own with the corpse, the nurse steals the woman's ring, but is shocked when a fly lands on the dead woman's finger where the ring was. She drops the ring, and while bending over to retrieve it, knocks over a glass of water and gets an almighty shock when the corpse's hand flops onto her head. On arriving back at her own gorgeously recreated hovel, she is haunted by the sound of dripping water, first in one room, then another. In a state of growing panic she sees the horrific corpse of the dead woman lying on her bed. Rushing into the next room, she is again confronted by it. She backs away, her face contorted with fear, only to find it behind her. Finally, she sees the dead woman approach, clawlike hands outstretched, reaching for her neck.

She is found in the morning, dead from fright, with her own hands around her neck. The ring, of course, is missing. As a short sharp little shocker, it's hardly the most original premise, but the moody atmosphere, coupled with a quite grotesque corpse, fashioned from wax by Bava's father, Eugenio, give it a memorable quality. Simple, but deliciously scary.

Karloff reappears briefly to introduce episode two, 'The Telephone', which is set in modern-day Rome, with a cool jazzy score. It's about a beautiful young woman, Rosy, who lives alone. She begins to receive calls from an old boyfriend of hers, Frank. Trouble is, Frank's been dead for three months. A letter arrives, with nothing on it. Nothing, that is, until she picks it up. Then a message appears to write itself: 'There's no way of avoiding it, Rosy. It won't be long now! Frank.'

Terrified, she tells a friend, Mary, who offers to stay the night. Mary makes Rosy some hot tea, with tranquillisers, and stays up to keep watch while Rosy goes to bed. Unlucky for her, because that's the night a man breaks in to murder Rosy, strangling Mary instead. A drugged-up Rosy wakes up to find Frank advancing toward her. As Frank lunges, she reaches under her pillow for a knife she'd hidden earlier, and she stabs and kills the intruder. The phone rings . . . it's Frank.

The final story is the best. Starring Boris Karloff as Gorca, 'the wurdalak' of the title, it has a moody atmosphere and some beautiful exterior locations. D'Urfe, a nobleman enters a peasant family's home. He is carrying a dagger, pulled from the back of a headless corpse, which they identify as belonging to their father, Gorca, played by Karloff. Gorca had left home five days ago to hunt down and kill a Turkish bandit who had been terrorising his neighbourhood. Many had thought the bandit was a vampire, a wurdalak, and for that reason Gorca had left his family with strict instructions: If he returned any later than five days, they should drive a stake through his heart and kill him.

Gorca limps over the bridge leading into town just a few moments after the town bell rings. His five days are up and his family are uncertain. Is he now a vampire? Should they kill him? The nobleman, who has stayed with the family because of Gorca's beautiful daughter, thinks they should. But despite a certain coldness toward them, Gorca still shows signs of humanity, wishing to hold his grandson. That night, as the family sleeps, Gorca prowls around the house and fetches his grandson. 'Grandpa, where are we going?' asks the child. 'I have a present for you,' chuckles Gorca. They ride through a night tinted an unreal, vivid blue. The next day the child is found and returned to the family – dead. Gorca has sucked his blood. The mother refuses to decapitate him, and buries him whole. In an especially chilling scene, the infant wurdalak returns to the house from his grave, imploring his mother to let him in. Soon, the entire family is cursed, and the nobleman D'Urfe finally succumbs to Gorca's daughter, rather than leave her.

Powerful and original as his work on *Black Sabbath* was, the best was yet to come. The first of Bava's true *gialli* films was the fabulous *Sei Donne Per L'Assissino*, or *Blood and Black Lace* (1964). It was an interesting taste of things to come for a number of reasons. The victims were all women, beautiful young ones at that. It was violent – shockingly so, in fact, with murders carried out by drowning, burning (faces and hands pressed to a hot stove) and even gouging, using a glove with sharp talons. The assassin of the title was faceless, or at least appeared that way for most of the movie, wearing a flesh coloured, featureless mask (very cool in a 1960s kind of way). The look of the film was influential as well – garish but also sensuous, washing the screen with swathes of colour and creating a beautiful, but unreal, deadly world that would have an incredible influence upon Dario Argento. Finally, and most disappointingly, the film's plot, which was thin, confusing and hard to follow, served as an unfortunate blue print for many of the *giallo* thrillers to follow.

It starts with the murder of a woman who, it turns out, had been blackmailing someone with information kept in her missing diary. One by one, other beautiful young women working in the same beauty salon are slain, until finally, of course, the killer is discovered. Not much of a plot, but at the time, the film's visual style and the graphic depiction of brutal murders throughout guaranteed it a sizeable audience.

Equally beautiful, and far more satisfying, was *Planet of the Vampires* (1965), Bava's one science fiction/horror film. Set almost entirely in one small room – the control room of the spaceship Argos – it featured Captain Markary and his small crew, wearing the coolest black leather space suits ever designed. They are searching for their sister ship, Galliot, and hence on their way to the mysterious planet Aura. Landing on the planet, they discover an alien craft and a huge alien 'pilot', dead at the controls. However, they conclude that

Mario Bava's low budget but powerful science fiction shocker – *Planet of the Vampires.*

despite the presence of the Galliot and the dead navigator, the planet is uninhabited. Uninhabited, that is, until the deceased crew of the Galliot rise from their graves. The final twist in the tale is that the crew of the Argos are not, as we assumed, human beings at all – and their next scheduled stop is . . . Planet Earth.

Hatchet for a Honeymoon (1969) began a rather lean patch for Bava fans, being a limp psychological thriller with only two killings and a schizo in a wedding dress to recommend it. A 'comedy Western' followed it, and Bava was not back on form until the visceral and trend-setting, not to mention near-legendary, *Twitch of the Death Nerve* (1971).

Like many of the 'stalk-and-slash' films that followed it in the 1980s, *Death Nerve* featured the sequential murders of mainly young people in a scenic setting. But Bava kept the whole mix fresh with murderers being dispatched alongside 'innocent' victims, without relying on quite the level of stomach churning mutilation that soon became *de rigueur* – the most shocking death being that which occurs when a youth has a live octopus attached to his face!

Baron Blood (1972) failed to match this level of inventiveness, but the film that followed it, *Lisa and the Devil* (1973), is the favourite of many Bava fans. It's a film for which the term 'dreamlike' could have been invented. Fantasy and reality merge throughout, and the presence of Telly Savalas, playing a demonic puppeteer while sucking on the lollipop that was to become his Kojak trademark, only adds to the weirdness. Elke Sommers plays Lisa, and she begins the film as a tourist, separated from her party, who keeps bumping into the sinister puppeteer. She's frightened by a strange man, Carlo, who looks exactly like one of Telly's puppets, and insists on calling her Elena. She hitches a ride out of town, but when the car breaks down agrees to spend the night in a gothic mansion nearby. During the course of a very long and confusing night she falls in love with a young stranger named Max, who in turn still loves his first wife, Elena. So much so, in fact, that he keeps her corpse in the attic. Various people are killed, including the chauffeur and Carlo, before Max drugs Lisa with chloroform and tries to make love to her next to the corpse of Elena. Max then kills his mother before falling from a window, impaling himself upon a railing.

In the morning, Lisa wakes to find herself alone in the house. The room that she had thought was full of Max's former victims – all dead and sitting around a table – is in fact full of puppets. As she leaves the house, she is taunted by some children who call her 'ghost' and tell her that no one has lived in that house for over 100 years. Somehow Lisa manages to find her tour group, and the film ends with her on the plane home, confused but safe. Until she discovers that the passenger next to her is actually the devilish puppeteer, and all her fellow passengers are puppets!

The film is a little confused, but the strange convoluted plot and sense of unreality only add to its power. If you allow yourself to go with the film, drift along with its strange twists and turns, it's an immensely rewarding experience.

Bava's next film, a gangster picture called *Wild Dogs* was never released, so we come to his last film, *Shock* (1978). A fairly standard spooky-house/possessed child kind of film, it nonetheless had enough unusual touches to keep you watching – in particular an odd dream sequence in which the child's mother appears to be floating upside-down and slowly turning, her long hair flowing around her in a most peculiar way. Like many of Bava's films though, by the time it reached our shores it was so badly dubbed as to be almost laughable.

Mario Bava died in 1980 at the age of 65. His son, Lamberto (who co-directed *Shock*), is himself a director, mainly of horror films, today. But in terms of skill and style, the heir to Bava's title of Italy's greatest horror stylist goes to Dario Argento.

MARIO BAVA FILMOGRAPHY

BLACK SUNDAY (1960)
HERCULES IN THE HAUNTED WORLD (1961)
ERIK THE CONQUEROR (1961)
THE EVIL EYE (1962)
WHAT! (1963)
BLACK SABBATH (1963)
BLOOD AND BLACK LACE (1964)
THE ROAD TO FORT ALAMO (1964)
PLANET OF THE VAMPIRES (1965)
DR GOLDFOOT AND THE BIKINI MACHINE (1966)
KNIVES OF THE AVENGER (1966)
OPERATION FEAR (KILL, BABY, KILL!) (1967)

DANGER DIABOLIK (1968)
HATCHET FOR THE HONEYMOON (1969)
ROY COLT AND WINCHESTER JACK (1969)
FOUR TIMES THAT NIGHT (1970)
FIVE DOLLS FOR AN AUGUST MOON (1970)
TWITCH OF THE DEATH NERVE (1971)
BARON BLOOD (1972)
LISA AND THE DEVIL (1973)
WILD DOGS (1974)
SHOCK (1978)

I confess that before 1985 I had never even heard of the movies being made and released in Italy by Mr Argento, even though most of them received a limited release in America and the UK. But when I stumbled upon *Suspiria*, Argento's sixth film, I knew I'd found my man. The moment the picture ended I raced down to the box office and, with what must have been a frightening gleam in my eye, demanded to know what else he'd made, when, with whom, whether they were as good, where he did his hair, etc, etc. Just every little thing a fan needs to know about their latest hero.

Like all great cinema, *Suspiria* (1977) loses much of its power when you try to describe the film. Shot in intense, vivid primary colours with an impossibly loud rock sound-track, it managed to create its own mood, its own reality. Like most of Argento's later films, the plot was thin, almost secondary to the main purpose of the film, which was to transport the viewer away from reality, even cinema reality, into a brand new, hyper-real world where sudden acts of seemingly random but outrageous violence can, and do occur.

Suzy Banyon, a young dance student, arrives in Germany where she will finish her ballet studies at the famous Freiberg

Suspiria – one of Dario Argento's earliest, and best, films.

Dance Academy. From the moment she leaves the quiet, controlled surroundings of the airport, she steps into the nightmare world of *Suspiria*. The music swells to a deafening crescendo and she finds herself in an incredible thunderstorm.

Hailing a cab, Suzy makes it to the academy, but is turned away at the door. Confused, she asks the cabbie to take her to a hotel, but on the way out of the academy, she sees a frightened looking woman running through the grounds.

Leaving Suzy, we follow the woman, a student at the academy, to a friend's flat, in an opulent turn-of-the-century mansion house with an ornate, coloured glass ceiling. The woman is terrified. She must get away from the school, but can't begin to tell her friend why; she wouldn't believe her anyway.

She goes into the bathroom to dry off, and the windows suddenly crash open – it's the storm. The soundtrack is now almost deafening, combining a gentle tune played on chimes with heavy rock guitars and the menacing sound of breathing and muttering. The noise alone is enough to scare you, but the girl is obviously frightened of something else, something outside. Taking a light to the window, she thinks she sees cat's eyes. It was a false alarm. The music dies down and she begins to step back – and then, to an even noisier surge of music, a hairy arm smashes through the window next to her, pressing her face against the glass pane. As her friend tries desperately to break into the bathroom, we see her face pressed harder and harder against the glass, until finally it smashes through.

Her attacker is inside. He stabs her repeatedly, almost leisurely, then ties a length of rope around her – in gruesome close-up we see the knife actually entering her heart. Almost dead, the woman throws her head back, and it smashes through the decorative glass roof. Her friend, trying to fetch help, stops as she sees the head appear – and then the roof gives under the dying girl's weight. It smashes and she falls in a shower of glass, until the rope around her waist slips up her body and stops her short – she hangs. As the noisy soundtrack continues beating on, the camera tracks down her body, following the blood dripping off her feet to the floor. There, amongst the broken glass, lies her friend – huge shards sticking out of her chest and face.

The next day, Suzy, unaware of all this, arrives at the academy. She meets the rather cold women who run the place, Miss Tanner and Madame Blanc. The rest of the girls are a tad malicious, but she befriends a girl called Sara. Suzy collapses, apparently from exhaustion, and is prescribed bland food and a glass of red wine with each meal by the academy's doctor.

While swimming together in the academy's beautiful pool, Sara admits to Suzy that it was she who had told her to leave on that first night. Sara was a friend of the brutally murdered girl, who had whispered to her of strange things at the academy; things to do with ancient witchcraft. That night, after drinking her prescribed wine, Suzy finds herself unable to stay awake. Sara, on hearing some strange footsteps, investigates. Something or someone chases her, and in an attempt to escape she falls into a pit of razor-sharp barbed wire. The more she tries to escape, the worse she is cut. Finally, her assailant slits her throat.

The next evening Suzy avoids the drugged wine, and follows the sound of footsteps into the heart of the academy, where she discovers a secret labyrinth. At the centre she finds a centuries-old witch, Helena Marcos, who controls the teachers and uses the school as a base to spread evil witchcraft into the world. The witch summons others to kill the girl, but Suzy grabs a glass feather from a bird with crystal plumage and stabs the witch in the neck. As she flees the academy, it is consumed by cleansing flames.

As you may have gathered *Suspiria* has no real message to impart, and attempts to say nothing whatsoever about the human condition. But it succeeds admirably in its intention to thrill and shock the audience in ways which, at the time of its release, were fresh and surprising. Much of the film's intensity comes from its look and the soundtrack, neither of which were accidental. The music was performed by the Italian rock band The Goblins, in conjunction with Argento. And to get the garish colours he wanted, Argento tracked down

The witch gets it in the eye at the end of *Suspiria*.

old film stock and used techniques that had been abandoned by technicolour in the 1950s – techniques which favoured and enhanced one of the three primary colours at any time.

Argento's earlier films were, to my taste, even better. Less vicariously violent than *Suspiria*, they were more firmly within the horror/thriller genre, avoiding the supernatural tone of *Suspiria* and its sequel, *Tenebres*.

His first film is in fact my favourite. *The Bird With The Crystal Plumage* (1970) is based on a classic *giallo* story – *The Screaming Mimi* by the American author Frederick Brown. In the film's incredible opening scene, Sam, an American writer working in Rome, witnesses a brutal attack in an art gallery. He tries to help but cannot get in through the thick glass window. Watching, horrified, as the victim tries to crawl away from her knife-wielding attacker, Sam is trapped unawares between the glass front and a second glass security window that slides silently shut behind him. It's a horrible situation – being forced to watch helpless, while a woman bleeds to death in front of you and you pray for the police to arrive.

The hero, trapped and helpless, in *The Bird with the Crystal Plumage*.

The woman, Monica, recovers from the attack, but her would-be murderer finds new victims. Sam, against the wishes of his girlfriend, Julia, becomes obsessed with solving the crime. But the killer has clearly seen Sam, and begins to terrorise him and Julia with phone calls, and nearly gets to Julia by hacking through several locked doors before the police arrive.

The film is full of exciting surprises, like the scene in which Sam pursues the killer into a convention hall, where he is lost among a sea of identically dressed people. Finally the mystery is solved: the killer is actually Monica. What Sam had seen in the art gallery was her trying to murder her husband, rather than the other way around.

It's an incredibly confident and assured first film, and the lush music by Ennio Morricone serves to heighten the horror by playing against it. Argento's next film, though similar, was not quite as good. *The Cat O' Nine Tails* (1971) starred Karl Malden as a blind ex-reporter whose hobby is completing crossword puzzles with the help of his sighted young niece. The film unfolds in standard *giallo* style, with the audience present at each of the murderer's brutal killings, and often having more information than the cops and the ubiquitous amateur sleuth. For the first time, Argento used the camera to give us the killer's subjective view – a technique that was to be much imitated in the 'splatter' or 'stalk-and-slash' movies of the 1980s.

Once again, a believable plot took back seat to style and a series of highly inventive set pieces, culminating in a spectacularly violent finish in which the killer plunges through a skylight, grabs a rope to save himself, and then has his hands shredded to a bloody pulp as he continues to fall, unable to stop or let go.

Four Flies on Grey Velvet (1972) was about a jazz drummer who believes he has killed someone, although in fact he has not. The explanation given for the title was that, according to this movie at least, we record on our retina the last sight we see before death, and one of the victims saw four flies on grey velvet.

Argento took a break from horror films in 1973 with *The Five Days of Milan*, his only comedy thriller. But his return to horror thrillers with *Deep Red* (1976) was well worth the wait. This complex and tightly plotted movie started, typically, with a dramatic and violent scene. An idyllic family Christmas is shattered by a brutal murder – we see the stabbing only as shadows on the wall. But the instrument of murder, a large bloody knife, falls at the feet of a young child, witness to the whole thing. In the background we hear a nursery rhyme tune, a theme that recurs immediately prior to each actual murder and murder attempt.

The film then appears to begin again, with a totally unrelated scene, a lecture at the Institute of Parapsychology, where Helga, a German psychic, is demonstrating her powers. As she scans the audience's thoughts, she recoils in horror; there is evil in the crowd, pure evil. Argento cuts to the subjective point of view of this evil person, as he or she rises and goes to the toilet, even stopping to look in the mirror, which is too scratched for the audience to clearly make out his or her features.

Later that night, while Helga is on the telephone, a visitor calls. As she goes to answer the door, she once again recoils; she knows that the evil is outside! A meat cleaver comes splintering through the door and Helga is hacked at twice before she crawls to the window. As she screams for help, another blow sends her face smashing through the glass, slitting her throat and ending her screams.

The only witness to this horrible crime is Helga's downstairs neighbour, jazz pianist Marcus Daly, played by David Hemmings. He is drinking with his friend Carlo in the square below when he hears her screams. Racing up to her apartment, he pulls her free from the smashed window, and sees the killer escape across the square below. Witnesses to murders in Argento's movies never leave it to the police. Daly becomes obsessed with the thought that he has missed something, some vital clue that will lead him to the killer.

Daly returns to Helga's apartment, and discovers that one of the pictures in her hallway is missing. Did the killer take it? If so, why? He thinks it may be an important clue, but wants the advice of his friend, Carlo. Daly seeks him out, first visiting Carlo's eccentric mother, Martha, to get his address.

Meanwhile, a photograph taken of Daly at the police station is printed in a newspaper, identifying him as the only eyewitness to the crime. In a particularly chilling scene, the killer returns to the apartment and attempts to kill Daly, but Daly hears the strange nursery tune that the killer plays before each murder and locks himself behind a thick sliding door. The frustrated killer whispers to him to give up his investigations.

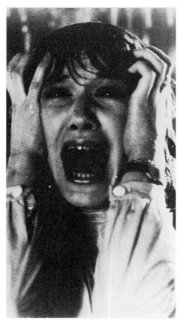

The films of Dario Argento tend to have this effect on people.

The tune reminds someone of a local legend, concerning a haunted house, where the sound of nonexistent children singing has kept people away for years. Daly arranges to visit a writer who described the house in a book, but the killer strikes first, drowning the writer in a scalding hot bath of water. Before she dies, she writes a message in the steam on a mirror in the bathroom, but the killer leaves a window open, and as the room cools off the message disappears.

Daly eventually identifies the haunted house, and discovers a painting hidden behind a fake wall, of a grinning child standing above a body holding a bloodstained knife. Daly continues his complex investigations and the killer just goes on killing. But then Daly discovers that the drawing he had seen in the house had been drawn by Carlo as a child. Is he the killer? Before he can be caught, he is knocked over, a car crushing his head like a ripe tomato.

Finally, Daly remembers what he had seen that day in Helga's apartment. The missing picture was not a picture after all, but a mirror! He had seen a reflection of the killer's face; it was Carlo's mother, Martha. In the final showdown, she attacks Daly in an old-fashioned elevator, but her necklace gets caught in the grill. Daly pushes the button, the elevator goes down and Martha is decapitated by her necklace.

Deep Red was followed by *Suspiria*, which in turn led to *Tenebres* (1982), another mystery thriller that dealt with a violent and random killer. Although beautiful to look at, it failed to match the inventiveness of either *Suspiria* or *Deep Red*.

Phenomena (1985), released in Britain and America as *Creepers*, combined many of Argento's pet themes: violent murder, of course; psychic powers, in this case the ability of a young girl to control insects; and an unseen killer. Once again, despite the crisp photography, powerful music and inventive murders, the film failed to reach the heights of his earlier work. Sadly, it was cut by about 25 minutes on release, adding to its problems. It's the only one of Argento's films in which the more implausible aspects of the story overwhelm his visual skills to the extent that the film is actually laughable.

Perhaps because of the lukewarm reception given to *Phenomena*, Argento did not make another film for two years. Finally he returned with *Opera* (1987), yet another beautiful but bloody, overly complex murder/thriller which promised more than it finally delivered. Argento proved he was as inventive as ever with murders – including one in which a knife enters a young man's neck and slices through his tongue – but the violence seemed more gratuitous and therefore more unpleasant than in his earlier work. However, if you have a strong stomach, there are one or two exceptional moments – in particular, a scene in which a pursued woman looks through a keyhole to try to identify a visitor, just as the killer fires a bullet. In extreme close up, we see the bullet travel through the keyhole before bursting through the back of her head.

Although Argento's earlier films are without doubt his best, it's rather fitting that this late full-length feature chose opera as its theme. Argento's talents are rather like that of an opera diva. Capable of creating remarkable, powerful emotional responses in the audience, his virtuosity can sometimes overshadow the film as a whole. Even his weakest films have moments of genuine terror and incredible cinematic beauty, but all too often they are grafted onto convoluted and often rather soppy plots. But what can I say? I'm a fan, and if you like your horror served up stylishly and with lashings of gore you will be, too.

DARIO ARGENTO FILMOGRAPHY

THE BIRD WITH THE
   CRYSTAL PLUMAGE
   (1970)
THE CAT O' NINE TAILS
   (1971)
FOUR FLIES ON GREY
   VELVET (1972)
FIVE DAYS OF MILAN
   (1973)

DEEP RED (1976)
SUSPIRIA (1977)
INFERNO (1980)
TENEBRES (1982)
PHENOMENA (1985)
OPERA (1987)
TWO EVIL EYES (1990)

24 Totally Deranged Movie
Carnival of Souls

Filmed in gritty black and white, two old jalopies in a small town pull up alongside each other. One is full of boys, the other, girls. The kids flirt and talk, and agree to have a race. Off they go, leaving the town and driving into the countryside. They come to an old bridge and race over, neck and neck. But the bridge is weak on the girls' side. It gives way, and the car flies off into the river below.

The river swallows the car and all those inside it, and over shots of the water flowing peacefully, the credits appear. Eerily beautiful organ music plays in the background. Welcome to the *Carnival of Souls*.

The car has disappeared, and we see the local sheriff questioning the boys, while others dredge the river. It appears that all the girls are lost, dragged away by the strong currents. But then someone shouts, and they all rush over to see a single figure clambering out of the river in a dazed state. She's recognised as Mary Henry, a local girl who plays organ at church. The other girls are never seen, and Mary remembers nothing.

Her behaviour, cold and distracted, is put down to the shock of the accident, and Mary leaves town for Utah, to take up a full time job as church organist. Driving through the night to get there, she passes a huge abandoned amusement park and pavilion, and, as she does, she sees the reflection of a strange, ghoulish man in her car window. He then appears directly in front of the car, causing her to swerve off the road.

Arriving at her destination, she meets with her landlady, a funny old duck who either acts in a very convincing stilted way or can't act at all. Looking out of the window of her new room, she imagines the ghostly face again, but of course there is no one there when she looks closer.

Candace Hilligoss rises from a watery grave at the beginning of *Carnival of Souls*.

At the church where she will be working she is introduced to their organ, 'our pride and joy'. Mary immediately puts the minister's nose out of joint by declining to meet any members of the congregation. She persuades the minister to take her out to the abandoned amusement park, but he won't accompany her inside the pavilion 'What attraction does this place hold for you?' he asks. Mary can't answer, but it is clear that she will return.

Back at the boarding house she meets her slimy neighbour, John Linden, a wolf who lives across the hall. He accidentally disturbs her in the bath, and asks her out for dinner. She refuses.

Stranger and stranger things happen to Mary. On a visit to a local department store, she senses something unusual, and then discovers that she has become invisible to everyone else in the shop. No one can see or hear her, and she can't hear them. Leaving the store, it's the same story outside, and she makes her way to a park, where gradually things return to normal. Or as normal as things are for her. Running from another sighting of 'that man', she bumps into a well-meaning doctor, who suggests she come to his office to talk. After telling him her story, he attempts to explain the sightings away as the after-effect of the crash, or perhaps the man represents a feeling of guilt, guilt over her surviving while the other girls died.

She returns to the amusement park, this time going inside the pavilion, where she sees nothing. But later, while playing the organ in church, she slips into a trance where she imagines the man and other phantoms dancing, summoning her to return.

Linden, the jerk from the boarding house, is waiting for her outside the church. She does go out with him and allows him into her room. As he comes up behind her to kiss, she sees the man in his place and screams. Linden, understandably miffed, leaves.

The next morning, she packs and leaves her room. Her car starts to break down, but she makes it to a garage, where she insists on staying in the car while it's being serviced. She shuts her eyes to sleep, but immediately opens them again when she hears the familiar sound of the man's footsteps. Running from the car, she heads for the bus station, desperate to leave town. But once again, no one can see or hear her. Running for a bus, she boards it to find it full of white-faced ghouls. She runs again, finding the park and normality. Visiting the doctor, she tells him of her fears:

Herk Harvey — a director and lead ghoul in *Carnival of Souls.*

> I don't belong in the world. That's what it is. Something separates me from other people. They're everywhere, they're everywhere! They're not going to let me go. Everywhere I turn, there's something blocking my way. He's trying to prevent me from living! He's trying to take me back somewhere. I can't fight anymore. I don't know what's real anymore. Thank you, Doctor. You're my last hope. If you don't help me, I'll have to go back there. He's trying to take me back somewhere. Doctor, you have to tell me what to do.

The doctor turns in his chair. He is the ghostly man. She screams, and then wakes up in her car. She did fall asleep after all. Didn't she?

The *Carnival of Souls* in full swing.

Driving away, she is drawn back to the abandoned pavilion. As the wind howls and a ghostly organ plays, she walks in. The dead rise to greet her from the sea, spectral couples dancing around her. She sees a ghostly version of herself, dancing with the man. Screaming, she runs, but they follow, chasing her under the pier and finally overwhelming her on the beach.

The next morning, investigating her abandoned car, the doctor and the minister find her footprints on the sand. They lead away from the pier and then disappear. Back in her home town, they've finally rescued the automobile from the river. Her corpse is inside with the other girls.

This remarkable low budget feature which has acquired a healthy following over the years due to its dreamy, haunting quality, was the one and only film to be produced and directed by the oddly named Herk Harvey. Working with writer John Clifford, Harvey had decided on a horror movie as his first foray into film-making because he figured it would stand a much better chance of earning some money. The year was 1962, and there was still a healthy audience out there, especially at the drive-ins, for horror films with a snappy title, even if they were in black and white and didn't have a monster in them. Harvey, whose film experience consisted solely of working on educational geographical films, hoped to make enough money with his first feature to be able to move on to other, non-horror projects. He alleges that the film was inspired by its main location, the Saltair Pavilion, a huge, decrepit, weird-looking building that had once been a famous and popular ballroom. It was located on the outskirts of Salt Lake City, and had been built by Mormons back in the 1890s. Over the years, an amusement park had been added to the facilities, but it was deserted by the time Harvey stumbled upon it.

Other key elements in the film were also dictated by what was available. Harvey knew that they could shoot part of the film for free in a nearby organ factory, providing the film not only with its beautiful and distinctive soundtrack, but also suggesting a profession for the lead character and providing the unsettling religious overtones – a soulless woman working for the church! Unable to stretch to much in the way of make-up, egg white was used on the faces of the 'dead' actors, proving to be all the more unsettling and effective precisely because it looked so different from standard monster make-up. In a further effort to cut costs, the lead ghoul was played by Herk Harvey himself.

The influence of *Carnival of Souls* can be seen in many of the more interesting horror films to follow. In particular, the look of the zombies in George Romero's *Night of The Living Dead*, and the strange music, disjointed relationships and stilted acting styles in David Lynch's *Eraserhead*, both remind me of Harvey's one-off.

Strange to think that a little film, written around a couple of key locations and with a first time cast, writer and director should be one of the most lyrical and memorable horror films ever. But it is.

25 Video Nasties

Cannibals and Zombies

Many of the films and directors dwelt upon in this book owe their survival, in the hearts and minds of my fellow low-budget sleazy cinema-loving friends, to an invention which, initially, seemed to pose an almost insurmountable threat to their existence. Just as many in the film industry in the early 1950s feared that television might steal audiences away and sound a premature death knell for the big screen, so too did it seem that the birth of affordable home video would irreparably damage and weaken the power and dominance of theatrical films as a source of cinematic entertainment.

In reality, of course, the opposite is true. The infiltration of VCRs into a huge percentage of homes has given movies a far longer shelf life, and introduced a new and incredibly lucrative way to help recoup the costs of movies long after they've been released and done the rounds. They have also performed a far more interesting and less obviously profit-driven action.

If you cast your mind back to the launch of home VCRs in the UK, then surely one phrase will come to mind: Video Nasties. I'm talking about the late Seventies and wonderful evocative titles like Scavolini's *Nightmares in a Damaged Brain*, the controversial *Driller Killer* and, of course, the unforgettable *Cannibal Holocaust*. Whole genres of which the general movie-going public, myself included, had been completely unaware, were suddenly sprung, encased in irresistibly garish and unpleasant boxes, and ready to insert into our new toys.

Cannibal flicks, Gestapo death camp movies, Kung Fu pictures, third rate slash 'n' hack thrillers, and a mountain of films produced on the most ludicrously tiny budgets were

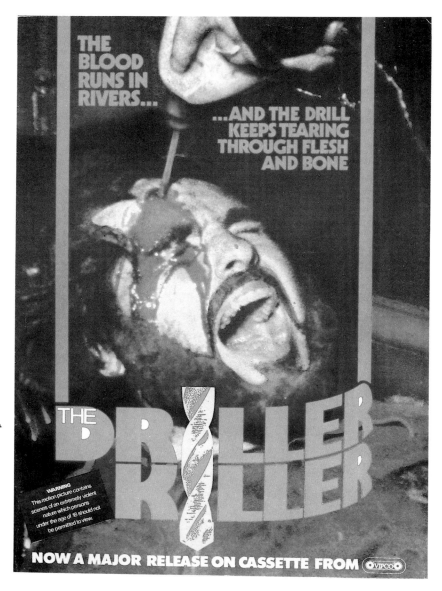

THE BLOOD RUNS IN RIVERS...

...AND THE DRILL KEEPS TEARING THROUGH FLESH AND BONE

THE DRILLER KILLER

WARNING
This motion picture contains scenes of an extremely violent nature which persons under the age of 18 should not be permitted to view.

NOW A MAJOR RELEASE ON CASSETTE FROM (VIPCO)

The Driller Killer —
sadly not available on
video in the UK.

soon all jostling feverishly for attention in the corner of what was probably just a few weeks previously a newsagent or local grocery store. Admittedly you had to be of a certain temperament to fully appreciate and enjoy much of the junk that was served up. But if you could overcome your squeamishness over the concept of humans pretending to eat each other on a very low budget, then much fun was to be had.

More scholarly film historians than I might well be able to screw a thesis worth of material out of the link between the growth of video as a source of entertainment and the boom in low-budget, gratuitous trash with flashy titles. In fact, if it was in the 1950s that unscrupulous film-makers discovered the art of making a quick but substantial buck from churning out low quality but titillating movies for the drive-in crowd, then it was in the 1970s that their even less scrupulous descendants rediscovered that art. Never before had so much trash been so quickly repackaged to be so eagerly consumed.

Quality thresholds had to be lowered substantially if maximum enjoyment was to be obtained, and inevitably many failed to make the adjustment. But for the few of us who greeted the avalanche of bizarre, esoteric, ultra-violent, camp, trashy or just plain bad films that appeared on tape in those golden days, it was very heaven to be alive. For those of you who, whether through ignorance, peer pressure or just an unfortunate attack of mature good taste, missed out on the cream of this bumper crop, here are the high and low lights.

The Golden Age of cannibal movies was without doubt from 1978 to 1981. The low-budget nature of both the production and distribution of this stuff makes it very hard to give a comprehensive list of those produced, further complicated by the many different titles that each single movie seems to have had. Sure, the grisly attraction of watching people chomp down on other people, whether through revenge (*The Cook, The Thief, His Wife, and Her Lover*), cultural differences (*The Running Man*), or just plain hunger were around before then, and continue to crop up today. But it was during the fertile, exploitative Seventies that the real goodies were churned out, and it was in the early Eighties that they turned up, via the wonders of video, on our doorstep.

A cannibal movie is not, of course, to be confused with a zombie flick. The similarities begin and end with the consumption of flesh. The difference is that zombies have the advantage of being dead, and are therefore more easily excused their strange taste for living human meat than your common or garden cannibal. But it is surely no simple coincidence that the boom in zombie flesh eaters coincided with the trend for films starring man-munching cannibals.

The all-time classic must be *Cannibal Holocaust* (1981) by the Italian Ruggero Deodato. Deodato is often lumped together with a group of like-minded Italians – Lucio Fulci, Luigi Cozzi, Umberto Lenzi and Michael Soavi, to name a few. No distinctive cinematic style is apparent in any of their works, but their willingness to rip off ideas in other, far better, movies, borrow from each other's lumpen work and unflinchingly dwell on the most gruesome of scenes give them an endearing quality that encourages folk like myself to seek them out.

Although Deodato is, like his brethren in the low budget extreme of Italian cinema, a clumsy hack, *Cannibal Holocaust* manages to be a curiously powerful and unsettling viewing experience. In *veritè* style it follows a crew of documentary film-makers as they embark on a trek into the South American jungles to capture on film a lost and primitive tribe. Of course, they are captured by said tribe and generally treated rather impolitely (castration, a disembowelling and even the skinning of a crocodile!) before the director figures we've had our money's worth.

Not quite in the 'classics' section occupied by Deodato's opus but charming in its own way nonetheless, is Antonio Marghereti's *Cannibal Apocalypse* (1980). Not content with ripping off the cannibal films that preceded him, Marghereti also attempted to benefit from the success of Coppola's *Apocalypse Now*.

Cannibal Apocalypse spends just enough time in Vietnam to justify the title and persuade unfortunate videophiles to hire this in the mistaken belief it might have Martin Sheen pursuing an undead Marlon Brando. A missing GI, Charlie, is discovered by his commanding officer. He's sitting in a pit with his buddy finishing off what's left of an unfortunate Vietcong soldier. From the look of things he was very tasty too. We then jump cut back to the States, where Charlie is released from a hospital for mental disorders. Presumably the doctors think

*Cannibal Holocaust –
not a nice movie!*

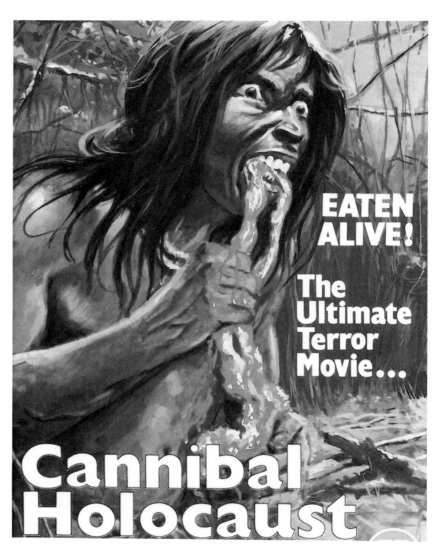

he's cured. Either that or they're deliberately helping out an Italian film-maker in need of a cannibal-on-the-loose.

He heads straight for a local flea pit and, despite what must have seemed like a fairly healthy prognosis when back in the ward, reverts immediately to the anti-social behaviour of his past by biting a tasty chunk out of a young woman's neck. After hiding out in a local shopping mall he is apprehended and returned to his buddy in hospital. They then eat most of the staff.

For no apparent reason, it seems that cannibalism is catching. Soon there are a whole lot more of these human-meat eaters making things tough for the local police. In fact, some of them even are the local police. The best line in the movie, if not in all of these cannibal films, is when the police captain discovers one of his men chowing down on a woman's breast. His response? 'Oh my God! Put it down son.'

After an all-out battle with some anti-social Hell's Angels (an idea lifted shamelessly from George Romero's *Dawn of the Dead)* the cannibal horde heads off to the sewers for a last stand, allowing Marghereti to fully exploit what little imagination he has in killing them all off. The most pleasing is the death of head cannibal chief Charlie, who is blown open by a shotgun, giving Marghereti a nice shot through the hole in his body. In the hackneyed tradition of just about all these movies, the end shot contains the big 'surprise' ending. Far from being over, cannibalism still lurks in the city, as we see a group of kids storing the dismembered parts of their mother in the fridge.

Special mention in the flesh eating category must also go to Umberto Lenzi's *Make Them Die Slowly*, also known as the less unsettling but equally tempting *Cannibal Ferox* (1981). For sheer deranged loopiness and illogicality, this one takes the biscuit. A drug pusher who falls out of favour with some gangster pals of his must leave New York. Where does he head for? Another American City? One of the drug capitals of Western Europe, Amsterdam maybe? No, of course not. He heads straight for the cannibal infested jungles of South America. He meets up with a team of anthropologists, intent on studying the natives in order to prove that cannibalism no longer exists. Seasoned video fans can't help but gloat; if only they'd watched a few more Italian movies they wouldn't need to head out to the jungles! We know that cannibals not only exist, but in huge quantities, and not just in jungles, but in all major cities as well.

In what almost passes for an unexpected plot twist, it turns out that the first evidence of cannibalism encountered by the group is actually the result of our drug pushing hero. Strung out on cocaine one night he had butchered a handful of natives. The natives understandably feel that they have a score to settle, which they eventually do in grand style.

The ludicrous atrocities include a woman suspended by hooks through her breasts, and the junkie-guy having his dick chopped off after spitting in the eye of the native's chief. He then escapes, is recaptured and has his hand chopped off, escapes again and is again recaptured before having the top of his head sliced off so his captors can eat his brains nice and fresh. One of the party of anthropologists does escape, and the film closes back in New York as she presents her findings. 'Cannibalism does not exist.' That's what she says! Cannibalism does not exist. What kind of proof was she looking for?

I don't know what the opposite of the phrase 'an embarrassment of riches' is (perhaps 'a pride of impoverished third-rate imitations'?), but if one exists it should be applied forthwith to the legion of Italian zombie flicks that rose, well zombie-like I suppose, from the cinematic grave of their altogether classier American inspirations. As mentioned earlier, the more interesting and clever films of George Romero were a great source of ideas for our Italian friends, and you can see at least a couple of his ideas in all the films mentioned here. And like all Italian rip-offs, what they lack in budget or style or even competence, they make up for with shocking, tasteless, over-the-top gore. In no particular order, here are the top few to look out for.

First up is Lucio Fulci's *The Gates of Hell* (1980). In the vernacular of modern American youth exists a phrase which, better than any other, sums up the impact of this particularly choice item. It is a 'chunkblower'. That is to say that the film will encourage you, gentle cineaste, to 'blow chunks', rather than that the movie itself does. (In which case the correct modern terminology would be that the movie 'sucks'.)

To detail the plot would actually be self-defeating. It is rambling, bizarre, difficult to follow and ultimately rather pointless. But within this shabby framework the director manages to squeeze in several scenes of such unspeakable and vivid unpleasantness that, even by Italian standards, it's truly memorable.

As far as I can work it out, this is what happens. For some dopey reason, the Gates of Hell are opening on earth. There are terrible goings on around the world, most notably in Dunwick, where a certain Bob (played by Fulci regular John Morghen) is hanging out in a hovel with only a blow-up doll for company. His hovel is gungy to the extreme. Aside from the doll, he shares it with the decomposing, worm-riddled body of a dead baby. Nice.

Despite his unpleasant lifestyle, Bob still manages to have friends, one of whom happens to be the daughter of the local sheriff. On discovering Bob sharing a marijuana cigarette with his daughter, the sheriff takes a very large electric drill to Bob's head. Presumably this is the way Italians think that American law enforcement officers carry on.

Predictably, losing most of your head at the same time the Gates of Hell are opening on Earth gives you a pretty good chance of returning as a zombie, which is exactly what happens to Bob. What's more, he returns very hungry, and gets to eat many people before the film reaches its confusing, unsatisfying conclusion.

Another walking-dead-on-the-loose Italian style is *Seven Doors of Death*, also from Fulci. And special mention must go to his *The House by the Cemetery*, a positively evil zombie flick in which a family moves into a spooky house, fear that there might be something in the cellar, discover that they're right and then all die. Gaping knife wounds, bursting sores and human flesh eating are the order of the day here.

The pattern of these Italian gross-outs is actually depressingly predictable, so I won't inflict any more on you. Just trust me that if it has 'Zombie' or 'Cannibal' in the title and was made in Italy during the late Seventies and early Eighties, it will be stomach churning. But, if you're in the right mood for it, fun.

Sources

Contemporary Erotic Cinema William Rostler, 1973

Re-search Incredibly Strange Films Editors Andrea Juno & V. Vale 1986

Cult Movie Stars Danny Peary, 1991

Horror Holocaust Chas Balun, 1986

Horror Film Directors 1931–1990 Dennis Fischer, 1991

Drive-in Theaters Kerry Segrave, 1992

3-D Movies R.M. Hayes, 1989

Black Action Films James Robert Parish and George H. Hill, 1989

Russ Meyer – The Life and Films David K. Frasier, 1990

The Rock and Roll Movie Encyclopedia of the 1950s Mark Thomas McGee, 1990

Fast and Furious – The Story of American International Pictures Mark Thomas McGee, 1984

Universal Horrors M. Brunas, J. Brunas and T. Weaver, 1990

Shock Xpress Edited by Stefan Jaworzyn, 1991

The Psychotronic Encyclopedia of Film Michael Weldon, 1983

Step Right Up! I'm Gonna Scare the Pants Off America William Castle, 1976

How I Made a Hundred Movies in Hollywood and Never Lost a Dime Roger Corman with Jim Jerome, 1990

Flying Through Hollywood by the Seats of my Pants Sam Arkoff with Richard Trubo, 1992

A Youth in Babylon David F. Friedman, 1990

The History of World Cinema David Robinson, 1981

Toms, Coons, Mulattoes, Mammies & Bucks Donald Bogle, 1989

Broken Mirrors Broken Minds – The Dark Dreams of Dario Argento Maitland McDonagh, 1991

Nightmare of Ecstasy – The Life and Art of Edward D. Wood Jr. Rudolph Grey, 1992

X–Rated David McCumber, 1992

For One Week Only Richard Meyers, 1983

Cocaine Fiends and Reefer Madness Michael Starks, 1982

The Aurum Film Encyclopedia of Horror Edited by Phil Hardy, 1985

Sexuality in the Movies Edited by Thomas R. Atkins, 1975
Dirty Movies – An Illustrated History of the Stag Film Al di Lauros
  and Gerald Rabkin 1976

The following periodicals have proved to be an entertaining and
reliable source. Most are available from comic book stores and
some of the bigger record shops. All are heartily recommended.

Psychotronic Magazine
Ungawa
Filmfax
Starburst
Fangoria
Cinefantastique
Midnight Marquee
Sight and Sound
Cinefax

Picture Credits and Sources

182 *House on Haunted Hill* (British Film Institute)
184, 192 & 193 *The Tingler* copyright Columbia Tristar. (British Film Institute)
186 *Homicidal* copyright Columbia Tristar. (Clare Wheatley)
197 *The Creature from the Black Lagoon* Universal International Pictures. (Flashbacks)
200 *Parasite* Wade Williams Productions. (Flashbacks)
209 *Jungle Captive* copyright Universal Films. (Flashbacks)
216 *Nosferatu: A Symphony of Horror* copyright Friedrich Murnay. (The Ronald Grant Archive)
220 *The Phantom of the Opera* copyright MCA Universal. (The Ronald Grant Archive)
223 *The Spiral Staircase* copyright VIACOM. (The Ronald Grant Archive)
224 *The Killer Shrews* copyright Hollywood Pictures. (The Ronald Grant Archive)
228 *The Wicker Man* copyright Lumiere Pictures Ltd. (The Ronald Grant Archive)
229 *Carrie* copyright United Artists. (The Ronald Grant Archive)
231 *The Evil Dead* copyright Renaissance Pictures. (The Ronald Grant Archive)
237 *Two Thousand Maniacs* (The Ronald Grant Archive)
238 *Colour Me Blood Red* (The Ronald Grant Archive)
239 *The Gruesome Twosome* (The Ronald Grant Archive)
239 *She Devils on Wheels* (The Ronald Grant Archive)
251 *Planet of the Vampires* (Clare Wheatley)
254 & 257 *Suspiria* copyright Surf Productions. (British Film Institute)
258 *The Bird with the Crystal Plumage* copyright Surf Productions (British Film Institute)
260 *Tenebres* copyright Surf Productions (British Film Institute)
264, 265 & 266 *Carnival of Souls* copyright Surf Productions (The Ronald Grant Archive)
269 *The Driller Killer* (The Ronald Grant Archive)
272 *Cannibal Holocaust* copyright GO Videos Ltd. (The Ronald Grant Archive)

Colour Sections

Flesh Gordon copyright Entertainment Film Distributors (Flashbacks)
Supervixens copyright Russ Meyer. (The Ronald Grant Archive)
Mondo Topless copyright Russ Meyer
Emmanuelle copyright Trinacra Films. (Flashbacks)
For Your Height Only copyright HGQ/Liluw Productions. (Clare Wheatley)
Shaft copyright Turner Entertainments Co. (British Film Institute)
Mamie Van Doren (The Ronald Grant Archive)
The Evil Dead copyright Renaissance Pictures. (The Ronald Grant Archive)
Psycho copyright MCA/Universal. (The Ronald Grant Archive)
The Gruesome Twosome (Clare Wheatley)
Suspiria copyright Surf Productions (British Film Institute)
Tenebres copyright Surf Productions. (British Film Institute)

Index

Figures in italics refer to captions.